Memphis and Shelby County Public Library and Information Center

For the Residents
of
Memphis and Shelby County

EVERY
EFFORT

EVERY EFFORT
A TRUE STORY

Barbara Mullen Keenan

St. Martin's Press / New York

Design by Madge Schultz

Library of Congress Cataloging in Publication Data

Keenan, Barbara Mullen.
    Every effort.

    1. Vietnamese Conflict, 1961–1975—Missing in action.   2. Keenan,
Barbara Mullen.   3. Missing in action—Family relationships.   4. Marine
Corps wives—United States—Biography.   I. Title.
DS559.8.M5K44   1986   959.704'38   86-1973
ISBN 0-312-27129-8

First Edition

10 9 8 7 6 5 4 3 2 1

To Bill

Acknowledgments

It would have been impossible for me to write this book without the help and support of other people. I would like to acknowledge some of them.

First, I want to thank my sons, Sean and Terence, for always being there when I needed them and for the patience they displayed during the long hours I spent at my typewriter behind a closed door. I also want to thank my husband for understanding why I felt compelled to tell this story.

I am grateful to Sheila Cronin for her contribution to the content of the book, and to Julia Thacker for her editorial assistance and invaluable guidance.

I also want to express appreciation to the people who gave me constant encouragement: my mother, Ruth Thomas, John Hayes, Mary Mullen, Carly and Ken Rosenlund, Bob and Carolyn Sherman, JoAnn Connor, Shirley Culbertson, Sally and Delia Alvarez, Alice Cronin, Celia Hennessey, Marilyn Lane, Deane Warner, Les Whitten, Maryanne Smarsley, Estelle Loleas, Kay Baldinelli, Helen Harris-Dawkins, Kathy Golden, Fred Wertheimer, members of Writers Unanimous and the Lesley College Writing Program, and my loving family.

Finally, this book is my personal tribute to others with whom I shared an experience called Vietnam: the prisoner-of-war/missing-in-action servicemen and their families, the gold-star wives, mothers, fathers, sons, and daughters, and all the veterans of the Southeast Asia conflict.

PROLOGUE

There was no indication during my growing-up years in Michigan that I would one day publicly oppose the President of the United States. In fact, I remember the day I first learned about patriotism in grammar school. Lydia Thompson, my third-grade teacher, was a tall, stiffly slender woman. Her hair was of so little consequence I simply remember that it was there, brushed neatly back from her face, tucked behind the silver wire rims of her glasses. She seemed ageless, as though she had always been exactly as she was then, standing at the head of our class, meting out assignments, rewards, and punishments. She did things in a level, straightforward way, her moods never varying. But then I didn't think of her that way—as human enough to have moods.

She referred to us by description rather than name: "You, boy, in the fourth row in the blue shirt, come up to the blackboard and finish this problem." I dreaded that she should ever call on me. The last thing I wanted was to be singled out for any reason. Fortunately, I had two things in my favor. I was small for my age and my last name (Thomas) had placed me in the back row. All that year I sat in a perpetually slumped position behind Wally Thibideau.

I was prepared to hide myself for another day the morning

Miss Thompson stood in front of us and smiled. "Today," she said, "we're going to talk about patriotism." Her eyes, which I'd never noticed before, glistened through the crystal lenses of her glasses. This sudden awakening in Miss Thompson took me by surprise. For the first time, I straightened up in my seat and peered up over the top of Wally's slicked-down hair.

"This is Charles Lindbergh's birthday," Miss Thompson said. Her voice cracked and became more high-pitched as she told us how the handsome young aviator had flown across the Atlantic in 1927 in his single-engine plane. Her passionate description rose to a crescendo until I felt I was there with Lindbergh in the cockpit of *The Spirit of St. Louis*. When she came to the part about landing at Le Bourget Air Field in France, I could see and hear the crowds of Frenchmen cheering.

I was caught up in the Lindbergh story, but I could tell Lydia Thompson was working up to something more important. When she had told us about Washington and Lincoln, it was with the same voice she had used to explain long division. But this was different. Finally she got to the point. "You are the luckiest children in the world," she said. She paused and dabbed the corner of her eye. Could I believe what I was seeing? Was she brushing away a tear?

"You are American," she announced. "God has blessed us all. Everyone in the world wishes he were American. And we are the fortunate ones. Honor this privilege, children. Never take it for granted."

After our brief moment of excitement, Lydia Thompson faded back into her dull real self and I slumped back behind Wally's torso. All through lunch, though, I thought about what she'd said and wondered why someone as ordinary as I should have been chosen along with Charles Lindbergh to be an American.

I was surprised at the end of that school year when Miss Thompson handed me a promotion slip with my very own name on it. To my memory she had never acknowledged my presence. But that didn't matter: She had told me I was somebody. I was an American. Until then I had had no idea why I'd been placed on

earth, the fourth child in a family of six, in a small town in
Michigan.

I kept my American dream carefully hidden in the body of a
skinny little girl who slid anonymously from one grade to the
next. Success in school in the 1940s depended upon two things:
one's ability to study hard and not call undue attention to oneself.
It was just as important, however, to be "well adjusted" socially. I
remember overhearing a teacher describe a classmate as a
"maladjusted child." It sounded like an incurable disease, as bad
as syphilis maybe. I vowed that no one would ever call me maladjusted. When plaid skirts, baggy sweaters, and bobby socks gave
way to ballet slippers, flowing black skirts, and middy blouses, I
threw away everything in my closet. I was embarrassed to win
the American Legion scholarship award in the eighth grade because I had to walk across the auditorium stage to receive it.

"She's smart but you'd never know it" was the way people described me, and I knew it was a compliment. I was part of the
silent generation and proud of it. I could do anything I wanted, I
was sure, if I just pointed myself in the right direction. I had no
intention of not "making something of myself" and little sympathy
for those who didn't have the gumption to do the same.

According to the rules, good behavior paid off. In my case, the
reward was a job with the Voice of America. I packed my untar-
nished ideals, shift dresses, and high heels into a suitcase and
boarded a Pan American clipper ship. We refueled at Wake Is-
land, Japan, and Hong Kong. Bursting with duty and purpose, I
landed at my final destination: Bangkok, Thailand.

In the late 1950s we were zealous as missionaries. There was a
sense of urgency and camaraderie among those of us representing
America overseas. We were battling against time and the spreading evil of communism in order to bring the hope of democracy to
backward countries. We were teachers of the underdeveloped: if
everyone on earth couldn't be American, they could be like Americans.

It was in Japan two years later that I met and married Bill
Mullen, a young Marine aviator. My pulse raced with pride and

envy whenever I watched his A4D Skyhawk jet screech down a runway. I would squint my eyes until the plane became a speck in the sky and watch it disappear from view a few seconds later. I felt that between us we were doing our part to keep the Free World secure. Our love seemed imbued with a sense of destiny. I would glance at Bill or touch him in the night and marvel at our good fortune.

I thought about all this on an October afternoon in 1971 as I walked back and forth in front of the White House shifting my picket sign from one shoulder to the other. The vision of Lydia Thompson loomed before me, her one-time smile lighting up her face. "God bless us," I could hear her say. "We are American."

EVERY
EFFORT

1. BRUSH FIRE

I was pushing a cart loaded with groceries through our supermarket as I always did on Friday afternoons when Georgia Murphy came flying down the aisle, past boxes of Fruit Loops and bags of sugar.

"Barbara," she said, gasping a minute to catch her breath, "you'd better get home. We just found out. The squadron is shipping out in three days!"

I threw the car keys on the hall table and ran up the stairs to the bedroom where Bill was rolling things up and shoving them into a duffel bag. "Is it true?" I asked. "You're leaving on Sunday?"

"Yes, the squadron's being sent to Japan," he said. "We found out for sure this afternoon."

He dropped what he was holding, came over, and put his arms around me. "Maybe it won't be for long," he whispered. After a few minutes he gestured toward his duffel bag. "I have so many things to do before leaving. And we have to talk."

"Let me help you pack," I said.

We folded things: khakis, green fatigues, then a leather flight jacket and an orange flight suit.

Suddenly I stopped long enough to notice other articles spread across the bed. "Why is the flight suit orange?" I asked.

"So it can be seen if you go down at sea."

"Bill, what are you packing anyway?" I asked. I bent over the duffel bag and sifted through it. "My God, this looks like battle gear."

"Taking these things is routine," he said.

"For Japan? Aren't you taking your dress uniform?"

"I don't think I'll need it. I don't think we'll be there more than a month or so."

"And then what, Bill? Vietnam?" I asked. "Is that where you're going? Are they sending your whole Marine squadron to Vietnam?"

"It looks like it. But I don't want you to worry. It's just a show of strength, they say. To prove we back the South Vietnamese government. That's all."

I looked back at the duffel bag lying there on the soft white tufts of shag carpet. "A show of strength. Not combat? Are you saying it's not going to be dangerous?"

"Hell, no. Who's going to fool around with a bunch of raggedy-ass Marines? Hey, don't look like that. Everything's fine."

"What am I supposed to do if you don't know how long you'll be gone? There's so little time."

"Maybe you'd like to go to Michigan while I'm away. I could have orders cut tomorrow before I leave," he said. "We'd only lose a month's rent on this place. The kids would like it and you'd be near your sister. Just think about it."

"I don't know," I said. "So you're sure this is temporary? It's not a regular year's overseas tour then?"

"I don't think it will turn into that."

"God, I hope not."

"I tell you what. Get a baby-sitter for Saturday night, Barbara. We'll go out to dinner. Just the two of us. Wear your slinky black dress. Candlelight, dancing, the works. We'll talk it all out."

He seems calm, I thought. I'm probably making too much of this. "Yeah, why don't we do that," I said. "Sounds good. Very romantic. We'll be June Allyson and Van Johnson. Soft music.

Starlit night. The next day they kiss and he leaves for the South Pacific." I walked toward the door and then stopped for an instant. "Would you mind moving the duffel bag? It's sort of in the way," I said. "Maybe you could put it in the trunk of the car when you finish packing."

He glanced up. "Sure, I'll do that."

Bill's gray suit hung over the back of a chair; my best black cocktail dress was tossed over the suit. Two tiny Kahlua glasses sat side by side on the nightstand, and my favorite nightgown was lying on the floor alongside the bed. The talk had been intense the night before, but not dreary, and we'd laughed a lot. Bill wouldn't let me be gloomy about the separation. He was acting almost too casual, but perhaps this was best. If it had been up to me, we'd have moped around all evening. As it was, we'd had a fine time, one we could unwrap like a little gift to cheer us up in the coming months.

I'd been awake an hour or so, and the first morning light was just beginning to show through the slats of the venetian blinds. Bill was still asleep. He looked younger when he slept: His high cheekbones were more pronounced, his eyelashes darker and more noticeable, and his mouth was gentle and relaxed. I lay still, watching him until I heard Sean shuffle down the hall to the bathroom. I slipped out of bed and pulled on my robe.

"Mom," Sean whispered outside the door, "ask Daddy if I can come in."

"Come on in," Bill answered, half in his sleep.

Sean walked around to his dad's side of the bed and squeezed in beside him, pulling the covers up to his chin. The door flew open again, and Terry ran across the room and leaped up on the bed. "Daddy, get up," he bellowed, bouncing up and down as if the mattress were a trampoline.

I left the three of them to their wrestling. I needed a cup of coffee. Down in the kitchen by myself I didn't feel quite as courageous about Bill's departure as I had the night before. No matter—I would try not to get depressed. There wasn't time for that anyway. I looked at the dozen roses in a vase on the counter and smiled. When had he found time to order those during the past two hectic days?

The commotion upstairs quieted, and I heard the three of them bounding down the stairs. "Pancakes, Mom," Sean shouted at Bill's prompting.

"Pancakes, pancakes," his two-year-old brother repeated.

I took a quick gulp of coffee. I wasn't quite ready for this.

"Terry's using all the syrup," Sean complained as soon as he sat down at the table.

Bill took the bottle from Terry's clutched fist, and Terry let out a screech. Bill laughed, tousled Terry's blond hair, and handed the bottle to Sean. "Big four-year-olds have to teach little brothers how to act, you know."

Sean's round hazel eyes gave his dad an incredulous look. "He's the one who was slopping the syrup all over. Anyway he's crazy. Really crazy. Nobody can teach him anything. Not even me."

Bill smiled. "Just be good boys for your mom while Daddy's away. OK?"

Sean nodded without enthusiasm. Terry screamed for more syrup.

It was noon when we piled into the little blue Tempest to drive to El Toro Marine Base. The Marine guard whipped a white glove up to his forehead in a snappy salute as we drove through the main gate. Sean looked pleased. Spit and polish. Even the trees, clipped square and tall, seemed poised in a perpetual salute. Today the orderliness was reassuring. We drove down a straight road through the center of the base past rows of rectangular buildings and pulled into a parking place in front of squadron headquarters.

Nothing was out of the ordinary except for the green canvas-covered trucks that were parked in the lot. The men and their families and girlfriends were gathering in groups near the trucks. Bill pulled his duffel bag out of the trunk, slammed the lid shut, and carried his bag over to the trucks. The boys jumped out of the car and chased after him. Some friends waved and motioned for me to join them, but I waited for Bill to return. I could see it was not an occasion for hysterics—on the other hand, I wasn't prepared for small talk either. I tried to relax. Marines are supposed to be sent here and there, I told myself, and something is expected of an officer's wife.

Terry was darting from place to place. Bill scooped him up, kissed him on the cheek, and slid him back down to the ground. Then he crouched down, wrapped his arms around both boys, and held them close and whispered something to each one separately. Terry wriggled away and hollered back with a swing of his hand, "Bye, bye, Daddy."

Sean tugged at his dad's hand. "Will you be back next week, Daddy?"

"No. Not that soon, Sean. I hope not too long, though." He patted Sean's curly brown hair, bent over, and kissed him on the top of his head.

Bill had kept his dark glasses on. I could see he was trying to appear calm. He put his arms around me and said, "Remember, Barby, I love you. We're going to have a hell of a good time raising these kids." He kissed me on the cheek and then softly, longer, on the lips. I didn't want to move, but he gently pulled my arms away from him and cupped my hands between his. "I've got to go now."

He turned and walked toward a group of officers near the trucks. "I'll write you tonight on the ship," he shouted before he leaped into the back of one of the trucks. As they drove off, he edged toward the open end and waved until the truck was out of sight.

"Take a nice nap, boys," I said. "Mommy has a lot of things to do." I closed their door and went downstairs.

The apartment was quiet. Three o'clock. I should clean up the lunch dishes, I thought. I put the salt and pepper back into the cabinet and carried silverware over to the sink. Then I picked up Bill's plate where he'd been sitting just two hours earlier, and suddenly it all seemed real: He was gone. I set the plate back on the table and slid into the nearest chair. A sense of emptiness swept over me. Now what, I thought. How could I possibly think about movers coming in three days?

I reached for the phone on the kitchen counter and dialed Larry Robinson, Bill's best friend. I had to talk to Ginny and Larry. The phone rang three times, four times, before Ginny answered. "I'm so glad you're home," I said. "I just got back from the base. The squadron's gone."

"You don't sound good. Are you all right, Barbara?" Ginny asked.

"I don't know. The reality suddenly hit me, just like that. I feel panicky. Honest to God."

"Just a minute. Here's Larry. He wants to talk with you."

"Hold tight, Barbara," Larry said. "Ginny and I will be right over. Get the boys ready. You're coming over here for dinner tonight."

Ginny stood in the doorway of the pale pink California ranch house. She held the baby in one arm and waved with the other. Sonja squeezed around her and ran down to meet Sean and Terry. I felt better already, as if Bill hadn't left at all.

We sat down at the dinette table in front of the sliding glass doors and I looked out at the patio where the four of us had had so many good times. "We'll be out of there in a few weeks," Larry said. "We'll call their bluff with some combat troops. You don't think they're crazy enough to take on the entire American military, do you?" I didn't answer. I didn't even know who "they" were. Maybe "they" were fanatical, suicidal. But Larry did make sense. We would certainly scare the hell out of this lunatic fringe of rebels in a tiny country.

"They'll back down like the Russians did in Cuba, when they know we're serious," he said. "Hey, Barbara, once the Marines have landed, that's all she wrote for those Commies in the rice paddies." I laughed and felt better.

Larry drove us home about midnight. He helped me carry the boys upstairs and we tucked them into bed. Then he stopped at the door before leaving. "Don't worry," he said. "Driving on a California highway is more dangerous than that piece of cake over there."

*   *   *

I hadn't expected to be in Marquette, Michigan, that summer. But I wasn't sorry I'd come. I walked on sidewalks where I'd played hopscotch and drove by the two-story frame house on Front Street where I'd grown up with my sisters and brothers. Just a few blocks north was my old high school where I'd rooted for the "Redskins."

My sister teased me about "returning to the womb."

"Sure," she said, "you make fun of the little hick town, but you're back at the first sign of trouble."

We'd stayed the month of June with my sister, Shirley, her husband, and their six children in their large house on a quiet tree-lined street. Bill's letters came regularly. He was still in Japan, but hinting that his squadron would be leaving soon for Vietnam. Realizing he'd be away more than a few months, I'd found a little cottage, just right for the boys and me, on Silver Creek Road, a few miles out of town.

By September we were settled in our new home. Bill was flying daily combat missions in Vietnam and I was enrolled in the university. Besides earning credits toward my degree, I hoped that attending classes and studying would help time to pass more quickly.

Our town seemed unaffected by what was happening over there. The local newspaper, *The Mining Journal,* printed news of Vietnam on page 3 or 4, if at all. For the most part, people didn't discuss that thing in "Veeetnaaam," as my postman pronounced it. As an item for conversation that fall and winter the next snowfall took precedence, and it snowed every day.

Once or twice a week the national news did a "situation in Vietnam" spot. One night on the TV screen in living color an A4E Skyhawk was shot out of the sky. As I watched the report, I was overcome with an increasing sense of terror. Shaking, I drove over to my sister's.

Shirley was only a few years older than I, but when we were growing up she seemed unapproachable to me. I was the kid sister; she was a tall, slim brunette beauty, far too glamorous to bother with me. And here I was years later needing her and knowing she'd clear out a houseful of teenagers in order to share a few quiet moments and a cup of coffee.

She met me at the door. "Come on in," she said. "Out to the kitchen. Let's put on the pot."

I tagged after her. "Shirley, I'm scared. How could a woman my age have a husband at war? Everyone thinks of young men marching off to war. Bill's thirty. People give me strange looks when I tell them he's in Vietnam."

She poured the coffee into our cups. "Look, you have a right to be scared. Most people don't even know there's a war going on. I might not either if it weren't for you."

"You know all Bill's friends were peacetime officers. There we were just living a good life. I don't even know what this is. Nobody calls it a war. You say war and people think of D-Day or Iwo Jima and John Wayne, even Korea. I heard one newscaster call this a skirmish. Another one referred to it as a brush fire. What the hell is that? In Washington they say it's a police action."

"What do you care what they call it? It's war if you're the one involved. I'd be terrified. Believe me, you're doing better than I would be."

"You just don't know. Every afternoon I get the cold sweats during class. I know it's early morning in Vietnam and Bill is flying missions."

An hour later we stood at the door and she put her arms around me. I touched her hand and said, "Thanks, I'm OK now. I've got to get back home. I'll be over on Sunday."

Larry Robinson was now in Vietnam with Bill, and more of Bill's friends were arriving in Chu Lai and Da Nang each week. I wondered myself why the Marine contingent was growing so large. At the same time, when Senator William Fulbright questioned the military buildup, I resented it. My sister and her husband assured me that our President and the generals wouldn't risk Bill's life or any others if it weren't essential to the security of the United States. I said I agreed and hoped Fulbright would be impeached or whatever it was we did to traitorous senators.

In October the Young Republicans and the American Legion staged a rally at the university to back our country's efforts in Vietnam. About twenty of us showed up in front of the student union. Though the war wasn't often discussed around the campus, I was surprised there weren't more students there. The rally, if you could call it that, broke up after a speech or two, and we all wandered off.

It was a long cold winter, even for northern Michigan. Lake Superior froze over by the end of November. Snow piled to eight-foot heights, and icicles grew until they covered the windows of our cottage. Sean broke a shoulder doing acrobatics off the sofa, Terry drank furniture polish one morning, and both boys came down with scarlet fever during a freak epidemic. I made hospital runs in zero weather.

As the winter progressed, I became aware of a change in myself, a sense of underlying darkness and anxiety that wouldn't go away. I tried to hide this from the children, lose myself in chores and studying, but it was always there, an expectation of disaster. If bad news were to come, I didn't know how it would be delivered. Near a Marine base, an officer of the day and a chaplain would come personally. I knew about that. Even in peacetime disaster was no stranger to a jet squadron. But this was different. The planes were being shot at day and night. I'd heard or read somewhere that pilots in Vietnam flew more missions in a month than World War II fliers did in a year. And here, three hundred miles from the nearest Navy base, the telephone might be the only communication. Even Western Union was closed after 6:00 P.M., which is why I was more anxious at night.

One evening I was so afraid the phone would ring I thought about going to a motel—anywhere where "they" couldn't find me. If the boys hadn't been asleep and if it hadn't been so cold outside, I might have gone. Instead, I took the phone off the hook and hid it under a pile of pillows and blankets so I couldn't hear the beeping sound of the recorder.

It was a solitary terror, and it snuck up on me unexpectedly. I knew I had to make a plan to control it, so I called the local priest and asked if I could have a talk with him. He said to come the next day.

"You see, Father, if the telegram should come, I don't want to receive it all by myself in that house out there in the woods," I said. "So I wondered if I could ask the Marine Corps to deliver it to you first?"

The war seemed removed from the rectory with its velvet sofa and lace curtains. The priest sat calmly watching me, his head tilted to one side, like a parent listening to the rantings of a frightened child. When he spoke, there was a shade of condescension in his tone that made me wish I'd never called him.

"Now, dear, there isn't much chance of that, is there?" he asked. "Your husband will be back soon. I'm sure. We all feel overburdened now and then. Just have faith. Taking care of those children by yourself is bound to make you nervous." He glanced at his watch. "Come in anytime to talk. I'm afraid I have to cut it short now. I'm sorry. But remember, you can come back anytime."

I got in the car and turned on the radio full blast. Johnny Mathis. "A Certain Smile." I was an hour late picking up the boys at the baby-sitter's. It was already five o'clock, and they ran down the steps from the porch when I pulled up. I heard Sean's foghorn voice all the way from the car. "Mom, where were you? We've been waiting ten hours."

I stopped at the end of our driveway and pulled a small package from my mailbox while the boys scrambled out of the car. I sat for a minute looking at Bill's familiar lettering on the package. Good, I thought, it's a tape, not a letter. I needed the sound of his voice. He'd be cheerful as usual. To hear him, you'd hardly have known there was a war going on.

When I sent the boys to their room to play, Sean protested. "Can't we listen, too?" he asked. "We want to hear Daddy, too."

"Yeah. My daddy will talk to me," Terry said.

"Mommy wants to listen to it first, alone. Then it will be your turn. Please, fellas, go to your room. It won't take long."

I wasn't in the mood for sharing Bill, not even with my own children—I wanted him to myself. I made a cup of hot coffee and

settled into the big chair in the living room. I wound the tape
onto the recorder and pressed the button. "Hey, Barbara. I love
you. You know that?" His deep Boston accent excited me somewhere in the center of my stomach. "The time is growing short.
I'm almost home. Guess what happened today? The barber on the
base who cut my hair yesterday was arrested today as a Viet Cong
informer. I hope someone knows who the enemy is. I'm having a
hard time figuring it out. I wish the Communists would call this
damn thing off so we could all go home. I can't wait to leave this
place. . . . We'll get our two-year tour in Hawaii, have parties,
lie in the sun, and teach the kids to play the ukulele. . . ."

Play the ukulele. I curled up more comfortably in the chair and
played the tape over again. Out the window I could see that it
was still snowing, but for the moment, with his voice wrapped
comfortably around me, I was lying in the sun with Bill.

Bill and I met in Japan in 1959 at a time in my life when
becoming involved with a Marine aviator was not in my plans. I
was busy with my job at the embassy in Tokyo. My free time was
organized: I was studying Japanese history, sight-seeing, and attending embassy functions. Then one night my roommate asked,
"Do you mind if Jack brings some friends from the squadron over
Saturday afternoon?"

I said I wouldn't mind, but I did. The last thing I wanted was
a bunch of bad-acting Marine Corps officers around, especially if
they were as nutty as the one Maryanne was dating.

They burst into our apartment as if the world were holding its
breath waiting for them, and I wished I had said no. I wanted to
run out the back door. I hadn't been around American men, except at the embassy, for more than two years. They seemed too
tall and loud and, as I suspected, a little brash. Bill was the third
to come through the doorway. Bright blue eyes and good-looking.
He had a pizza in one hand and a bottle of champagne in the
other.

"You didn't tell me your roommate was an Irish lassie," he
said. "I know a colleen when I see one." They'd obviously stopped
somewhere along the way for a spirit or two.

He practically swaggered over to me. "Bill," he said. "Bill Mullen. And you?"

"Barbara," I said. Lord, he thinks he's God's gift, I thought. How am I going to get out of this one?

He handed me a piece of pizza. "Want some champagne?" He didn't wait for an answer; he handed me a glass and poured. I was annoyed at myself for not leaving. They were worse than I had anticipated. How could anyone really be that overbearing? I sipped my champagne. He refilled my glass. He was funny, though, and making me laugh in spite of myself. I finished the second glass. And there was something appealing about him, I had to concede.

Someone had gone out for more champagne. I was drinking my third glass. I looked at Bill again. Charming maybe, under the flamboyant cover, but of course he's too young, I concluded. I was used to more mature men, serious, much more polished.

"I had a nice time," I said later, disbelieving my own words and wondering where the hours had gone. Maryanne was laughing and shoving the other three out the door. Suddenly Bill whipped his arms around me and gave me a breezy good-night kiss. "See you next weekend," he said. It wasn't a question.

I was ready the following weekend; in fact, I thought about nothing else all week and for the succeeding weeks. Bill was stationed at Iwakuni, a Marine air station in southern Japan, near Hiroshima. It was easy for him to hop a military plane up to Tokyo, but our weekends in the south were fun, too. I often took the overnight train from Tokyo.

It arrived at 8:30 A.M. Bill was always waiting on the platform, and I was the first off the train. He'd slip an arm around my waist and whistle for a taxi. Our inn was outside of town, six miles from the base. The innkeeper's wife would greet us at the door with a smile and a bow. "Barbara-san, the room is ready. How was the train ride? Tell us if you need anything."

We'd toss our bags on the floor and push back sliding panel doors to have a view of the garden below with its rocks and sand and miniature trees. Then we'd change clothes and hop onto Bill's Honda cycle. I'd wrap my arms around his waist and we'd ride out into the country, up and down dirt roads winding around rice paddies and farms. We'd end up on the highway by the sea. And come home exhausted.

In the evening we'd meet Bill's friends and their Japanese companions at the officers' club. Bill and I would sneak off early. Our room at the inn seemed all the more quiet and intimate after the blaring music and activity at the O'club. Futons would be laid out on the tatami mats, the sliding panels would be closed, and one tiny red light lit at the head of our bed. I couldn't imagine being in that room and not being in love. After soaking in a hot bath down the hall, we'd slip into kimonos and paper slippers and return to our room. Limp and relaxed, we'd curl into one another's arms under the futon.

Those romantic times seemed far away that winter, but it didn't matter. Soon we'd be together again. I'd pictured his homecoming in my mind so often it was almost as if I'd already experienced it. At last April came and the sun broke through the gray sky. Icicles began to drip, and the streets of Marquette turned to slush. I watched as the sun's warmth transformed the crusty layers underneath and the recent fall of powder into a thick watery substance. Eventually it would cover all the roads and sidewalks. It was an uncompromising promise of spring, and I felt a sense of triumph. We had done it. Bill and I. We had beat the odds—he in his steaming jungle and I in Dr. Zhivago land.

They couldn't keep him any longer. His extended thirteen-month tour was over, and our meeting in New York was three weeks off. No patriotic speeches, no parades, but still my returning hero. How could any woman in 1945 have been prouder than I? Our celebration would be private. I'd never have to think about Vietnam again.

2. ALMOST HOME

MARQUETTE, MICHIGAN, APRIL 1966 Green Bay is as exciting as San Francisco, London, or Paris to people who live in the small towns of northern Michigan and Wisconsin. My sister and I were going to spend the weekend there, shopping and trying out new restaurants. She deserved it more than I did, having held my hand through days and nights of anxiety about what could have but hadn't happened.

We arrived in the city about noon. "I can't wait to get started, Shirley. It's such a beautiful day. I've got so much to do," I babbled breathlessly as I hung things in the closet.

"Hold tight, Barb. Give me a minute to catch my breath," she said, and collapsed on the bed.

That afternoon at Prange's Department Store I headed straight for the lingerie counter. I picked up a black lacy negligee, held it up to my shoulders, and twirled around. "This is it, Shirley," I said. "Look, the layers peel off."

"Sexy as allowed by law," Shirley said, eyeing the salesclerk, who was watching me with amusement. "If you want it, Barb, pay the woman, please," she said, darting a look around to see who else was watching the spectacle.

A couple of hours later we were on our way to the train station to meet my other sister, Jean, who was coming up from Chicago. "You and Jean are going to have to hold me down, Shirl," I said, squeezing her hand. "I'm so excited I want to stand on a street corner and scream. I thought this year would never end."

"Well, enjoy it, Barb," she said. "You deserve it."

The train was just pulling into the station when we arrived. "There she is," Shirley said, pointing to one of the train windows. Jean was already waving wildly.

A minute later she appeared in an exit door. Shirley grabbed her overnight bag and I threw my arms around her. "So great to see you," I whispered in her ear. "My God, your hair is blond. I've never seen it blond."

"We're going straight to the restaurant," Shirley said. "I've decided we should drink a toast to Barb. And Bill. It's been a long winter."

Later in the hotel room, stretched out on the beds and comfortable in our robes, we talked for hours. "It's as if we were kids again," Jean commented.

"You know what?" I said. "There's no one else I'd rather be celebrating with this weekend."

"I hate to put a damper on the festivities," Shirley said. "But maybe we should get some sleep. We're going to have a full day tomorrow."

"I suppose you're right," Jean said. "It's nearly midnight."

"We'd better decide now how we're all going to get in and out of that bathroom in the morning," Shirley said. Then rolling her eyes and nodding her head in my direction, she added, "We'd better let our little princess go in first, Jean. You know how long it takes her to get beautiful. Twice as long as it takes us."

We were all laughing at the old joke when someone knocked at the door.

"Who could it be at this hour?" Shirley asked.

"Three Paul Newmans, if we're lucky," I said, laughing. "I'll get it." I walked over to the door and opened it.

There were two Marine officers standing in the dim hall light. They looked like a photograph: unmoving, in dress blues, high-necked, white belts, red stripes down the sides of the pants, white gloves. The taller of the two had a mouth that was moving, mechanically, as if a tape recorder from under his jacket were really producing the sound, but I was only aware of the splendid uniforms.

"Mrs. Mullen, we must inform you of the following message which was received by the Defense Department tonight," he said. He was reading aloud from a sheet of teletype machine paper. A lot of words. Words I couldn't understand. I leaned against a closet by the open door.

"Come in, please." Shirley was talking to the uniforms. Their words faded away and came back; I tried to concentrate.

"Radio contact with the plane was lost on a flight over Southeast Asia. They tried to contact him but don't know why he didn't answer. We have few details yet."

What plane, I thought. Bill's on his way home. There's been a mistake. The taller one had walked over to Shirley and was now speaking directly to her as if I were no longer present. "He's lost and hasn't returned with other members of the flight. Rescue planes and helicopters are searching."

"Searching!" I heard myself scream into the room. "God, his plane has crashed; he's been shot down!" Whatever strength I had left drained from my body. The wall hit my left shoulder. I sank to the floor in a limp pile. For a second I tried to pull myself back up.

When I came to, I heard a scream, "No," coming from somewhere in the distance, and then again, "No, no," louder and closer. I realized it was my own voice repeating itself, but I couldn't stop it.

Then I heard Shirley speaking. "Jean, we've got to get some tranquilizers for her. Maybe there's a hotel doctor."

Jean was in bed with me, and I was icy cold. I pulled the blankets tighter and tighter around me. Jean was holding me in her arms, and Shirley was sitting on the edge of my bed; the Marine officers had gone. "The Marines will wait up all night for messages," Shirley said. "They'll tell us the minute they hear anything."

I could see her and hear her, but it was as if she weren't really there. Nothing seemed real—the room, the bed, the blankets around me. If I numb myself, yet stay awake, I thought, I'll take hold of this nightmare—or whatever this is. I wanted to remain alert. I was sure if I slept I'd lose control and something terrible would happen. My shivering finally stopped, and I lay in the silent room. My sisters didn't speak for the rest of the night.

Daylight came and the phone hadn't rung. I could see the clock on the table. It was 5:00 A.M. Shirley picked up the telephone and dialed a number. She spoke a few words, put the receiver down, and said, "They've heard nothing more, Barbara. They say we should return home, where they'll contact us."

"No, it's a mistake. I'm not going to leave this room," I said. "They'll find out. They're wrong. He's on his way home. He wasn't flying any more missions. Maybe he just had plane trouble. He'll be found. I know he's safe. We have to stay here. Bill wouldn't want me to leave. It takes a while to hear. I won't leave this hotel! I won't go!"

Two hours later my brother-in-law arrived. He stood motionless in the doorway. Maybe I'd never looked at him before. Rugged, handsome, good-natured Bill Flanigan, father of all those kids, Shirley's husband. He'd driven all night. I wondered why he didn't speak, and then I saw tears in his eyes. Slowly but assuredly he walked toward me. He reached an arm around my shoulder, eased me up from the bed, and then led me to the door. Each step across the room brought details into focus. Sharply, outlines began to appear—the carpet, a table, a lamp. It was real after all. My sanctuary was being destroyed. I hid my face under his jacket, looked only at the floor, and followed him out of the hotel.

I lay down in the back seat of the car, stared up at the blue sky through the window, and tried not to think. The trip back would be six hours. They stopped to eat, but I stayed in the car and shoved the sandwich they brought me into my purse.

Our car entered the driveway of the little yellow cottage, which to my surprise looked unchanged. I was glad Shirley's teenage daughter had kept the children at their house. I found the instant coffee on the counter where I had left it the morning before and methodically heated the water. Clutching the warm cup, I gazed out the window and suddenly remembered the black negligee. I hoped we hadn't left it in the hotel; it seemed terribly important.

Bill Flanigan left. He said he'd check on the children and be back. "Jean and I will stay all night, Barb," Shirley said.

"Of course, we'll be here as long as you need us," Jean added quickly.

"I don't want to be alone," I said. "We'll hear something soon. I know we will. Just wait. It won't be long."

At 11:00 P.M. the Michigan State Police rang the doorbell and handed me a telegram:

MRS. WILLIAM F. MULLEN. DELIVER. DON'T PHONE.

452 SILVER CREEK ROAD, MARQUETTE, MICH.

I DEEPLY REGRET TO CONFIRM THAT YOUR HUSBAND CAPTAIN WILLIAM F. MULLEN USMC ON 29 APRIL 1966 BECAME MISSING WHILE ON A FLIGHT MISSION IN THE REPUBLIC OF VIETNAM. EXTENSIVE SEARCH OPERATIONS ARE IN PROGRESS AND EVERY EFFORT IS BEING MADE TO LOCATE HIM. IT IS SUGGESTED THAT YOU REFRAIN FROM FURNISHING ANY PERSONS OUTSIDE OF YOUR IMMEDIATE FAMILY WITH ANY BACKGROUND DATA REGARDING YOUR HUSBAND'S PERSONAL HISTORY AND MILITARY SERVICE. RELEASE OF SUCH DATA COULD ADVERSELY AFFECT HIS WELFARE SINCE IT MAY BE USED BY HOSTILE FORCES FOR COERCION AND PROPAGANDA PURPOSES. YOU ARE AS-SURED THAT ANY SIGNIFICANT INFORMATION DEVEL-OPED CONCERNING YOUR HUSBAND WILL BE SENT YOU PROMPTLY. I EXTEND TO YOU ON BEHALF OF THE UNITED STATES MARINE CORPS OUR SINCERE SYMPATHY DURING THIS PERIOD OF GREAT ANXIETY.

WALLACE M. GREENE, JR.
GENERAL, USMC, COMMANDANT OF THE MARINE CORPS

Missing. It overshadowed all the other words in the telegram, demanding attention, explaining nothing. It produced no images, like a mirror without reflection. It had been twenty-four hours since his plane was lost, and still they hadn't found him. My mind shifted quickly. A kaleidoscope of guerrillas, machetes, and guns flashed across a screen in my head: he had ejected from the plane; he was now in enemy territory, perhaps being surrounded by enemy troops this minute. Be calm, I repeated to myself. I must be calm. I'm imagining the worst. I don't have to do that. What I have to accept is bad enough. Wherever he is, he's on his own, and I can't do a thing to help him.

Contrary to my solemn intentions, I dozed off sometime in the middle of the night, curled up on a sofa, the telephone strategically placed six inches away. By some grand mistaken order of things the sun arose that morning as usual. With it came the grim acknowledgment that another silent night had passed. I pulled the curtain aside and watched a woman across the street open her front door to reach for a newspaper.

At ten o'clock a potted lily plant was delivered to the front door. The card began, "In your moment of grief," and was signed by my landlord. Every natural instinct called out for the comfort of tears. But I couldn't give in. Mourning was for loss, for death. Again I reached for the telegram. It said "extensive search operations . . . every effort is being made to locate him."

"Got to hold together, girl," I ordered aloud. "And get that goddamned lily out of here."

My sisters came into the living room, but I walked directly past them to the telephone and dialed a number the officers had scratched on a piece of hotel notepaper.

The voice at the other end of the line answered in a deep, rapid manner, "United States Marine Corps Headquarters, Casualty Branch, good morning, sir."

I caught my breath and spoke quickly. "I'm calling to find out, do you have any information about my husband—is he alive?"

The sure, positive voice asked me, "What is his serial number?"

Serial number? They don't know his name, I thought. That's

why I haven't heard. "The number. I can't remember. His name is Captain William Mullen."

"I have no information now," he said. "Be assured, though, that you will go on receiving your allotment and as soon as we know anything you will be the first to hear of his fate."

"Yes. Thank you, sir. Good-bye," I said.

He was gone. In his place was a dial tone, but I still clasped the receiver to my ear. *Fate.* It was worse than I'd imagined. That person didn't know about Bill, that he was just missing. "Missing" was a better word than "fate."

3. BONA FIDE HOPE

MAY 1966 The boys burst through the door. "Mom, Mom, did you have a good time?" Sean hollered. "We had fun at Aunt Shirley's." Instinctively, I held out my arms and gathered them both up at once, but at the same time something in me wanted to run from them. They looked so small and helpless to me; I felt unequal to the responsibility.

I told them they could play outside until lunchtime, and when they were gone I turned to my sister. "Please, Shirley, keep them a little longer?" I asked.

"Honestly, Barb, I think they should be with you," she said. "Let them help you."

"I'm scared to death," I said, dropping into the nearest chair. "I don't know if I can take care of them."

"Just take it an hour at a time," she said, putting an arm around my slumping shoulders. "I'm only ten minutes away— night or day. You know that."

I crawled through the next few days. Feeling too shaky to drive, I asked Shirley to bring us groceries. I did only what I had to do. I cooked meals for the children in a dreamlike state. For the most part, I was glad when they were playing in the yard and out of sight. Then suddenly I'd be aware that hours had passed.

Fear would overcome me, and I'd run to the window to be sure they were still there. I'd call them to the back porch and squeeze one and then the other until they'd ask what was wrong. "I can't breathe, Mom," Sean said one morning as I held him to me. "Let me go." He ran back to his baseball pals in a field behind the house, and I sank back into a chair and stared out the window again.

Nine days had come and gone when I heard that Vice President Humphrey was going to speak at our university. "To bring glad tidings of the Great Society," the newspaper had said. For the first time in ten days I dressed, absently used a lipstick, and brushed my hair.

I unfolded my telegram and showed it to Secret Service men at the airport gate. They told me to wait near the runway where his plane had just landed. Wind whipped across the small airfield. I shivered and pulled my coat tight to my sides. The plane door opened, and the Vice President came out and down the stairs. He walked straight toward me, smiled, and extended his hand. Before he could speak, and before I lost my nerve, I blurted out, "My husband's plane was shot down ten days ago. I haven't heard a word since then. Could you find out for me if he was captured? There must be information by now."

His smile quickly faded. "I'm sorry, so sorry," he said. He took my hand and clasped both of his around it. "You should have heard something by now. There should be some information. I promise you'll have some word tomorrow, Mrs. Ahh . . ."

"Mullen, Mullen. Captain William F. Mullen, United States Marines." I pronounced it clearly.

He scratched Bill's name on a piece of paper and stuffed it into his suit coat pocket. He touched my hand again, hesitated a moment, and then walked toward the terminal building. For a few seconds I just stood there and stared after him and wondered how I'd remembered Bill's name.

Shirley came over early the next morning to wait with me for the promised "information." At eleven o'clock a telegram was delivered. She took the envelope, ripped it open, glanced over the page, and then read out loud:

MRS. WILLIAM F. MULLEN. DELIVER. DON'T PHONE.

I REGRET TO INFORM YOU THAT YOUR HUSBAND CAPTAIN
WILLIAM F. MULLEN USMC CONTINUES TO REMAIN IN A
MISSING STATUS. ALL SEARCH EFFORTS HAVE BEEN UN-
SUCCESSFUL. YOU WILL BE INFORMED IMMEDIATELY
SHOULD ANY ADDITIONAL INFORMATION BE OBTAINED
CONCERNING HIS STATUS.

R. C. MANGRUM
LT. GEN., ACTING COMMANDANT OF THE MARINE CORPS

Shirley put her hand on my shoulder. "You'll hear something,
Barbara. I just know you will."

"'Status,' Shirley. 'Missing' and 'fate' don't mean anything, but
something about 'status' gives me a chill. It sounds so official."

"It's just a word, Barbara. It doesn't mean anything either."

I walked around in a daze for two more weeks. If I hadn't had
to take care of the children, I might not have gotten out of bed at
all. Their immediate demands, however, were frightening to me.
The spreading of a peanut butter sandwich was a major achieve-
ment. At night when they were asleep, requiring nothing of me,
I'd stand at the foot of their bed and look at them and be thankful
I had them. I knew if it weren't for them I wouldn't bother with
tomorrow. They were both my burden and my solace.

Then one morning a letter came from Larry Robinson in Vietnam. I was afraid to read it because I was alone and I knew Larry
would tell me the truth. I held a piece of paper over the page so
that I could read only one line at a time. If I needed to stop, I
could.

Dear Barbara,

The grief I feel when contemplating the worst that may
have happened to Bill is as wrenching an emotion as though
I had lost not only a true friend but a close-to-the-heart
brother. By optimistic rationalization, however, I am able to

keep my spirits buoyed. I believe there is a chance Bill is still alive—a prisoner of war.

I will relate the situation on the day of Bill's disappearance and give details of the ensuing search. I think your questions will be answered, Barbara, and the basis for my opinions revealed.

The target we were hitting that day had considerable antiaircraft fire protecting it. Ten aircraft were hit and two knocked down during our attacks. My present squadron had two hit, one severely and almost lost. Of the two that were downed, one was an Air Force aircraft; the other was Bill's.

According to other members of Bill's flight, Bill was pulling up and away from the target after completing his run. Because of flak, the flight leader did not circle the target after they completed; rather, they moved out of range of the guns to rendezvous for the return to the base. Bill was last man in the flight and, as he was seen in a normal recovery from a bombing run, was assumed to be without problems until he failed to check in on the radio.

His flight leader turned back to search, but, of course, they were by this time some ten miles from the target area. Because of the distance involved, it is not likely anyone in the flight would have seen a chute. Also, because of the large area, the tremendous height of the trees, and the density of the jungle mass, the wreckage was not found and will probably never be found.

Bill's flight was short of fuel, but his flight leader did direct a prop aircraft into the area to control rescue operations before they departed. We started to send protective cover aircraft from Da Nang immediately after he went down and continued to do so for the rest of the day, all of the next day, and most of the day following. I heard Bill was down, and I got into the rescue cover flights.

At this point, you are probably wondering how we knew where to go for the rescue. Each pilot carries a small radio that emits an emergency signal or transmits and receives. The usual technique for the downed pilot is to go to emergency signal or "beeper" until an aircraft is overhead, then switch to transmit and receive to tell the rescue aircraft of any injuries, etc. Sometimes, however, some portion of the radio is damaged on ejection or landing. More importantly, there is *no way* the radio can work *unless* the pilot escapes the aircraft before it crashes.

Shortly after Bill was missed, a "beeper" signal started to come from an area well away from the target on a line toward Bill's base. The obvious conclusion is Bill at least ejected and landed, although he may have been wounded or injured. Rescue aircraft tried to get to the "beeper" area but were driven back by enemy fire. Three more were hit during this attempt, and one crash-landed trying to return to base. A very important factor in continuing the rescue attempts occurred during these first tries. When asked by the rescue coordinator to turn the "beeper" off and turn it on, the person running the radio would respond immediately. It is not felt that the Viet Cong could respond to commands given in English as rapidly as was done; therefore, when darkness fell on the first day, opinion was that Bill was alive, running his rescue radio, but the radio had a bad transmitter and he was unable to communicate.

At daylight rescue attempts were resumed. Shortly after we started, the "beeper" came back on the air. This time, however, there was no response to commands. Rather, all during the day the "beeper" would come on and go off. When attempts were made by the helicopter to get to the "beeper" position, a torrent of enemy fire would erupt, driving them back. The following day found no change. Opinion now was the VC either had a radio of their own trying to draw in the rescue aircraft for an ambush or they were using Bill's radio. If they were using Bill's radio, the best that could have happened to Bill was capture. I think he was captured. Rescue attempts were called off on the third day.

As I have mentioned, I don't think we will ever find the wreckage. Also, I am sure the ejection seat and Bill left the aircraft as the radio would have been smashed in a crash. If Bill was not badly wounded or injured and if the enemy troops followed their orders to take American aviators prisoner, Bill is most likely a prisoner. A lot of "ifs," but it does give hope.

Ironically, when Bill and I were talking approximately a week prior to the accident, he was worried about me being shot down after he had heard that I had been hit two or three times on night missions in the same area. Joe Homer, myself, all of Bill's many, many friends keep saying he'll come out of it in the usual grand style. There exists a bona fide chance he is still alive.

Barbara, I hope this letter, as badly written as it is, answers some of the many questions you must have. If my handwriting is illegible, please excuse; I am rushing to get it in the early mail pickup after a late, late night hop.

Please write again on any topic or for any advice I may be able to assist with. I do have access to the Hanoi releases a few days before they become public and will forward any information I may come across.

Keep those guys thriving, for the world would indeed be a forlorn place if it were not for people like my buddy Bill Mullen, and, God willing, his offspring, who will develop to be like him. God, give us hope!

Sincerely,
Larry

Even as I read the last sentence of Larry's letter, I felt a change come over me. A warm surge of energy passed through my body, and I took a deep breath. Larry thought Bill was alive. He said there was no way the radio could have worked unless the pilot had ejected and landed. It would have been smashed in a crash. I repeated this over and over to myself. I'd never really believed Bill was dead; it didn't matter about the black jungle, rescue planes that never returned, possible injury. Bill's plane had not blown up in the sky! There was every reason for hope. The next day, for the first time in a month, I got out of bed with eagerness. I was full of plans. The movers had been scheduled to come the following week, and I let them come as planned. I couldn't remain in that house in the woods where I'd counted the days through the icy winter.

My mother had been pleading with me to come to Illinois. Before Larry's letter I hadn't had the energy to drive that far, but now I was sure I could do it. I looked forward to seeing her and my brother Bill and my sister Jean again. If I felt up to it, I'd go on to Massachusetts to visit Bill's family.

All morning the movers loaded our belongings into a van, and I kept thinking—this should be carrying our possessions to the West Coast en route to Hawaii. Now they would find a home in the corner of a storage warehouse, and I wondered when I would see them again.

I gave each boy a plastic bag and told him to take what he wanted out of his bureau drawers before the men came back for the bedroom furniture. Then I threw some clothes for all three of us into two large suitcases. From the back door I waved to the boys, who were now leaning against a tree in the backyard. "Put your things in the trunk of the car now, boys."

Terry sauntered over to the back porch. His blue eyes peered up at me through tangled strands of blond hair. He had stuffed a Tonka truck into the pocket of his jeans; he took it out and ran it up and down the sleeve of his sweat shirt. "Where the heck are we going, Mom?" he asked.

"I told you we're going to Uncle Bill's, sweetie," I said. I walked over and patted him on the shoulder. "We'll have fun at Uncle Bill's, Terry. Everybody will be there, Aunt Shirley, Aunt Jean, your Uncle Danny." Then I put my hand under Sean's chin. He'd been withdrawn all morning. "You OK?" I asked. He nodded yes. "You and Terry can get in the car now," I said. Before backing the car out of the driveway, I took one last look at the little yellow house.

As our blue Tempest carried us southward through the northern Michigan woods, past miles of neat and orderly Wisconsin farms, I pictured the family waiting to welcome us. Just a few more hours, I told myself. At last I rounded a corner and caught sight of my brother Bill's rambling Midwest home. "Hi there, fellas," he hollered from the doorway. He raced down to the car, hugged me, and then took each boy by the hand. "Come on, guys. Your Aunt Pug has a big slice of chocolate cake for you in the kitchen. Go on into the living room, Barbara—everybody's in there. I'll get the bags."

I greeted everyone and then went straight over to where my mother was sitting on the sofa in front of the bay window. "Don't get up, Mom," I said. She reached a hand out to me, and I grasped it eagerly. I leaned over and kissed her and sat down in a chair next to her.

I had interrupted Jean, who was laughing and telling a story about her youngest son. I listened but somehow this was not the scene as I'd pictured it earlier in the car. My brother Bill came back from the kitchen. He was smiling and carrying a martini pitcher, which he set on the coffee table.

An hour passed, and every subject but the one that seemed to lurk in corners and dangle in the air was being discussed. I felt like a plastic mannequin propped in my Danish modern chair until Jean startled me with a question. "Don't you remember that time, Barbara?" she asked. "Your Bill was always such a good sport about those things."

Suddenly I bolted to my feet and screamed, "What do you mean *was*—*is, is, is!* He's alive. Don't you know that? Don't you believe that?"

"Barbara, please sit down," my mother said. "We know what you're going through."

"Jean didn't mean anything," Bill said. "We're just trying to take your mind off it."

"It. It," I screeched. "How callous are you? I can't take my mind off him for a minute. How can any of you? Look at all of you sitting here talking about old times as if nothing had changed!"

"We sympathize, honestly, Barbara," Jean insisted.

My young brother Danny nodded agreement. Shirley got up from her chair and started toward me, but I screamed, "Sympathy! There you go again. He's not dead!" I darted from the room and ran up the stairs. I slammed the door to the bedroom, fell onto the bed, buried my head in the pillow, and sobbed. Later I lay there by myself, thinking, they don't know how to act. This isn't a wake or a funeral—there's no name for whatever this is.

Early the next morning my brother found me drinking coffee by myself at the dining room table. He poured himself a cup, ruffled the top of my hair with his fingers, and then sat across from me at the table. I thought how tired he looked. I guessed he hadn't slept much. "Is there anything I can do to help?" he asked.

My brother had always seemed invincible. Ever since I was a little girl I'd turned to him with my problems, but now I felt sorry for him. He was used to making decisions, taking charge; he'd never learned how to be helpless. "Maybe I could lend you some money to get you through."

"Thanks," I said. "I'll take you up on that."

Later that morning my mother and I took a long walk together. We sat on a bench in a nearby wooded park. "How am I going to keep going, Mom?" I asked, the tears already forming in my eyes. "If only I'd hear that he's alive."

She handed me a handkerchief from her purse. "You have no reason to think he's not alive," she said.

I looked into the warm brown eyes that had comforted me so often as a child. "It isn't fair, Mom," I whispered. "I love him so."

"Try to be stubborn like you were when you were a youngster," she said. "Sometimes you were exasperating. Remember when you insisted on having a room of your own even if it had to be that closet with half a window behind the chimney? Be tough about this, too. Just say he's coming back."

I pictured my tiny room on the third floor, wiped my eyes, and smiled. "You're right, Mom. Larry said there was bona fide hope."

4. CONFLICTING REPORTS

<u>JUNE 1966</u> I buttoned the boys into their new blue-and-white checkered coats as the train pulled into South Station, Boston. They wore the long navy pants and caps I'd chosen so carefully a couple of months back. This is how they were going to look when Bill saw them for the first time: I had planned it to the last detail.

I saw Mary's blond streaked head down at the end of the platform and told the boys to come to the window and wave to Gramma. She still looks young, I thought, too young to be Bill's mother. The boys scampered down the steps, and Mary threw her arms around them. Then she straightened up. "Hello, Barbara," she said gently, and reached in her purse for a tissue. She dabbed her eyes quickly, took my hand, and smiled. "Come on. Let's get a taxi and go home."

Brockton is a suburb of Boston that over the years lost prestige as the shoe factories moved in and the political character changed from Republican-Yankee to Democrat-labor. The Mullens lived in the lower five-room flat of a thin four-story home they purchased during the 1930s. Bill grew up in this old house, which the family had stubbornly kept in good repair. His room on the third floor gave every indication that a seventeen-year-old would be back in half an hour. The hockey team pictures remained on the table by a single bed, which, as if in a state of readiness, was wrapped in clean sheets and warm quilts. A tennis racket leaned in one corner, and ice skates were tossed on the floor of the closet. Old textbooks were neatly piled on the desk, the drawers were strewn with girls' phone numbers, school assignments, and printed joke sheets.

The family was middle-class, and for the most part, Irish. His dad was the son of Irish immigrants who did whatever was necessary to buy a home and raise the four children "God gave them." Bill's dad had been a lobster fisherman before World War I, but he contracted a bronchial condition in France that prevented him from resuming the harsh life of a New England fisherman.

Bill was born in 1935. Six months after that, his dad was forced to leave his wife and child and move to Arizona for his health. Bill's mother, a pretty hazel-eyed blonde, had expected, as did most young women then, to fill her days caring for her husband and children. Instead, out of necessity, Mary Mullen had begun working in the office of the WPA when her son was two weeks old. Three years later she was hired as a bookkeeper by an ice and coal company where eventually she worked herself up to office manager. Bill's grandmother, a handsome, no-nonsense Scots lady, took care of the young boy throughout his childhood. Gram, as everyone called her, still lived with Mary and Bill's dad.

There was always a sense of warmth and caring in Bill's home. I'd felt welcome there from the very beginning when Bill and I first came back from Japan. Irish relatives ensured that parties and holidays were fun, noisy, drinking (more than Gram ever knew) occasions. I loved those times myself: Bill at the piano surrounded by first, second, and third cousins, and aunts, uncles, and neighbors.

The family believed that Franklin Delano Roosevelt had saved them and the nation. They were sure that no place on earth was as good as the United States, and the election of John F. Kennedy had simply verified it. JFK's picture hung over the color TV, and Gram, at eighty-six, still referred to him as "my boy."

I looked at Gram now, sitting in her spot at the end of the sofa, where she'd been most of the two weeks since we'd arrived, and wondered what agonizing thoughts were hidden behind those old violet eyes that never cried. What had happened to her Billy, who used to bound through the door with a shout: "Hey, Gram, I think I smell custard pie." Billy, who drove his tricycle off a ledge at age four and insisted on having a ride in a single-engine bi-plane at twelve. Who stayed out too late with high school friends. Who with a hug or a favorite piece on the piano or a word of flattery found his way back into her graces. Where was he now?

Bill's dad spent his days praying in an upstairs bedroom. When he came back downstairs, he would state emphatically, "Bill will be back. God won't let us down; you'll see, Barbara." He refused to consider anything else. The one thing that had gone right in his life was his robust, healthy boy. God would keep him safe.

Bill had also been the core of his mother's existence, making sense of all the years of work. Without him the family seemed to have lost its purpose. Now they were three individuals, the mother, father, and grandmother, harbored in separate hells. On the surface we all shared our worries and hopes, but we hid the real pain, each of us telling the other to bear up, that we must be strong for Bill.

I had hoped the grandchildren would transform us into a co-hesive unit, but after we'd been in the house a week or so, I suspected that the opposite was happening. Grampa, out of breath, chased after the boys all day, issuing warnings of immi-nent danger, until exhausted, he would go back upstairs to rest. Gram insisted that the boys' eating habits were poor: They ate too much of this, too little of that. The spilling of a glass of milk could sour dispositions for hours.

Sean and Terry were sitting at the kitchen table one evening arguing with one another about which one of them had eaten the most cookies when I glanced into the living room and noticed Gram. She had picked up a color photograph of the two of them, laid it across her lap, and was smiling down at it. I poured some more milk into Terry's glass and asked him to please be quieter. I wanted to add, "so Gram can stare at your pretty picture in peace." But somewhere under my protective haze of numbness, I was beginning to realize that four generations living under one roof was taking its toll on everyone.

During those brief moments of passage from sleep to consciousness, the truth swept over me each morning. If I could live until one o'clock, the mailman might bring word from somewhere. At ten-thirty I started to pace, hoping the phone would ring. After the mailman had come and gone, I scanned the afternoon newspaper for anything pertaining to the war in Vietnam.

I listened to the radio, filling time until the national evening TV report. One afternoon an announcer reported that a Navy lieutenant had escaped from his captors in the jungles of Laos. An Air Force officer had gotten away with him, but he'd been caught and beheaded by Laotian guerrillas. This first public acknowledgment of prisoners of war brought both a sense of horror and a momentary taste of bittersweet excitement. Out of contact, *but alive*—there were men in enemy hands.

"Another day conquered, Mary. Tomorrow we'll hear something," I'd say before going to my room at night. She'd just nod. I seemed to be crawling into bed earlier each night. I pulled the sheets over my head and rolled into a ball. Wrapping my arms around my knees and clutching them close to my body made sleep come quickly. Gratefully, I slipped into its soothing black nothingness.

Words that trickled in from Southeast Asia and Washington confused us. A positive opinion was canceled by a negative one a few days later. Mary folded a letter from Bill's commanding officer back into its envelope and laid it in front of her on the kitchen table. "He says the pilots and crews share the sorrow of this sad event with us. I almost wish he hadn't written at all," she said. "It's worse than the one from Westmoreland offering his 'deepest sympathy.'"

The teapot whistled and I got up and poured water into our cups mechanically. I wondered how many hours we'd already spent at the table rehashing the letters. "I think it's even worse when it comes from a chaplain," I said, as if making one worse would make another better. "I can't get over Chaplain Hammerl telling me, 'Whatever may still be asked of you, I know you'll accept it and God will be your strength.' He doesn't know me— how does he know what I'd accept?"

"Maybe we should just stop reading the letters altogether," Mary suggested. She ran her fingers through her hair. Her pretty face looked drawn; I noticed tight little lines around her mouth I hadn't seen before. She smiled up over her cup. "Let's go out for pizza with the kids tonight and cheer ourselves up."

In July the Marine Corps sent me instructions explaining how to write to prisoners of war. I could send a letter to Bill through the International Red Cross or in care of a National Liberation Front representative who was in Algiers, they said, but they couldn't guarantee the success of either method.

In a month's time correspondence had offered us sympathy for the loss of a loved one and instructions on how to write him. I stared at this latest letter from the Marine Corps lying in my lap. The more I thought about it, the funnier it seemed. I smiled to myself. Then, all alone in the living room, I started to giggle. I couldn't stop myself. I carried the letter with me into the bathroom so Bill's dad and grandmother who were in the kitchen wouldn't hear me. Then I held my hand over my mouth to stifle what had become hysterical laughing. I grabbed the sink with both hands and focused on the image in the mirror. "Who could write a letter to a dead man?" I asked. Then I sat down on the lid of the toilet and leaned my head on the wall next to it. Only a crazy person, I thought. I have to believe he's alive and write it fast, before the next blow—before the chaplain writes again, for instance.

I went straight into the bedroom, where I could be alone. He's alive, I kept telling myself. I took a pen and a stationery pad from a nightstand drawer and chose the words carefully. I didn't know how many strange hands would hold the letter or how many un-friendly eyes would read it before it reached Bill.

Dear Bill,
    We all pray for you and think of you every day and won-der where you are and how you are. I hope someday we will

hear from you too. But it doesn't matter as long as you are well.

The children are fine. I believe they've each grown two inches this summer. We go to the cottage with the folks and Aunt Lil, Aunt Maude, and Uncle Eddie every Sunday, and they love it.

The little one carries on with his lively antics. Thank goodness the folks have maintained a sense of humor thus far. Sean is so excited about starting school next fall. I hope he'll always be that way about it.

People have been wonderful. I keep hearing from Paul and Barbara, Kay and Ed, Ginny, Larry, Estelle, Maryanne, etc. Have seen Joe Homer, Bob and Nancy and Georgia and Andy.

Our families too have been great. My brother Bill is driving our car out from Illinois next weekend for me. Don't worry about us, Bill. We are well taken care of. We'll just wait until you're back with us no matter how long that takes. Sean and Terry and their mother miss you very much. God seems to give us strength when we need it. Keep the faith.

All my love as always,
Barbara

I had made a handwritten copy of the letter, addressed one to the International Red Cross and the other to a person with a strange-sounding name in Algiers. I clutched the two white envelopes in my hand and then walked to the mailbox at the end of the block. The sun streaked through tall trees onto the sidewalk. The old neighborhood was pleasant and peaceful on this balmy afternoon. Suddenly, standing in front of the mailbox, I wanted to scream, "Listen, people, something terrible is happening here. I am a Jewish woman in 1942 whose husband has been dragged off by storm troopers. I don't want any more of your sound advice. Don't tell me to go home, take a tranquilizer. Stop telling me to get out of the house more often. Go out to dinner. See a movie. In all the hell and chaos of World War II, would a Jewish wife have felt better getting out to more movies?" Hardly, I thought, yet that's what people were telling me. It seemed to me right then that I could have taken the siege of Britain, bombs and all, anything but the serenity of that quiet sunny street. I slipped the letters into the mailbox and wandered back to the house.

Gram, Dad, and the boys were all napping. I felt numb, almost nonexistent. I poured a bottle of Coke into a glass and flopped into a lawn chair in the backyard. There was something unreal about what was happening to Bill and me. Nothing had ever gone wrong for us, our kids, or our friends.

"Why us, Bill?" I asked into the air as if an answer would come from the unmoving trees. "Think how we always bounced from one good time to the next. Remember St. Patty's Day when I dyed my hair green? The Irish songs, the jig, the green beer?"

I took another sip of Coke. There wasn't a sound, not a breeze blowing in the little patch of backyard. I thought about the time they asked me to be Miss July in the Playboy Pageant at the officers' club in Pensacola. Bill didn't think I'd do it. I marched down the runway in those red satin shorts and blue satin halter covered with sparkling white sequins, while my Uncle Sam top hat bobbed to the strains of "The Stars and Stripes Forever." Finally Miss December emerged and there we were—all twelve months perched on our tall bar stools, legs crossed and smiling out at a ballroom full of officers and their ladies. Just as the band broke into "A Pretty Girl Is Like a Melody," Bill wiped a hand across his forehead. I saw him out of the corner of my eye and was pleased that he'd been so nervous for me. I strutted back to our table after the program. "I didn't fall on my fanny after all, did I?" I asked, poking him gently in the ribs.

He burst out laughing, his eyes crinkling at the edges. "No, but I was ready to run out the door if you had."

I could suddenly picture his face clearly. I felt as if he were standing by my lawn chair, bending over me. I could almost feel his strong arms around me. "I know you're here, Bill," I said. I felt his hand stroke my face; he kissed me and whispered, "Hang on, Barby. We'll be OK."

"Please forgive me for mailing that letter," I whispered back.

"Those sterile words weren't from me—to you. None of this is happening to us."

That night the ringing of our telephone jolted me awake at 2:00 A.M. I groped my way through the dark toward the nearest phone on the stand in the living room, but Bill's mother had already picked it up.

"He's what?" she said. "Are you sure? How do you know he's dead? You're a Marine officer?"

She handed me the phone. Her hands were shaking. "Who is this?" I asked. "I'm Captain Mullen's wife."

"I'm a Marine lieutenant, Ma'am. Jack Harris is my name. I served with Captain Mullen in Vietnam. I have some information that shouldn't be kept from you any longer. I'm calling from San Francisco."

"You're just back from Vietnam? Why isn't Washington calling? Why should you be calling?"

"Ma'am, listen to me. You have to know, and they won't tell you. That plane went down in a ball of fire and he couldn't have gotten out. I feel it's my duty to tell you the truth. Also, please, let me extend my sympathy."

"This is not what we heard from others. They said he used his radio on the ground. Why should they lie? Officers in his flight wouldn't lie. Why are you calling?" I gasped for breath. "Keep your sympathy! I don't want it."

I hung up and then began to shiver as I had the first night in the hotel room. Mary stared blankly at nothing and lit a cigarette. Bill's dad looked shaken for the first time. He made a weak attempt to object. "I don't care who says otherwise; he's alive. He's OK, I tell you." He got up and walked into the adjoining parlor. Pulling the lace curtain back, he looked out at the dark street.

At 8:00 A.M. we called Marine Corps Headquarters in Washington. The Marine captain who answered was horrified by the incident. He said he would find out if there was an officer by that name on leave in San Francisco. When he called back twenty minutes later, he said, "I'm sorry to admit that the call you received was from a Marine officer all right. I was hoping to tell you it was a crank protester or something. He spent most of his tour in Vietnam filing casualty reports. We understand you're not the first next-of-kin he has contacted."

"But what about the information he gave us—what he said about Bill's plane?" I asked.

"It seems he has the phone numbers written down, but he confuses the facts when he calls, especially after he's had a few drinks."

"Can't you stop him?" I asked.

"I wish we could stop him," he said. "But it's difficult. Sometimes these men who return without injury feel a terrible guilt that they've come back at all. It doesn't make sense. But try to understand, the man needs help."

"I understand," I said. "Thank you, sir. We'll try to forget it happened."

Mary hadn't moved from the sofa all night. She was lighting another cigarette. Dad had gone back upstairs to pray. "I guess we're fair game for all of them," I said. "Optimists, pessimists, commanding officers, friends, chaplains. And now, disturbed veterans."

5. THE SEARCH

Gram was nestled in her place at the end of the sofa. Her lips moved slightly as she fingered the rosary beads in her lap one at a time. Dad was upstairs praying, I supposed. I walked past Gram into the parlor and over to the corner where the upright piano stood as it had for twenty-odd years against the wall by the window. Running my fingers absently across the closed lid, I glanced numbly at photographs spread across its top. Familiar faces smiled as they had through good times and bad—this afternoon in defiance of all reason, it seemed.

The quiet house made me restless. I strolled down the hall and stopped in front of the mirror just to be sure that I was real. There was a new haunted look in my eyes that startled me. I recognized the face, but felt as if I were looking at a stranger. It was as though I'd lost the notion of myself as a person.

We couldn't go on living the way we were, me with no sense of direction, the children wandering aimlessly as they chose, and all of us crammed into a six-room flat. Until that day it hadn't occurred to me to move or plan beyond the moment, but now I hurried to the kitchen, found the newspaper, and began to study ads for apartments in the area. I felt certain that a strong woman

would take some sort of action. Since I nearly burst into tears at
the end of each ad I read, I doubted I was that strong woman,
however. I was glad I had time to compose myself before Mary
came home.

I let her put away a bag of groceries, flop into a chair, and light
a cigarette before I told her of my decision. I was thankful that
my voice sounded as if it belonged to a sane person. If Mary were
to detect my true emotional state, I was afraid she might not
want to set me loose in the world with two helpless youngsters at
my mercy.

A week later we moved into a small apartment in a complex of
identical duplex buildings. I bought a stiff-backed green sofa with
a matching chair and two end tables that were sold as a group.
When Mary saw them, she commented, "I hope they'll last the
six months it'll take you to pay for them."

We resurrected a kitchen table, three chairs, and an antique
metal bed from the folks' cellar. I bought two foam mattresses at
a discount store and laid them out on the floor to use as beds for
the boys. We picked up some cardboard boxes at the supermarket
to serve as bureaus, and I borrowed four towels, four washcloths,
and some pots and pans from Mary. I never bought more than
two days' worth of groceries at a time. After all, it's just a temporary arrangement, I told myself.

I found that carrying on for the sake of the children was a
double-edged sword. I was now solely responsible for them again.
There was the burden that came with putting up a front of cheer-
fulness and normalcy, while I was distracted with worry about
Bill. When the children's peace of mind was threatened, however,
I realized just how crucial their adjustment was to my own well-
being. Terry was having difficulty orienting to the new place. He'd
wake up during the night, leap out of bed, and run from room to
room, screaming, "Manthas are after me, Mom!" I'd scoop him up
and carry him back to my bed, where he'd snuggle close and tell me
about the praying mantises that were trying to chase him out of the
house. "They're bigger than me, Mom, and green, real green,"
he'd whisper breathlessly until he fell back to sleep.

In the morning he would seem to feel better. I'd feed the children, take them for walks, and read to them. Then at night, by myself, I'd pray to anyone listening to please get us through another day.

On sleepless nights I plotted searches I would undertake to uncover information about Bill. Someone, somewhere, had to know about him. Who, I'd ask myself. The Marine Corps? Our intelligence agencies? If they knew, then why wouldn't they tell me? Perhaps they would tell someone else, someone they trusted more than me, and I could squeeze the information from that person or organization or authority.

I made a list of the most likely recipients of such information; I decided I would investigate them one at a time. Each week I followed up on another hunch dreamed up in the early morning hours. Settling the boys down with a baby sitter or Grampa, I would drive off in my blue Tempest bent on securing that precious bit of information that would confirm Bill's whereabouts or condition or both.

I started with the local Red Cross, only to be greeted by an elderly lady who told me a long story about the remains of a young man killed in World War II which had just been returned. I shouldn't give up hope, she said. One by one, I crossed the possibilities off my list: a Marine recruiting officer in Brockton, a Marine reserve detachment at Otis Air Force Base on Cape Cod, a Marine chaplain at a nearby Navy Reserve base.

Then one morning I woke up and realized I had nowhere to go. In a frenzy I drove back to the Navy Reserve station and burst into the chaplain's office. He quickly sent me to the medical dispensary, where a young doctor issued me a bottle of tranquilizers.

That evening I faced the truth. All my ideas had been used up. As a military wife, I'd contemplated the most terrible possibility: My husband might one day give his life for his country. But never had I imagined the horror of simply being out of touch with him, having no means of contacting him and no one on earth who could tell me anything about him. I had always had confidence that the Marine Corps would stand by me through any adversity. I hadn't bargained on their silence.

About this time I began to consider the likelihood that there was no information about these missing men because they were all dead. Perhaps this enemy didn't believe in taking prisoners and we were all fooling ourselves. And then a film was released by Hanoi and shown on U.S. television. I watched captured American pilots being dragged through the streets of Hanoi by North Vietnamese soldiers. The men, some wounded, bandaged, and limping, were forced at the end of bayonets to walk in a humiliating bowed position through jeering crowds. I tried to get a glimpse of their faces, but with their heads bent it was difficult. The film was over quickly, and the news went on to another story. I was stunned by the inhumanity of the exhibition, but still, racing through my mind was: "Thank God, there are some alive."

One of the pilots identified was Commander James Mulligan of Lawrence, Massachusetts, whose story along with a picture of his wife, Louise, and their children appeared on the front page of the *Boston Globe.* That same day, having read the article several times, I wrote a letter to Louise Mulligan, in care of the newspaper. She telephoned as soon as she received my note and, after a brief chat, we planned to meet for lunch the following day.

It was with a feeling of both eagerness and trepidation that I drove to the restaurant we had agreed upon. What would she look like, I kept asking myself, this woman who was sharing my nightmare? I pulled into Monroe's crowded parking lot at noon. A woman, perhaps in her mid-thirties, was standing by the front entrance. A bright print dress offset her shoulder-length blond hair, and her face seemed unperturbed. If I had expected that Louise Mulligan would appear haggard or exhausted, I was wrong. I locked the car door and walked over to her.

"I'm so glad you wrote me," she said, stretching her hand out to mine. "Let's go in."

We sat down in the front of the dining room, where green plants overflowed from baskets before a large bay window. I hadn't been in a restaurant like this in a long time, and I suddenly wished we were there for a more pleasant reason. I ran a finger down a crystal vase in the center of the table and looked at the woman across from me. Her deep blue eyes were intense and serious. "You can't imagine how alone I've felt," I said. "When I read about you and Jim in the paper, I couldn't wait to meet you. No one else, no one can understand what it's been like—except another woman who's been through it."

"That's true, but I don't know how much help I can be right now," Louise said. "The past few days have been so hectic."

The waitress had come over to our table. "Why don't we order a drink first," I said.

"Let's do that," Louise agreed, managing her first smile.

When the waitress had gone, I said, "Tell me everything. How have you made it through the past months since Jim's plane was shot down? You didn't know any more than I—until the other day, did you? I haven't had anyone in our situation to talk to. I've thought I was going crazy at times—that this couldn't be happening. I just can't find out what's happened to Bill. . . ." I seemed to be raving and she was sitting there looking serene and in charge and just listening. My God, I thought, why can't I be like that? "I'm sure Bill was captured," I said more calmly. "Everything points to that."

"The worst is not knowing," Louise said. There was something straightforward and reassuring about her voice. "Those nights of doubting and days of hearing nothing are an indescribable horror. I can't tell you how I've gotten through it. But I do have some other missing-in-action wives near me in Virginia. I know that has helped. Reporters are calling at all hours now, but when I begin to feel sorry for myself, I think how lucky I am to know for sure that Jim is alive."

"I'd give anything for that—anything," I said, realizing that this woman was the only person I knew who would understand exactly what I meant. I asked if she knew anyone I could contact for information, and she said she was sure channels would open up now that some POW names had been released.

We talked about places we'd been stationed, our husbands and children. I was astonished to learn that this composed and youthful-looking woman was the mother of six sons. My admiration for her seemed to grow by the minute.

I placed my fork under the smallest possible portion of shrimp salad, knowing my stomach would resist more than a few bites. "Do you think they're being tortured?" I asked her.

"I suppose so," she said. "The Defense Department seems to know very little about their treatment. We can assume that the enemy is trying to get statements out of them, though."

"I'm sure it's worse in Laos," I said. "The Communists are on the move along the Ho Chi Minh Trail, and then there's the U.S. bombing. I suppose I shouldn't be mentioning Laos, really. The military hasn't told me that's where Bill went down. I heard it from Bill's friend, who said he'd be in trouble if the Marine Corps found out he'd told me."

We finished our glass of wine and sat at the table as long as we could. I knew Louise would be returning to her home in Virginia the coming week, and I suddenly felt more alone than ever. "We'll keep in touch," she said, as if she'd read my thoughts. "Call me anytime you want. If I hear of any new channels to pursue for information, I'll let you know."

I sat in my car for a minute to collect my thoughts before leaving. The lunch had gone well. As I watched her car drive away, though, I wondered if we were really just twins deceiving one another.

I decided to write *Life* magazine that afternoon and ask for an enlargement of their picture of the captured pilots in the streets of Hanoi. Spurred on by Louise's good fortune, I daydreamed that Bill might be in front of one of those bayonets, too. When the photo came, I studied it with a magnifying glass. The outlines of bodies were fuzzy and facial features were blurred, but I knew none of the men was Bill.

In the coming weeks I heard often from Louise in Virginia Beach, Virginia, where a small but growing enclave of husbandless wives were congregating. The Navy was bombarding the women with do's and don't's, which Louise passed on to me by phone and letter. An air of authority came with the knowledge that one's husband was alive, and I accepted Louise's declarations as gospel.

She wrote:

> When you're talking to the press, the Navy says to give nothing that could be used adversely toward your husband. Have your neighbor or friend play telephone secretary. In fact, we shouldn't talk to the press ourselves at all. The Navy reminds us that we won't be our real selves in our present emotional state.
>
> The Navy says no one can help us—not the Defense Department or miscellaneous organizations. We shouldn't write to Communist leaders or heads of state. It could upset possible negotiations or serve propaganda efforts. When you write Bill, don't mention names of the children, your friends, or events, and above all, don't write your troubles. If you hear from him, send the letter immediately to Washington for analysis.

Louise conveyed a sense of stability and control which I envied. She believed in prayer, for one thing. She sent me a powerful novena to be said each hour for nine consecutive hours. She was certain that prayer, along with having met Senator Ted Kennedy, had been the reason for public identification of Jim. I didn't dare question her reasoning; I wanted to believe something worked. I followed her instructions to the letter. I prayed and prayed, with no result. Insidious recriminations gnawed away at me. Doesn't Bill possess the ingenuity to surface somewhere? Aren't my prayers intense enough?

All the while, Louise's spirits remained high. "I'm certain you'll hear something soon, and then you'll be in a position to make decisions," she wrote. Another dispatch began, "Please let me explain. The reason I haven't written is that we've lost three very dear friends, two off the *Oriskany* and another off the *FDR*." But farther down the page she insisted, "I'm still very optimistic about this whole situation, and the feeling is the same among most of our military friends. I definitely feel that about November or December you will see some big changes being made; this purge in China is being felt all over."

A purge in China. I hadn't felt it at all, especially with regard to Bill's being alive or not. I was now sure my present geographic distance from the military was leaving me at quite a disadvantage. Try as I might, I couldn't divert my attention to China.

Though her advice sometimes eluded me, Louise's friendship made me feel I was not a lonely freak in a world of normal people. There was an indisputable difference in our situations, though. She no longer shared the uncertainty of life or death in the same way I did. She had seen Jim whole, walking down a Hanoi street—and the Communists would have to produce him at the end of the war. I needed that same assurance in the form of a tape, a photo, or a name released. And I was determined to get it one way or another.

The days fell one into another. Often it surprised me that the events of man and nature continued to evolve. Lucy Johnson had been married in fairy-tale fashion, Martin Luther King, Jr., feverishly pursued his dream, and now the leaves were turning color.

Sean went off to kindergarten, starting his school career with a show of courage. "Don't tell the teacher I'm scared, Mom," he said. "I'm going to try it out. If I like it, I'll stay. If I don't, I won't." I gave him a hug, but he shrugged me off and ran outside to the waiting VW van. He climbed in and looked straight ahead without turning back to wave.

That afternoon he slammed the apartment door and made a run for my arms. He let me hold him for an instant, and then he planted a wet kiss on my cheek. He wiggled away and made a dash for the kitchen. "What's to eat, Mom? Hey, next time you write Daddy, tell him school was neat and I was the biggest kid in the whole kindergarten!"

On another autumn afternoon Sean and Terry were riding up and down in front of the apartment on tricycles with new friends.

It was a glorious day of yellow sunshine, crisp air, and brown and orange leaves. The spirit of the day seemed to cry out for some kind of action. I would dial Marine Corps Headquarters, I decided, and this time I wouldn't be ignored.

"Yes, Mrs. Mullen," a sergeant answered, "we'll try to locate your husband's file, but I'm sure if you haven't heard from us it's because we have newer cases than yours to take care of. Calling Marine Headquarters only uses our valuable time, you know. And it serves no purpose."

"No purpose, Sergeant?" My tone was full of disbelief, and suddenly I was angry. "I haven't heard a thing from headquarters for months. I want to speak to Colonel Abblitt. He's head of Casualty Branch, isn't he?"

"I'll see if I can find him. Just a minute," he said.

A few seconds later I heard the colonel's businesslike voice. "Yes, Mrs. Mullen. We'll be getting a letter off to you in the next few days."

"I don't want a letter, Colonel," I said. "I've been waiting five months for a letter. Why can't you just answer my questions? I want to hear something officially. Did Bill get out of the plane? Was his radio heard on the ground? For how long?"

He cleared his throat before speaking. His words came slowly. "This is off the record, remember," he said. "Radio beacons on the distress frequency were heard. My personal rationale is that it was your husband operating the radio. Then, later on, the radio fell silent, at which time we presumed he was entrapped. When it was heard again, the radio seemed to be in the hands of the enemy."

"Is that all?" I asked.

"Yes," he answered.

"Thank you, Colonel. I suppose that's really what I wanted you to tell me. A friend of my husband's told me that a long time ago, but I wanted—I needed—to hear it officially. I only wanted you to verify what he told me."

"Sorry that it took so long, Mrs. Mullen," he said. "There are some things that are classified. But we are understaffed. And we're busier every day. Really, call back whenever you want. I'll try to talk to you personally. We are trying our best."

"Thank you for the information, Colonel," I said, but I was still angry when I got off the phone. Why had it taken five months to squeeze those few precious words out of them? Why hadn't they trusted me with such personal, vital facts? What harm could there have been in that?

I had believed all along that Bill was alive, and my conversation with Colonel Abblitt left me feeling more anxious than ever to confirm it. I sat at the table long after I'd hung up the phone, thinking about past fruitless visits and other telephone calls and letters. My plea to the Vice President had gotten me a vague reply from the Commandant of the Marine Corps; my letter to a senator had brought the same response from the Deputy Director of the Corps. Perhaps I'd just been aiming too high. This time I would write to a congressman, I decided. A representative might take a more personal interest.

I dashed off a note to my Michigan congressman quickly, before I lost heart. "Dear Congressman Cleavenger," I wrote. "My husband is a fine officer, devoted to the Marine Corps, who always performed his duties willingly, regardless of risk. I have not wanted to spoil his record by acting in a manner unbecoming to an officer's wife. Nevertheless I am asking you to help me. I must contact my husband somehow. . . ."

I tossed the congressman's answer on the kitchen table where Mary and Dad were sitting a few weeks later. "What's the use of contacting anyone?" I said. "He sent my letter on to the Marine Corps, the same as all the others we've written. You'd think I was mailing out letter bombs, they get rid of them so fast. I'll have to find some other way to get through to Bill."

"I hope you can, Barbara," Mary said doubtfully. She kept stirring the coffee in her cup. "I've run out of ideas, and energy, too."

The next day I read in the Brockton newspaper that a Marine pilot from Bill's old squadron in Vietnam had returned and was based at nearby Weymouth Air Station. When I called him, I was surprised that he sounded so excited, really anxious to see me. I should come that same afternoon, he said.

I hadn't seen anyone from the squadron since the day of Bill's departure, so I dressed carefully, putting on a new blue sweater and a matching skirt. I was grateful that Mary had forced me to buy some new clothes. Also, that the sweater was bulky, disguising the weight I'd lost. I brushed away at my shag hairdo—grown shaggy beyond its original intentions—until I gave up, threw the brush on the bureau, and ran out to the car.

Reality had a way of sweeping over me, unexpected, hot, and suffocating as a Santa Ana wind. Just being on a military base again, seeing the short hair and the uniforms, had this effect. I parked in front of a building marked "U.S. Marine Corps Reserve," flopped the visor down, and took a last look in the tiny mirror.

Major Haley had seen me drive up. He came out to the hallway and shook my hand. "Come on in, Barbara. It's good to see you." I was relieved to see that he looked unchanged. He introduced me to a young lieutenant who was in his office. The lieutenant took my coat, and Major Haley offered me a chair. I was at home. It was so ordinary and natural; I expected Bill to stroll in the door any minute.

They started right in talking about Vietnam, news of the squadron and how it really was over there. The lieutenant's first story was about a pilot who, sixty miles from his base, with his plane torn up by enemy fire and his legs mangled and bleeding, had flown home, rather than eject. As the men talked and I listened, I noticed that most of their stories were about comrades who had made it home safely.

Maybe this is how they sustain themselves in battle, I thought. If one had the will, one could survive. But what about those who didn't manage to return, I wondered. Were they placed in a "less than" category? What of those who merely vanished? Was their behavior considered to be unprofessional?

I glanced at my watch. "Can you tell me where Bill went down exactly?" I asked.

"Where Bill went down," the major answered, "is one of the worst possible areas. Heavy, heavy enemy concentration. He must have landed right in the middle of their camp. It was five miles from the target; he got that far, which was good. That's where the radio signals were heard."

The lieutenant broke in. "We had three guys killed in that area in a week. One radioed that he was hit, straight through his thigh. He was told to go over the sea but decided he could make it home. He was never heard from again. Must have been so weak he just crashed. If he'd gone down at sea, it wouldn't have mattered anyway. With his bleeding the sharks would have got him. Sharks out there are as long as a room."

"About Bill—" I purposely addressed the major, who I thought more likely to stick to the subject. "Exactly what do you know?"

He waited several seconds, long enough for my heart to move into my throat. "Bill was on a snake-eyes run. Major Hornsby, the flight leader, saw a flash under his plane as they both were turning up into the clouds. He told Bill on the radio that his plane had been hit."

"Was a parachute ever seen?" I asked.

"A forward air control prop plane saw a flash and smoke on the ground. It must have been Bill's plane going into the trees. He was flying at treetop level. You can bail out in an A4E at that altitude going ninety knots an hour. It has a good seat. Nothing was unsafe about his bailing out at that altitude. A fluorescent yellow panel was seen in the trees. That was the color we were using that day."

"And the radio, what about the radio? I heard there was radio contact." I stared at the major so the lieutenant wouldn't try to answer.

"Bill's beeper signals were heard immediately from the ground," the major said. "Some sort of voice, but not identifiable, was heard. There was something wrong with the voice transmitter. He answered instructions immediately, though. He was told, 'If you hear me, turn on the beeper.' The radio went off, and then he was told to turn it on for two minutes. Each instruction he was given he followed exactly."

The lieutenant interrupted. "The Commies probably had already spotted him when he was using the radio, but let him continue in order to bring down other chickens in the rescue mission. Flares are no good in those jungles. The pilot sees the helos in the distance and tries to head a flare in their direction, but he wouldn't send one up until the helo was close enough to drop a ladder he could jump onto. Usually before he can send the flare, though, the helos have headed in a different way. Those damn mountains in Laos are higher and more rugged than those in Vietnam. The jungle cover is a hundred and fifty feet near the Mia Gia Pass. Flares won't even penetrate that jungle canopy, and the helos can't see a thing on the ground."

"Do you have any idea when I might hear that he is a prisoner?" I addressed the major, but the lieutenant answered again.

"They use all their tricks as soon as they capture them. It used to take us days to get all the information we wanted out of our prisoners; now we know how to get it within hours. I imagine they have their means also."

The major gave him a withering look. "In Laos," he said, "we never hear unless they move them north. Lieutenant Dengler— you must have read about him this summer—was near the North Vietnam border when he escaped. We hope they take Bill up north where he'll be safer. We know where the camps in North Vietnam are. They're all supposed to be off limits to bombing. Of course, B-52s can't pinpoint that well in Laos." He paused for a few seconds, and then as an afterthought he said, "Maybe our government knows more than they divulge about who is held where."

While I savored that possibility, the lieutenant began another story. "An Air Force plane went down at night the same day as Bill in the same area with two aboard, the pilot and a radar interceptor," he said. "Their voice transmissions wouldn't work. They didn't use the beeper's signal either because they were afraid it might not work well. They should save it, they figured, for morning. That night they moved away from the enemy and came to a clearing. When a helo went over, they turned on the beeper and were picked up. One had a broken shoulder, but otherwise he was OK. They were clever all right."

52

Though I was sure the men didn't mean to be insensitive, I almost felt I should apologize for Bill's failure to escape so smoothly. I got up from the chair and held out my hand to the lieutenant. He grasped it firmly. "I'd better go now," I said. "Thanks so much. Both of you."

Major Haley walked down the hall with me. "Good luck, now, to you and the boys. Come back out again if you like," he said.

"Good-bye. Thanks," I repeated. I felt sorry for him. I imagined him going back to the office where they would resume telling their stories. What will they do with their grim memories when they tire of relating them to one another, I wondered.

When I got home from the Navy base, there was another letter from Larry Robinson in my mailbox:

I flew to Thailand this week in order to talk to the rescue coordinator for our part of the country. Everything the coordinator said reaffirmed the likelihood of Bill being captured and being a prisoner of war. He said Bill was probably surrounded by enemy troops during the afternoon and captured just prior to dark. The last positive radio response was received at about 5:00 P.M. We all believe Bill was captured, Barbara. Colonel Gray says he will come back with two thousand Vietnamese singing "Danny Boy."

The versions of what happened, contributed by those few who'd been there, were beginning to fit together, and the stories all ended at 5:00 P.M. But what really happened at 5:00 P.M. when Bill was discovered and surrounded and entrapped? Sitting upright in the old brass bed at two in the morning, staring out my curtainless window, I envisioned the rest of the story. At first it was blurry, but with practice I polished off details. The drama unfolded on a screen inside my head. I saw him caught and mistreated by men who hated him. He was beaten, tortured, dragged off, put in a cage, then moved to a campsite where buildings were ruggedly constructed of wood strips, thatch, and bamboo. Finally taken from the cage, he was fed something white and mushy from a bowl, put in a shack, and chained to the wall.

Soon the guards also became real to me. They acquired personalities. There were three—one cruel, one stupid, and one noncommittal. Noncommittal was best. I was glad when he was on duty. I gave them names one night, but I discarded that—how could I have known their names?

Filling in Bill's thoughts was the only good part. It lent newness; I could put something different in his mind as often as I wanted. He could be nostalgic, resentful, resolved, tough, or whatever I needed. In pain, neglected, suffering, BUT ALIVE!

6. DISCONNECTED

ADDISON, ILLINOIS, DECEMBER 1966 A sliver of December sun slipped through the uncovered windows. In the corner of the bedroom Terry had rolled off his foam mattress and was curled up on the bare wood floor beside it; a few feet away, Sean lay perfectly straight on his mattress, arms at his sides, resting as seriously as he did everything else. Sean's clothes were carefully stacked in what was left of a cardboard container next to him. Terry's grocery carton, having lost its functional value, had been kicked into a corner. Next to the crumpled box, his socks, jeans, and underwear were tossed in a pile that was topped by one red and-white sneaker. A fire engine and a dump truck, prized presents from Grampa, guarded the foot of each mattress. I came into the room, picked up Terry's blankets strewn over the floor, and covered him. We're living like refugees, I thought.

The place was exactly as it had been the day we moved in. The walls were still bare, the floors uncarpeted; there were no curtains at the windows. My children needed a real home. All my instincts told me this, though the thought of settling into any kind of new life frightened me, as if it were an admission that Bill's disappearance was not a freak episode soon to be solved, but a continuing reality that we might have to live with.

My brother had been suggesting for weeks that we move to Illinois. He said he could find an apartment for us near him and his family. So far I'd avoided making a decision, but the more I thought about it, the more it seemed the best alternative. At least we could get our belongings out of storage and have our beds and bureaus, books and dishes and stuffed animals around us again. I could try to make a home for us.

I knew saying good-bye to Dad and Gram and Mary would be difficult. My leaving was an acknowledgment for all of us that our months of anxiety had ended without conclusion. "We'll keep in close touch," Mary said the morning we packed up. Leaning her head through the car window, she gave me a farewell kiss. "Call us soon as you get there."

The boys waved through the back window as we drove off. In the rearview mirror I watched Mary, Dad, and Gram blowing kisses until we reached the end of the block and turned the corner.

Two weeks later we moved into our third home in a period of six months. Our new apartment was located in Addison, a dreary industrial town outside of Chicago that bordered on my brother's bedroom community. Though a relatively new building, it had already taken on an air of grayness, the way a chameleon turns the color of its surroundings. Flimsy trees sprouting bare branches blended into a background of gray sky and dirty cement parking lots.

Three days before Christmas, on Terry's fourth birthday, the moving van unloaded our effects. I'd hoped that unwrapping the familiar items would bring me comfort, but I was surprised it had the opposite effect. Each object seemed to conjure its own memory. A butcher knife flashed a picture of Bill slicing a Sunday roast; a music box, a birthday party in a Quonset hut. I kept running to the bathroom to brush away tears.

By Christmas Eve I had unpacked the most needed items and hung some drapes. The boys had finally accepted my promises that Santa knew we had moved to Illinois and that he would find us. I kissed them good night and then collapsed into a chair in the living room. The only light came from a tiny Christmas tree in the corner that I had trimmed halfheartedly early that morning. As far as I was concerned, this would be just an imitation Christmas. The last real one was the one we'd spent together as a family in California. I thought back on it and was pleased I remembered every detail of the day.

I woke Bill in the morning by brushing my hand over his forehead and stroking his curly hair lightly with the tips of my fingers. Still half asleep, he'd pulled me gently toward him, his lips brushing against my neck and cheek. He kissed me softly on the lips. "It's early," he said. "Don't worry, the babies will sleep another hour." I smiled and snuggled closer. This was our time.

A couple of hours later Santa had brought his trains, trucks, and Lego blocks. The turkey was in the oven and Bill had dragged the boys off to the bathtub. They were now wearing short white pants, navy bow ties, and red blazers. "Look at those pouting faces," Bill said. "You'd think I'd just tortured them."

"Quick, let's take a picture," I said, grabbing a new camera from under the tree.

Terry's shirt had already come out of his pants, and his tie was twisted to the side. Bill patted his behind. "Please sit still, Terry—till Daddy counts to ten. And pretend you can smile, OK?"

The bar and hors d'oeuvres were set up in the TV room, and delicious aromas from the kitchen permeated the house. "The place looks beautiful, Barbara," Bill said, and he looked pleased.

I lit green candles and set the last red napkin on the table just as my brother Floyd, his wife Yolanda, and their two-year-old daughter, Annie, came through the front door. Ginny and Larry Robinson arrived a few minutes later with their two baby girls, and friends from the battalion dropped in throughout the afternoon until the house was full. Bill and Larry demonstrated a soft shoe number and Yolanda tried to teach us the Watusi as babies ran unharnessed from room to room. After we had eaten, with everyone in a mellow mood, Bill played the piano; we sang Christmas carols and talked for hours.

It was early morning before everyone had left. The children had been sleeping soundly for hours. Bill unplugged the tree lights while I blew out the last candle. He came into the dining room and slipped both hands around my waist, and we held one another for a long, quiet moment.

In bed I laid my head on his chest, snuggling into the curve of his neck just above the curly dark hair on his chest. He'd fallen asleep almost at once. I listened to his even breathing until it synchronized so perfectly with my own that I could no longer hear it.

I hoped Bill was reliving that day, too, wherever he was. Suddenly I felt revived and not quite so alone in our strange new home. I wanted to wrap the rest of the presents and assemble toys I had bought. If I searched, I might be able to find more tree trimmings, too, I thought.

When the boys woke me at 6:00 A.M., I was ready for them. Terry made a run for the rocking horse and climbed onto the saddle. "Yahoo!" he screamed, twirling one arm in the air and pointing a finger at the ceiling. Sean tore away at the packages. Ripping glittery paper off a long red racing car, he smiled and shook his head. "This is from Daddy, I know. Isn't it, Mom?"

"It's what he wanted you to have, sweetie. I'm sure of that," I said. Drained, but grateful, I whispered a thank-you into the air. "We made it."

Once we were settled and waiting in Illinois, I took a wider interest in the war, which until then had seemed more of a personal injury. Though I still hounded people for information about Bill, I slowly accepted the fact that I wouldn't see him until the war ended.

During December, before Christmas, peace rumors had run rampant. My optimism soared when President Johnson attended a Southeast Asia conference in Manila and presented his peace plan: The United States would agree to leave South Vietnam if the North Vietnamese did the same; the North would remain communist and the Saigon government would continue to rule in the

South; all the troops would go home and the country would be at peace.

By January I felt sure the war would be over in a matter of weeks. My moods swung from frantic to euphoric. I didn't see how I'd have time to transform our apartment into a home, but I attacked its blandness with fervor.

Though Bill had been captured for six months, I figured he'd be in fairly good condition. President Johnson and Averell Harriman had both said publicly that they thought the American prisoners were being well-treated. This comforted me, and I marveled that they knew how those men in prisons in North Vietnam, huts in South Vietnam, and caves in Laos were treated. I was thankful for whatever intelligence network our government had set up to come up with such positive information.

My anticipation, however, was short-lived. The rebels said they would gain nothing by agreeing to President Johnson's Manila plan, and General Westmoreland thought the United States was far from finished in South Vietnam. There was a great deal more to do, he said, "in order to root out the guerrilla infrastructure deeply embedded in the South Vietnamese countryside."

That winter the argument over the war grew more heated; the Senate had split more precisely into hawks and doves. Senators Mike Mansfield, Robert Kennedy, and others threatened to slow down President Johnson's request for 4.5 billion dollars in military hardware, while others said that doing so would deprive the half million Americans in Southeast Asia of food, clothing, and arms.

In a Senate speech, Bobby Kennedy declared, "We are not in Vietnam to play the part of an avenging angel pouring death and destruction on the roads and factories and homes of a guilty land."

But the same day, President Johnson informed the Senate that our bombing was "imposing a major cost" on North Vietnam. "We shall persist," he said, ". . . until those who launched this aggression are prepared to reinstall the agreements whose violation has brought the scourge of war to Southeast Asia."

I read the arguments and listened and grew confused. In a corner of my kitchen was a desk on which I wrote scribbled notes at odd hours to heads of state asking questions that they didn't answer. During more sensible moments I berated myself for this obsessive behavior the way a closet drinker would when sober. As the monster in Southeast Asia grew, I charted its development on a small bulletin board behind my desk. Each month the *Navy Times* devoted eight square inches to a cumulative accounting of casualties.

I hung the clippings in a neat horizontal row across the top of the board. January 1967: 6,319 dead, 374 missing, 94 reported to be prisoners. February 1967: 6,711 dead, 380 missing, 102 reported to be prisoners. April 1967: 9,226 dead, 395 missing, 153 reported to be prisoners. Looking at it made me feel more in control. They weren't putting anything over on me: I knew what the numbers were.

One evening pictures of a lovely white building in Vientiane, the Nationalist capital of Laos, flashed across my TV screen. A news commentator said that the structure housed hundreds of CIA officials. Visible within its compound were men in crisp white shorts energetically whipping tennis balls back and forth. I immediately wrote a letter to the CIA, in care of "Those Concerned with POWs in Laos," Washington, D.C. I suggested that between tennis matches or at the next cocktail party they could ask around for information on POWs held captive in that country. I knew it sounded disrespectful, but I no longer believed their claims that our prisoners were well-treated. If they knew that, why didn't they know more—who was alive, for instance.

Within two weeks, in a plain envelope, I received an assurance that the intelligence community understood its responsibility to these men.

Once I typed a letter, made a hundred copies, and sent one to each United States senator, asking what this war was all about. I also wrote the head of the Red Cross in Geneva, Secretary-General of the United Nations, leaders of neutral governments, and presidents of Communist countries pleading for information about Bill. Frustrated at their lack of response, I decided to circumvent all intermediaries. I wrote to Ho Chi Minh that I was coming to see him. Then I wrote the State Department requesting permission to go.

By return mail the State Department turned down my request to visit North Vietnam. I thought it would be difficult to top that effort until one night I glanced down at my sheet of stationery. I had perfectly and legibly written, "Dear God," and it struck me that my ideas were becoming too imaginative.

As we grew used to life in Illinois, I measured time in terms of news reports, loads of washing, and trips to the supermarket. I pushed my body out of the door to attend night classes at a local college and plodded through the studies. Without my family, I'd have had no adult companionship. My mother and sister Jean drove out from Chicago every week or so to visit, and every Friday night, unless someone was ill, I had dinner at the country club with my brother Bill and his wife, Pug. I viewed the beautiful people in the dining room from a distance as if I were invisible. Yet I looked forward to repeating the ritual each week.

I was a round peg in a world full of square slots. Married without a partner. Unattached but not single. Once I was invited to a party in the apartment building. I changed my dress three times, rechecked my lipstick, added mascara. I teased, pushed, and sprayed my hair, then brushed it out and began all over.

People began to arrive. There was laughter and the sound of music coming from above. The boys were asleep. I'd told them where I'd be. But when I stepped out into the hall, I suddenly felt woozy. As I started up the stairs, my head began to spin so badly that I had to stop and hold onto the banister. When the swirling stopped, I turned and ran back down to my apartment. I closed the door, secured the chain lock, and then stood still for a moment, my heart pounding. I removed my dress and wrapped myself in an old terry-cloth robe. The heart palpitations had slowed. I poured equal quantities of scotch and water into a glass, and in the dark I listened to the sounds from another planet.

My only clearly defined role was with my children. We were becoming pals. The three of us trotted off to just about every museum, zoo, and children's theater in the Chicago area. One Sunday I panicked until I found a Cinderella production we hadn't seen. I soon realized why it wasn't listed under children's entertainment. The stepsisters were jealous of a relationship between Cinderella and her stepmother that had nothing to do with sweeping the floor and cleaning chimneys.

On a Saturday afternoon, just a few weeks later, Terry securely fastened himself to a post in the lobby of a Chicago theater before announcing to everyone within earshot, "I'm not going to any more of these dumb shows that don't have any popcorn!"

I pried him loose with the promise of a hot fudge sundae, but prudently sat us near the rear of the theater. Intuition told me this was a smart move, and I was right. At the most crucial moment Terry leaped out of his seat, ran into the aisle, and bellowed, "Don't eat it, Peter Pan! The shit gave you poison!"

I whipped us out onto State Street, pulling Terry by the collar. "Damn it, anyway," I screeched. "John-John would never do this to Jackie Kennedy!"

Sean backed away from the two of us, looking aghast. Why does that kid always act so superior, I thought. I was about to ask him who the heck he thought he was when Terry screamed, "Who's John-John?"

They both stood still and stared at me. "Yeah, who is John-John?" I said. I put an arm around each of them, hugged them to my sides, and laughed. "We're supposed to be having fun. Let's go get that hot fudge sundae, guys."

"Hey, neat," Sean said, smiling for the first time, probably glad the whole day wasn't going to be a washout. "I'm having marshmallow on mine."

At the ice cream parlor I asked the boys if they'd like to take up ice skating. "There's a rink not far from home," I said. "Maybe we've had enough of museums and theaters for a while."

"Wow," they answered in unison, peering up from mounds of chocolate ice cream and fudge sauce.

"You too, Mom. Are you going to do it, too?" Terry asked, grinning and then aiming a sidelong glance toward Sean.

"I don't want you two making fun of me. Of course I'm going to ice-skate. I'll show you both."

For one month, terrified, I clung to the outside wall of the skating rink while they both whizzed by me. Then one morning, in a rare moment of fearless abandonment, Sean sped past his brother, lost control, stumbled forward, and fell face down on the ice. A large hulk of a man picked him up where he lay unconscious. We were in the hospital emergency room before Sean revived. "What's the matter, Mom?" he asked, blinking his eyes. "I beat Terry, didn't I?" After a few days of observation at the hospital, the doctor gave him a clean bill of health but suggested that I go home for a rest. I was happy to oblige.

The children chased each other around the parking lot for the next few weeks, waiting for summer to arrive. On the first warm day we switched to swimming lessons, which meant I could plop into a lounge chair with a good book for an hour of peace and quiet every morning while someone else took charge.

On the first day, the children were grouped according to height, which is why Terry ended up with the seven-year-olds. I had barely sunk into my chair outside the fence when I saw him streak past an organized line of boys and girls. In disbelief I watched him fly through the air and then disappear under the blue-green chlorine water.

A loudspeaker shrieked, "Get that kid going under at the deep end!" Within seconds he was fished out by one of the three lifeguards who leaped in after him. Two of the young bronzed bodies handed him back to me wrapped in a large towel and asked in an accusing way, "How old is that kid, anyway?"

As they stomped away, I heard one mumble to the other, "That's the biggest goddamned four-year-old I've ever seen."

Between quick breaths and gulps on the way home, Terry peeked out from his towel long enough to poke a finger into his brother's ribs. "Ha, ha, ha, Sean, I can even dive now and you're older than me, big sissy."

The pool director had told me on the way out that they could not assume responsibility for "a child like that," but the thought of a long hot summer and no place to dunk them was more than I could bear. Smothering pride, I drove straight back to the pool the next day to beg for another chance. I followed the head instructor around all morning until he finally succumbed.

In spite of the nitty problems of parenthood, I realized more every day that my children were a thin thread connecting me to the human race. I wanted the three of us to be a real family; I needed to draw on the strength that unity would provide. And yet I knew that couldn't happen until I told them the truth about their father. When they had asked about him in the past, I'd said he'd be home when the war was over. How much, I had asked myself, would a four-year-old and a six-year-old understand?

I dreaded telling them, but I knew I couldn't put it off any longer. One evening they snuggled up to me on the sofa for our bedtime reading, and I knew the time had come. I breathed deeply and started in. "Boys," I said, "I want to have an important talk with you tonight. It's about Daddy. I want to tell you why he hasn't come back to us yet."

"Yes, and why don't you show us his letters?" Sean asked. "You used to. A long time ago you showed us his letters and told us what he said. Maybe he doesn't want to write to us anymore or something."

Oh, God, I thought. Who did I think I was fooling? I should have done this months ago. Sean's anger hadn't been part of my rehearsal. I wanted to seem calm, but my heart was racing. Telling them made it more real; maybe I hadn't done it before for my own selfish reasons.

"This is what happened, boys," I began again. "Quite a while ago Daddy's airplane got shot at, and he had to get out of the plane and come down in a parachute. Our helicopters couldn't pick him up on the ground because there were a lot of Communist soldiers who were shooting at our helicopters. The Communists are the people we are fighting over there, you know. They are holding Daddy a prisoner, and so far they haven't let him write to us."

"Are the Communists really, really bad, Mom?" Sean asked.

"Our President thinks they are trying to take over the country of Vietnam and that our country should stop them."

"No," he said, and he banged a fist on the book in his lap. "I mean, will they be bad to Daddy?"

"I think they have to be good to the men they keep prisoner," I answered quickly.

There was a long moment of silence before either spoke again. Finally Terry asked, "Do you think he's dead, Mom?"

Sean answered him quickly, before I had a chance. "No, he's just hurt maybe or something. But he can't write to us. Right, Mom?" He tilted his head to the side in a way that would allow him to detect any change in my expression.

"I want you both to listen now, carefully," I said. "I believe he is still all right. When this war is over, I hope he'll come home. We don't know for sure. We just have to pray for him."

Suddenly Terry jumped up from the couch. "Don't tell any more till I get back," he said. "I'm going to get some cookies. Remember, don't talk now."

He ran to the kitchen, bumping a table on the way. He seemed to think our discussion was part of his bedtime story. Sean wiggled uncomfortably.

Terry returned with a handful of Oreo cookies and plopped them on the table. "How does he look, Mom? My dad, does he look like Timmy's dad across the hall?"

"No, he's bigger and better," Sean burst in. "He takes you for rides in the car and throws you in the air and takes you to airplane shows. Stupid, don't you remember nothin'?"

"I'm not stupid."

"You are too."

"Quiet, boys, please. Terry, you know what your dad looks like. You've seen lots of pictures. I can show you more pictures if you like. We can look at them anytime. But do you know what I'm trying to tell you about him now?"

"I know," Sean said, rubbing a hand across his forehead. "I'll tell Stupid. Our dad is OK. And when the fighting is over, then he'll come back."

He said it with such certainty. Sometimes he looked older than six and much too serious. I didn't want him to act older than he should; he was only a little boy. I patted him on the knee. He stared straight ahead. I wanted to cry, but I stopped the tears.

Terry stuffed another Oreo cookie into his mouth and mumbled, "Can't we have our reading story now, Mom?"

"Yes," I said. Picking up *Charlotte's Web,* I opened to the folded-down page and began to read.

7. MY COUNTRY RIGHT OR WRONG?

<u>JULY 1967</u> There were brief moments when it seemed Bill had never left. I would suddenly feel that he was standing in the kitchen watching me, or sitting beside me in the car or walking with me in the park. I didn't have to see him to know he was there. In my mind I pictured him perfectly. Above the high cheekbones his eyes were tilted at the corners, his mouth was relaxed as if he were about to smile. He was near enough to touch.

Other times I tried but I couldn't remember the simplest things: what he laughed at, what we talked about, how we made love. I couldn't conjure up a vision of his face and his features, and I felt as if he'd been gone forever.

In a two-paragraph letter the Marine Corps informed me that he had been promoted from captain to major. I was to call him Major William Mullen, rather than Captain, in future communications. On pieces of paper, he was a person. At night I crawled into an empty bed, a wife without a husband.

I'd lost track of old military friends, and I hadn't heard from Louise recently. I just waited. I waited to hear that the war was over. I waited for Bill to return. I waited to be rescued.

This particular afternoon was hot and sticky. The children

were out in the parking lot riding their tricycles, and I was inside pacing from the living room to the dining room and back to the kitchen. Finally I sat down in a chair near the window where a slight movement of air could be felt. I switched on the radio, a thing I now did out of habit to fill the vacuum of an empty room. A voice boomed out, "This is Dr. Holloway reaching you in the spirit over the airways of WBBM radio, Chicago."

He soon had my full attention. He talked about his ability to perform "out-of-body travel" anywhere in the world—10,000 miles had been his record. One after the other, listeners were calling in. They asked him to tune in on an aunt in Minnesota, a girlfriend in California, or a grandfather in Germany. He described people's arthritis pain, romances, and childhood homes in detail.

I thought about it all afternoon and then made up my mind to call him at a hotel he had mentioned on the air. To my surprise he answered his phone in a very ordinary human voice. "Come tomorrow afternoon and bring a picture of your husband," he said. He sounded matter-of-fact, as though it had been an everyday request. Or, I wondered later, could it be that he had known, somehow, that I would call?

My mother, who supported me in almost any endeavor, thought I'd gone too far this time. She told me so when she came over to baby-sit, but I finished getting dressed and ignored her looks of disapproval. The commuter train to Chicago took thirty minutes, and the bus from Union Station another twenty. The hotel was huddled among abandoned stores, a booming go-go disco, and buildings in various stages of neglect. In the dingy lobby two old men were slouched in a couple of plastic chairs. I made my way to the front desk, carefully trying not to touch anything. A balding man in shirt-sleeves was reading a newspaper behind the counter.

"Dr. Holloway's room, please."

He peered sharply at me over the newspaper. "Room 302. Elevator over there," he said.

The door at the end of the hall was answered by a woman with brassy blond hair who wore an immense diamond ring. She greeted me politely and asked me to follow her into an adjoining room. She left, and I sat for what seemed endless minutes before a tall, distinguished-looking gentleman entered. He stared at me for a moment and then asked to see the picture of Bill, which he studied intensely. When he looked up again, a voice like Charlton Heston's bounced off the walls. "This is Dr. Holloway reaching you in the spirit."

I began to ask him something before realizing he was no longer consciously present. His eyes were closed, he had slumped in a chair, and his legs were stretched out.

"It's my leg, my leg," he moaned as he grasped his thigh just above the knee. "People are cruel, cruel, I don't understand," he cried out, and buried his head in his hands.

He appeared to be in terrible pain. If he had reached Bill, I wanted to be there, too. I concentrated. I tried hard to empty my head of any other thoughts, but there I remained—just sitting in that old hotel room with a middle-aged man in a trance. I looked out over Lake Michigan and wondered how long he'd be under. Suddenly imagining what a dingbat Bill would think I was, I squelched an almost uncontrollable urge to giggle.

The Moses-like voice suddenly invaded the room again. "Your husband is most certainly alive now, in awful circumstances. The worst of his suffering is mental anguish. His prison appears to be some kind of stockade. He has been involved in an attempt to escape in which others were killed. His leg is injured, but his health seems good. I cannot, however, predict the future. I do feel a strong love force from him." Then he fell silent again.

I thought this was a sign for me to go, but when I stood up his eyes opened. "I hope I've helped you," he said. "Don't forget a contribution to our missionary work, please. The envelopes are on the table by the door."

On the way home I jotted down every word the doctor had uttered during his transfixed state. Then, gazing out of the train window, I whispered to my reflection, "Jesus, girl, you're becoming a certifiable loony."

The next morning in an instant of clarity it came to me that my lack of direction was not entirely my fault. It was the war. It wasn't ending; it was escalating. My future was in the hands of far-off people I'd never met: presidents of countries, generals, and guerrilla fighters. I was tied to circumstances over which I had no control.

It had been a year and five months since Bill's plane was shot down. Since the direction of my life was dependent on the outcome of the war, I suddenly felt I should be doing something other than sitting around on my hands waiting and visiting psychics. I decided to write Averell Harriman suggesting that the United States try a bombing pause in order to bring the Communists to the negotiating table.

His answer was a disappointment when it finally came. It also depleted my best idea. "The cause for which your husband was fighting cannot be achieved by unilateral restraint," he wrote. "We hope and pray that there will be definite information about men like your husband who may be in the hands of the enemy." The hoping and praying I could do myself. It made me uneasy to know our leaders could think of nothing more pragmatic.

Sometimes I regretted having left my military protectorate, where right and wrong remained separate and distinguishable, because my uncertainties were growing by the day. Almost against my will, I felt the public debate begin to challenge my own thinking. Could there possibly be some truth to the accusations? Could men be dying for no good purpose? Even if the Vietnamese had violated some international agreements, how many other countries had done as much without such reprisal from us? I didn't want to believe the growing criticism, but I couldn't understand why President Johnson opposed a bombing halt if there was any chance it would start peace talks.

I found myself reading everything I could get my hands on—books, newspapers, periodicals. Harrison Salisbury of *The New York Times* described firsthand accounts of the devastation of our bombs on civilians, which he said only strengthened Communist resolve to go on for another twenty years, if necessary. Tom Wicker, also of *The New York Times,* claimed, after an interview with a North Vietnamese diplomat, that President Johnson had misread a North Vietnamese peace offer as a sign of weakness.

Wicker reported that the North Vietnamese told him they would never talk "under bombs." Arthur M. Schlesinger Jr., in *The Bitter Heritage* warned that what might happen within our own society as a consequence of our Vietnam policy could be the most serious result of the Vietnam conflict.

There were days when I tried to bolster my support for the war, when I wished we would just win it as we had always won wars in the past? I wanted to feel some pride when President Johnson said, "The United States is determined to continue fighting in Vietnam in the face of great costs and agony." On those days I anxiously flipped through the *Chicago Tribune* in search of its editorials and cartoons that poked sarcastic fun at gloomy Guses who doubted our ability to win.

By the summer of 1967, however, between 500 and 600 Americans were being killed on the battlefield every month, the rate of wounded was more than 3,000, and the war was costing more than two billion dollars a month, and still we weren't winning. Though peace demonstrations were growing, a *Chicago Tribune* columnist dismissed them as "leftist rallies headed by admitted Communists. . . . The marchers crying 'stop the war' might impress the Communist chiefs in Hanoi," he wrote, "but they'll have no more impact on government policy than a snowflake on a hot stove."

The more I read, the more confounded I became. In spite of administration tough talk, I found it hard to believe that a country the size of North Vietnam was a real security risk to the United States. There was an inconsistency I couldn't accept. If Communism was the enemy, what would it prove if we mustered all our power and licked the Vietnamese Communists while détente with Russia was page-one news?

Christmas 1967: We'd been living in Illinois one year. It was a season in which peace groups trooped off to North Vietnam. Though my own conscience struggled with the meaning of the war, I was shocked by the barrage of criticism of American policy expressed by Americans visiting Hanoi. After seeing a few prisoners, the visitors announced to the world that the POWs were well-treated. With a handful of letters as proof, they praised the captors, not mentioning the hundreds of prisoners who were not allowed to write letters. They didn't ask that the North Vietnamese allow the International Red Cross to see the hidden American POWs.

In February I read that Dave Dellinger, of the National Mobilization Committee for Peace, had received a telegram from the North Vietnamese telling him that three prisoners were to be released. The local story mentioned that Professor Flaks at the University of Chicago was a member of that committee. Though I was skeptical of the group's motives, I decided to call Professor Flaks at the university. I briefly explained my "situation," as I had taken to calling it, to a young man who answered. I told him that I'd been hesitant about calling because I didn't believe the peace groups really cared about the POWs; I thought they were using them as a means of getting publicity.

"You're wrong," he said. "I'm sure Dave Dellinger will try to find out how they're being treated."

"Don't accept what they tell you," I said. "Most of us have heard nothing. Ask why they cruelly withhold information from us."

"This is the first time I've talked to one of the POW wives," he said. "Write me about your husband. We'll ask about him in Hanoi. I'll also give you my telephone number at home. Call there or at the university anytime. Ask for Rennie Davis." There was a pause. "I don't know what else to tell you. This war is so sad."

On a frigid January morning I pinned three more casualty clippings to my bulletin board. November 1967: 15,997 dead, 641 missing, 227 reported to be prisoners. December 1967: 15, 997 dead, 647 missing, 231 reported to be prisoners. January 1968: 16,880 dead, 750 missing, 232 reported to be prisoners.

The remnants of my ambivalence about our policy in Vietnam finally had to do with loyalties and people, not the war. Even if the government in South Vietnam was worth defending, it seemed we were unable to win this kind of war, and no number of new deaths would justify the deaths of those already sacrificed. I wanted to act on my kitchen-corner convictions, but I was immobilized with fear. What would Bill think? How would my family react? Would there be repercussions from the military?

Eugene McCarthy had done well in the January New Hampshire Presidential primary running solely on a peace platform, and I had been thinking about passing out leaflets or doing something for him in our suburb during the Illinois primary. I wouldn't have to explain my situation to the McCarthy people, I thought, and the military probably wouldn't find out what I was doing.

I drove around the block three times before parking in front of the little storefront headquarters where posters of Senator McCarthy were plastered across the windows. What if they ask me questions, I worried as I walked toward the building. The closer I got, the more I wanted to turn heel and run back to the car.

A woman near the entrance opened the door for me, shook my hand, and then gave me a name-and-address sheet to sign, and I felt more relaxed. I sat down at a table and talked with a group of people who were stuffing envelopes, and a young man asked if I could pass out leaflets in my neighborhood. On my way out I picked up a stack of pamphlets and said I'd see them in a few days.

I already felt like one of the group. I turned up the sound on the car radio on the way home. Al Hibbler was singing about love and the passing of time. I hummed along with him. "Unchained Melody." I felt good. I was actually doing something!

I'd been canvassing my neighborhood, passing out McCarthy antiwar leaflets for about three weeks, when I was invited to a family dinner at my brother Bill's. I was so excited; I couldn't wait to tell them what I'd been doing, yet I wasn't sure what their reaction would be.

My brother looked dumbstruck as I related my activities. "You should be ashamed," he finally burst out. "How could you let Bill Mullen down that way? And dragging those kids along with you is really lousy. Don't you know you're promoting the pinko propaganda of that chicken candidate?"

I was stunned by his explosive reaction. At first I couldn't speak. I was hurt, too. I wanted to run out to the car and have a good cry. But instead I heard myself scream, "We're not talking about a damn football game. Human beings—thousands—are dying! If there were any more troops in that country it would sink into the South China Sea. As many bombs have fallen on North Vietnam as were dropped during all of World War II. We can't win this one, whatever we do. And I'm not sure we should. You with your big red, white, and blue war and honest-to-goodness fascists wanting to take over the world. Well, this one is different."

"Communists are worse than fascists," Bill said. He tried to add more, but my brother-in-law interrupted.

"We should be fighting this thing like a real war," he said. "The President has his hands tied. That's where the trouble lies. What we need are more troops and more bombing over there, not people running around destroying the morale of our fighting men. You're telling them they're dying for no reason. Can't you see that?"

"Let's change the subject," Jean said, glaring at her husband.

"It's illogical," I said. "You're more concerned with people saying the war is wrong than discovering if it is wrong. Yes, Vietnamese are killing each other, but we're killing more of them than they could ever manage on their own! You both say we should give the commies hell, but your sons are safe at MIT and the University of Illinois. It isn't right. It'll be more of those faceless ones, those black ones and poor ones who can't afford college, who'll be coming back in boxes!"

I knew I'd better leave. I hustled the boys out to the car. On the way home I felt surges of remorse, relief, and then remorse again. I was surprised by my own emotional outburst.

The next morning it all seemed like a bad dream. Without my family's patience and support I felt that I might not make it. Yet I knew I couldn't have gone on deceiving them, covering up my opinions. Even if they reject me, I thought, I'm still glad I did it.

My brother called by ten o'clock to ask if I'd like to come over for breakfast, and I was grateful they weren't going to desert me. I knew, though, that the war would be off-limits for conversation from then on.

My mother, however, surprised me. After breakfast she followed me into the front hall and whispered, "You know I'm an old-time conservative, but I agree with you on this. This war is a bunch of nonsense, and we should bring them all home now." She said she had believed that for some time; now that she knew how I felt, she could be honest herself.

After that, my mother and I went to McCarthy political meetings together, she in her silk crepe dresses adorned with tasteful jewelry and I in a dull, nondescript garment that was usually gray. On the way out of one large rally in a downtown Chicago theater, she said, "I hope nothing goes wrong at the convention here in July. These nice young people are so sincere. You know there are people who are incensed by the war protesters."

"Stop worrying, Mom," I said. "McCarthy will be nominated. I just know it. Nothing's going to go wrong now."

8. SHATTERED HOPES

OAKLAND, CALIFORNIA, MAY 1968 Lyndon Johnson announced that he would not seek reelection, and I decided to move back to California. Somehow, over a period of time, the two events became imprinted on my mind as one. I wanted to shout, "Hallelujah!" when I heard the President's speech that Sunday afternoon. As far as I was concerned, we had won. Robert Kennedy or Eugene McCarthy would be elected President and the war would end. That spring I had planned and rejected the idea of going back to California a dozen times. Suddenly it seemed President Johnson had made the decision for me. When Bill returned, I wanted to be there where he and I had said good-bye.

I stuck a thumbtack into the last casualty list I'd hang there on my corner bulletin board—May 1968: 23,926 dead, 929 missing, 286 reported to be prisoners—and made plans to leave Illinois.

I carried my radio from room to room and hummed old songs along with Frank Sinatra and Peggy Lee and packed boxes until late at night. I tossed out a closet full of gray clothes I had accumulated article by article over the past two years. I bought a yellow dress, a pair of orange shoes and matching bag, and I cut my hair. I sold my little blue Tempest and then bought three airline tickets to San Francisco.

This was our fourth home since Bill had become missing two years earlier. It was an old pale green monstrosity nestled in the hills of Oakland. Ivy covered half of its outside walls. Thirty stairs led down to a wide porch and front entrance that opened into a long hallway. Small rooms branched off larger ones and blossomed into a living room in the center.

Kay, an old friend from Michigan, had found the place for us before we arrived. "Sorry, Barbara, it's a little weird," she had said, "but it's all we could come up with in your price range. And you said you didn't want an apartment this time."

I didn't mind, I told her. After my sterile apartments I loved the rambling disorder of the house. I ran from room to room, opening doors and looking out windows.

The neighborhood consisted of winding streets lined with green trees that supported a patchwork of pastel houses. The nights were sometimes cool enough for a fire in the fireplace. Mornings were warmed by a bright sun in skies of extraordinary blue. The children seemed happy.

On the morning of June 5 the telephone woke me early. It was Kay, and her voice was barely audible. "Barbara, did you hear? Kennedy was shot last night. I went to bed early. I just heard."

"My God," I said.

Just then Sean ran from the living room. "Mom, the man on TV—he says Kennedy got shot. You better come listen. Somebody tried to kill him!"

"Kay, I'll call you right back," I said.

"Maybe he won't die," Sean said. "The man on TV said he wasn't dead."

I grabbed my robe and ran to the living room and listened to the details in stunned silence. Sean had followed me from the bedroom. After a few minutes he pulled on the sleeve of my robe. "Come on, Mom. Make some coffee," he said. He took my hand and led me into the kitchen. "It will be better if you have coffee. Probably he'll be OK." I lowered myself into a chair without answering.

Sean dashed into the back bedroom. "Terry, Terry, wake up!" he hollered. "Kennedy got shot! And Mom's just sitting there. Hurry up. Come on."

"You're lying, Sean. I'm going to ask Mom. You're waking me too early, too, for nothin'." Terry shuffled down the hall. Pulling at his flannel pajama bottoms and rubbing his eyes, he stopped at the doorway. "Is Kennedy dead, Mom?"

"No, but he was shot, Terry."

"Terry, climb up on the cabinet and get the instant coffee," Sean ordered. They both scurried around. Sean heated water in a pan. A few minutes later they placed a cup in front of me, and I pretended to sip from it, but they had poured the milk in first and dark flecks of brown floated on top. They ate their cereal in silence, never taking an eye off me. They got up from the table, put their bowls in the sink, and went into the bedroom, where they dressed in a hurry without the usual wrestling match or search for last night's homework or hunt for a missing shoe.

I hadn't moved from the table. Sean stopped alongside my chair before leaving. "It's OK, Mom," he said. "You don't have to go to the game this afternoon if Kennedy dies."

"Thanks," I said, nodding. "I'll come. Don't worry. See you this afternoon."

The door slammed, and Terry ran back into the kitchen. He grabbed a forgotten baseball mitt, hesitated for a second, and then brushed a kiss across my cheek. "Bye, Mom," he whispered. The door banged again.

I sat at the table a long time. I couldn't focus on who had shot Kennedy or why. All I thought about was Ethel Kennedy. I kept wishing I could slip her a magic formula that would carry her through the next few hours, but I knew there was no easy initiation to our club.

On June 6, Bobby Kennedy was dead. His death and the statistics of his victory in the California primary were reported simultaneously. I felt they were a sore reminder of what could have been. I had been so sure Bobby Kennedy would be elected in November—I couldn't believe how perfectly we'd been set up. I couldn't believe that he was really gone.

*   *   *

I spent as little time as possible weighing the consequences of politics and war that summer. I was an instrument of constant motion. Keeping busy was the end, not the means. I made friends with the neighbors, drove children to and from swimming pools—anybody's children. I didn't ask names; they just piled in. For all I knew, they were pint-size hitchhikers, or maybe the word had gone out at the local boys' club. I'd scream fearsome threats into the air in transit: "Knock off that wrestling or I'm going to stop the car and toss you out into the gutter." Or, "I'm going to hail the first policeman I see and tell him to lock you up and throw away the key." I'd settle fights over who didn't get a hot dog or who must have eaten somebody's underwear because everybody had a pair when they came. I'd count heads, drive home, sweep out the car, and start out again the next day.

Then it was August. The political conventions had begun, and the truth stared back at me from my twelve-inch black-and-white television set: what happened out there in the larger world had something to do with me and my children.

Soon I was caught up in the drama; I lost interest in my daily charter to the swimming pool. There was a small people's revolution on the block, but I ignored it. I put on another pot of coffee and, flicking from channel to channel, took in the details. By the end of the day the speeches were as stale as my coffee. I watched nevertheless.

I bought a memo pad in order to really keep tabs on the Republicans. But they offered so little I filled only two pages. The delegates boasted, in fact, that there would be no debate over Vietnam at their convention. Thunderous applause broke out when Richard Nixon promised to bring an *honorable* end to the war. I switched off the set and looked glumly at the gray screen. I'd heard it all before from Johnson, Harriman, Rusk, McNamara, and Westmoreland. After a few minutes I got up, pulled a cord, and opened the drapes.

Daylight brightened the room, and Terry appeared in the doorway. "I can't believe it," he said, and bellowed, "Sean, come and see. The TV's off and Mom is moving. I think she's alive."

"They're all the same," I said. "Richard Nixon—ugh. Now he thinks it's his turn to win the war."

"Nixon—yuk," Terry said. "Now can we go swimming tomorrow?"

Sean poked his head around the corner of the doorway. "Is it over, Mom?"

"Thank goodness," I said.

"Yahoo!" Terry screeched.

I sat down again. "The Democrats are next week."

The next week I stationed myself in front of the set once more. I was a little hopeful that Hubert Humphrey would transform himself into a peace candidate until he told the delegates, "Our presence in Vietnam is to prevent the success of aggression. Regrettably," he said, "wars have their built-in escalation."

After that, chaos broke out in Chicago, and then nothing could drag me from my darkened room. By now the boys were overtly impatient. Terry let me know he was sick of seeing me sitting there staring at the TV. "We can't ever watch our programs," he complained.

"You can watch them later," I answered. "Go on out and play and give me some peace."

He turned a sulky look in my direction and then slammed the door on his way out, but I paid no attention. In front of me, antiwar protesters were swearing they would stay overnight in Lincoln Park against the orders of Mayor Daley. Later Chicago police burst out of the woods into the park, swinging clubs at everyone, and a police car smashed through a thrown-together barricade.

I stopped watching long enough to fix a hasty dinner for the boys, then, feeling guilty, uncovered a box of Twinkies to pacify them. "You going to watch that dumb stuff again tonight?" Terry asked. I nodded yes, and he shrugged. "Let's go out and play ball," he said to Sean.

By the next night I was so totally absorbed with the TV that I let the boys make themselves something to eat. They gave one another understanding looks as they slapped peanut butter and jelly on slices of white bread.

I dashed back to the living room. The situation had deteriorated while I was away. I felt responsible, as though I had shirked my duty. About four hundred people were huddled in the park when tear gas burst through the trees. Ministers tried to carry off a wooden cross they had constructed. People ran screaming through the woods. Huge trucks sprayed more gas, and young people began hurling pieces of the pavement at the police.

In the morning I greedily read the newspaper to find out what had happened during the night while I slept. Five thousand protesters, it said, had massed in Grant Park across from the Hilton Hotel at 3:00 A.M., where they chanted, "Join us, join us. Dump the Hump!"

I rooted for them because they were working out my own resentments. I believed that Humphrey had stolen the nomination from the real peace candidates: Kennedy and McCarthy. Down deep, I knew Hubert Humphrey would end the war sooner than Richard Nixon, but that didn't seem to matter. Revenge provided more immediate satisfaction.

On the last day of the convention people were trapped as they tried to join a march in the downtown area. Between twenty and thirty policemen with clubs began beating those who tried to flee. Demonstrators, McCarthy workers, and reporters staggered into the lobby of the Hilton Hotel, blood streaming down their faces from head wounds. A larger force of police charged into a crowd of between ten thousand and fifteen thousand in Grant Park. Some of the policemen headed straight for Rennie Davis, who was on the bullhorn urging the crowd to sit down and be calm. He was attacked from behind, his head was cracked open, and the young man from the University of Chicago fell unconscious to the ground.

By the end of the day I was dazed, as beaten as dreams of peace in Chicago. My own little world looked inviting again. I suddenly thought about the boys and wondered if they were still awake. I gently pushed their bedroom door open and heard them whispering and giggling in the dark. "Boys," I said, "get to sleep."

The day after Richard Nixon was elected in November, a South Vietnamese minister said, "With Nixon President . . . we will have more time. . . . Nixon will not be under the same kind of pressure that Johnson was to end the war."

I was sure now that nothing would change for four years. The present had to be tolerated; I lived for the future. I imagined a far-off reunion with Bill.

One afternoon a Marine officer from Alameda Air Station called. He wanted to show me some intelligence photos of POWs. From the window I watched him get out of a green sedan. The short hair and creased beige uniform stirred memories. He started up the stairs, and a familiar rush of hot air swept over me.

In the living room he placed a thick loose-leaf book on my coffee table and opened it. Pressed under its plastic pages were nearly two hundred pictures. Some were a couple of inches square; others nearly filled a page. The larger they were, the less clear. They were all photos of men held captive somewhere in Southeast Asia, acquired from journalists and other friendly sources.

Before I examined the pictures, the Marine officer asked Sean, who had been sitting quietly on the sofa, if he'd like to look at the book. Sean quickly nodded and jumped to his feet. "Come on with me into the other room," the officer said, taking Sean by the hand. "See if you can find a picture that looks like your dad."

They came back, and Sean handed the book to me. I spread it across my lap and flipped through the pages, stopping now and then to look at a certain picture, not because it resembled Bill, but because a fuzzy outline in striped pajamas or a torn flight suit seemed to call out for acknowledgment. He was someone's son or father or husband. Then I turned a page and looked at a picture that gave me a start. I didn't want to pin hopes on some damned photo that probably could never be identified for certain, yet there was something so familiar about the posture, the body build, the shape of the head. The features were blurred, but out of the dotted haze Bill's face seemed to form.

I turned the page without comment and continued looking at the rest of the photos. I wanted to hand the book back without saying anything, but I hesitated, and I noticed an expectant expression on the officer's face. I laid the book on the coffee table, turned pages until the eerie likeness was before me, and pointed to it. "I don't really think so," I said, trying to brace myself against disappointment. Perhaps there had already been positive identification of the picture. I didn't want to look silly or impressionable. "It does look something like Bill," I said.

The captain told me that Sean had chosen the same picture. "I don't know how he could remember," I said. "He was only four when his father left." The officer said it was amazing what they remembered and then told me that Bill's mother and father had picked the same photo when they were shown the book in Massachusetts a week earlier.

Before I was able to derive any significance from the photo, however, the officer warned me that the Defense Department had narrowed the picture to two possibilities: Bill and a Navy officer. But I easily convinced myself that it was Bill. One night I dreamed that Bill returned and together we attended the funeral of the Navy officer. Since there was no reality—no one knew the truth—I believed anything I wanted.

I was purposely sleepwalking through the days. Then one evening Sean's teacher called me. "I'm really puzzled," she said. "I hope you don't mind my calling you at home. I want you to know that Sean is a bright boy. But I'm having a problem with him. He refuses to give us his address. When I ask him for it, he insists that he doesn't know it. I give him a card for you to fill out and he doesn't return it."

I hung up the phone and marched into Sean's bedroom. "What's this all about, son? Don't you want people to know where you live? Your teacher says you won't tell them."

"If I learn it," he said, "we'll just move again. You're always talking to Kay about when Dad comes home. Then I suppose we'll have to move again. Even if he doesn't come home for a while, you might decide to move again anyway. I don't know what's going to happen." He leaned on his elbows, cuffing two hands to his forehead, and stared into an open math book on his desk.

"Look at me when I speak to you," I said. He looked up, and I said, "I'm sorry I got angry. Let's make a bargain. If you give the address to the teacher, I promise we'll stay here. Honestly."

"I'll bet," he said, darting a quick glance at me over his shoulder. "We'll see."

The episode with Sean forced me to think also about Terry. When his kindergarten teacher had described him as "hyperactive," I'd laughed and called him a spirited lad, but I suspected it was more than that. Sometimes he seemed bent on self-destruction. Startled neighbors periodically reported his imminent demise on rooftops, in trees, or doing bicycle wheelies downhill into traffic.

I wondered why I wasn't more strict with him. Perhaps because he makes me laugh when I least expect it, I thought. I smiled, remembering the morning he walked out from behind the aspirin counter in the supermarket with a monkey in his arms. "Where the hell did you get that?" I gasped. By then the monkey had leaped from his arms and disappeared out the front door. The police came, and Terry told them a wild story about how the monkey was riding on a Great Dane in the parking lot, and a red-bearded man named Inferno let Terry hold the monkey. He said the man had a purple van with yellow streaks down the sides. All the way home I tried to lecture Terry about disease and strange animals, but I kept bursting into fits of giggles. He was rolling on the floor laughing, too. It's how we usually ended up, he and I.

There was a spirit and enthusiasm about Terry that I didn't want to stifle. How precious that freedom was! But I was beginning to sense that he was getting out of hand and I had to come to grips with it.

Then one afternoon he was late coming home from kindergarten. Two hours went by. School was only four blocks away. After the first half-hour, I alerted the police. Five hours later he was found climbing a jungle gym in a park six miles away. When the police officer brought him up the stairs, they were holding hands. The officer was smiling.

Drained with relief, I should have reached for Terry. I wanted to hug him to me and never let him go, but I couldn't seem to touch him. Instead I screamed, "Get in the house! Go to your room and stay there!"

The police officer looked stunned. He shook his head and

started down the stairs. At the last minute I shouted to him, "Thank you," but he didn't look back.

I followed Terry into his bedroom and continued my tirade. "Don't do this kind of thing to me. Don't you know your mother's been through enough? Your father disappeared on me. And now you. I can't take any more!"

Later I heard him crying in his room, but I didn't go to him, and I didn't take him any dinner. "I'm a rotten mother," I kept telling myself. But I couldn't move. I held the coffee cup with both hands to steady it. I don't need this kid scaring the hell out of me, I thought. He's not going to make me feel guilty either. I remember how Bill used to laugh at his antics. He'd put higher and higher fences around the backyard, but even at two Terry climbed over all of them. And then Bill would roar, "He's quite a tiger, isn't he?" Well, he wouldn't be howling now, I thought. God damn it. This kid is a chip off the old block. Why did Bill have to fly that last mission and leave me with all this responsibility? How could he do that to me? I'll never forgive him if I find out he volunteered for that mission.

Christmas came and with it the end of 1968—the year of lost heroes and promises gone sour. I kept saying, "We made it to Christmas," as if someone were going to come along and pin a badge on me. Instead, at midnight on Christmas Eve, I poured myself a glass of sherry and sifted through a pile of unopened Christmas cards. Among them was a holiday greeting from ex-President Johnson. He appreciated my constancy, patience, and devotion to country, he said. I took a sip of sherry and threw the card into the wastebasket.

9. OFFICERS' WIVES AND LADIES

MARCH 1969 Late as usual, I ran down the stairs, juggling my books under one arm and wriggling into my sweater with the other. But I noticed that the mail had already come, and I couldn't pass it up without having a look. If I did, I'd only sit in class all morning wondering if there was something in that little black box that would change my life.

I set my books on a step and pulled out a letter. It was from Sybil Stockdale, a Navy commander's wife who I'd heard was trying to contact as many POW/MIA wives as possible. Her short note told me to call Maerose Evans, who lived in nearby Alameda; Maerose's husband, Sybil wrote, had been shot down in Laos four years earlier. I thought it was worth being late to get this bit of news and decided to call Maerose after my first class.

I needed more than ever to share my anxieties with another MIA wife. My suspicions of the new administration had grown rapidly during the few weeks Richard Nixon had been President. Four hundred deaths a week on the battlefield had brought the total in March to 34,000, already 10,000 more than the previous summer of the political conventions.

Almost overnight, it seemed, the President had aligned himself with the cause of the POWs, condemning their mistreatment and demanding their release. With no change in U.S. policy, it seemed like empty rhetoric, especially since the Geneva Convention stated clearly that "prisoners of war shall be released and repatriated without delay *after the cessation of active hostilities.*" There was something about the new campaign that was making me nervous. At last I could discuss my concerns with other wives.

I called Maerose from a phone at the school and told her how difficult it had been for me to locate other MIA families. "We didn't know about you either," she said. "And you're just twenty minutes away. Why don't you come over tomorrow and meet some of the other women?"

Maerose was tall and wiry; her huge blue eyes were full of life. She would be the leader of the group. I felt that immediately. "Hi, Barbara. Welcome to the secret society," she said. I followed her into the living room, where she introduced me to five other women. She found me a chair and then smiled. "Don't worry what you tell us," she said. "We've all thought it or done it, too."

The women chuckled in agreement. I relaxed. "Maerose, break Barbara in fast," one woman urged. "Tell her about our mannequin."

Maerose, who needed little encouragement, began the story. "You see," she said, "we want to rent this mannequin. We can have it on different nights. We can set it in the car seat next to us. Then we can dance with it in the evening. Have it send us flowers."

"God, that's beautiful. I love it already," I said.

Maerose's audience smiled appreciatively, and then she continued. "This could be the best part," she said. "We pull the drapes, keep the lights on, and imagine the neighbors straining to watch the silhouettes in the dark."

I tried to picture these women in another time, but I could see them only in the present, sitting there in their trim pants suits, offering personal confessions to one another between sporadic outbreaks of laughter.

"Now I want an honest answer," one woman said, swinging a

pointed finger in a semicircle to include everyone in the room. Then she patted the top and sides of her bouffant hairdo, a gesture that seemed to give her the confidence to go on. "What about when you're at a military base or in town conducting business and someone asks, 'And where is your husband stationed?' and you look them in the eye coolly and say, 'Oh, he's missing in action.' Now admit it," she said. "Don't you enjoy it?"

"I do," I said, laughing. "I don't know why. I like seeing people squirm as they grope for something tactful to say. I never told that to anyone before. I guess I thought it was a little unbalanced of me."

"If it is," roared a young woman from across the room, "you're looking at a whole group of weirdos."

The afternoon vanished in a continuous swirl of conversation. I was surprised that three hours had slipped away. "I hate to leave," I said. "It's the best time I've had in years."

"Not a word to anyone about this now," Maerose said, grinning. "We'll all be committed."

I was relieved that it had turned out so well, and I couldn't wait for the next get-together in two weeks. All twenty women in the Bay Area would be there. I supposed there would be a more serious discussion then and I would be able to share my apprehensions about the administration and the POWs and the war.

Finally the night of the meeting came; I placed the directions on the car seat next to me and set out for an apartment building in Alameda. Between stoplights and turns I rehearsed how I would present my concerns to the group, what actions I thought we could take.

The door was opened by a small woman with sandy red hair. "Hi, welcome to the luau," she bubbled, tossing a Hawaiian lei around my neck. I thought I was in the wrong apartment until I spotted Maerose across the room. The women were all wearing muumuus or other Hawaiian outfits. "Sorry no one told you it was a Kon Tiki party," the hostess said. "It doesn't matter. Come on in and meet everyone." I followed her into the living room as though she were a stewardess directing me to my seat.

The talk whirled around me: sweet-and-sour pork recipes, children, your apartment, my house, California. Not wanting to be dumped from the aircraft, I dredged up some stilted little contributions. I felt as if I'd been tossed back in time, to an officers' wives' luncheon in 1962.

It was nearly midnight when I got home, but there was no use going to bed. I wouldn't be able to sleep. This was life and death and we'd sat around eating pineapple and rice and barbecued pork. I sat in the dark and argued with myself. Maybe it was their way of coping; perhaps I was losing my sense of fun.

I knew it was late, but I decided to call Kay. I told her about the Hawaiian luau, and she woke Ed from a deep sleep. "Ed, Ed," I heard her say. "Those women Barbara was meeting tonight. All they did was eat Hawaiian food."

I heard Ed answer in a muffled voice, "What the hell are you talking about? For God's sake, Kay, tell Barbara to go to bed and count her blessings. She's not that loony yet."

"Really, Barbara, Ed says you're not the nutty one. Just get some sleep and don't worry about it."

I was still trying to sort out the implications of the Kon Tiki party when Maerose called with another invitation a few days later. How would I like to drive down to Palo Alto to meet Alice Stratton and "really get something done," she asked. I agreed, thinking that Alice might take a more serious approach. Alice's husband, Commander Richard Stratton, had received a lot of publicity earlier when the first pictures of prisoners bowing before cameras were followed by reports of abuse and accusations of brainwashing.

Four of us were sitting at the table in Alice Stratton's cozy kitchen. Her three sons were asleep, but samples of their nursery school artwork decorated the refrigerator. Alice was serving coffee and cake, and the other woman was relating a story about her own son when Maerose said it was time to get down to business. "Our project is going to be a mass letter-writing to get Congress to pass a resolution protesting the mistreatment of our men," she said. "I've really thought about this."

"But how is that going to help end the war?" I asked.

Maerose glared at me in disbelief.

"We are not political," she answered swiftly, emphasizing the word "political."

"What does that mean? You want the war to end so Jim can come home, don't you?"

"Of course, but we have no control over that. The war will end when the Communists agree to a peace proposal," she said.

"You mean we're helpless?" I asked. "We let the Communists decide when the war will end?"

"Barbara, we are military officers' wives. We are certainly not going to instruct the Commander-in-chief how to run a war. He knows much more about that than we do."

"You mean we're not going to tell our own government how we feel about the war or that we want the men brought home? We're just going to ask to have them treated better for as long as it goes on?" I asked.

"We are going to be ladies about this," Maerose said. "Don't forget this is a *humane* cause. We have to keep out of politics."

"Why?" I asked, my voice growing weaker.

"Because some of these politicians undermine our own government," Maerose said emphatically. "Ted Kennedy and Senator Fulbright don't care a bit about our servicemen."

"But they do care," I protested. "They're trying to stop them from being killed or captured."

"We're not going to betray our country's cause, Barbara. If you won't help make the world aware of the plight of our captured men, you don't have to," she said with an air of finality. She began passing out papers to the others from a neat stack in front of her.

I spent the next hour assuring them all that I really disliked Communists and thought they were rotten not to at least let me know if Bill was alive. I left carrying piles of mimeographed forms and drafted letters. God forbid that Bill should ever think I wanted him starved or beaten.

In California the passing of winter and coming of spring is not heralded as it is in most places. Sometimes, in fact, the transformation is barely perceptible. Events more often denote the change of a season than the weather. It was May, and the boys had finished their first full school year in Oakland, I had chalked up a few more college credits, and Richard Nixon had been President for five months. And it was time, he said, to disclose his secret plan to end the war.

It was curiosity more than hope or belief that compelled me to turn on the TV the night he explained why the United States could not disengage from the war in a hurry. "It might be easy and popular to simply abandon our effort in Vietnam," he said, "but the cause of peace might not survive the damage done to other nations' confidence in our reliability."

If it was our reliability that was on the line, I wondered why the "other nations" he mentioned had been so reliably absent in Vietnam. One thing is reliable, I thought as the President faded from television view: There will always be new reasons for staying in the war.

The plan had been no more than I had expected. I was not, however, prepared for what I considered the exploitation of the POW issue that followed.

Two days later, when Ambassador Lodge presented the Nixon plan to the Communists in Paris, he told the press that "the Communists should at least agree with the U.S. on POW treatment. I brought out the heartrending situation of the prisoners' wives who are uncertain as to the fate of their husbands. North Vietnam's refusal with regard to these humanitarian requirements cannot have a favorable effect on our negotiations here."

About this time, I started clipping everything from our local newspapers that referred to escalating casualties. It was as if I were keeping a scorecard on this President who had promised us peace. I pinned the clippings to my new bulletin board, which was twice the size of the one I'd had in Illinois. For eleven days in May the articles I attached to my board were about U.S. Army troopers who attacked a 3,000-foot mound of land they called Hamburger Hill. Fifty of them had died, and three hundred were wounded; the hill was abandoned a week later when North Vietnamese mortars slammed into the outpost. I was certain now that the war was completely out of control. If the loss of these young men could be rationalized, anything could. The prisoners championed today could easily become necessary sacrifices tomorrow.

If a family group was to take a strong independent stand, I was sure it could hasten the end of the war. An unsettling intuition, however, told me that this would not be the case and my first letter from the new POW family group Sybil Stockdale had been organizing confirmed my belief.

I pulled the white mimeographed sheet from the envelope and read with a skeptical eye. "I feel very strongly," Sybil wrote, "that public criticism of our own government would be detrimental to our purpose and would make Hanoi very happy. I know this is frustrating, but I believe it is also very true. . . . Hang on. We'll make it. We also serve who stand and wait."

The next letter from Sybil was more formal. "The National League of Families of American Prisoners in Southeast Asia" was printed at the top of the bond stationery. At the bottom was a footnote that indicated that information on the organization was being circulated by the Defense Department and reprinted in military journals. Somewhere in the middle of the page, Sybil urged us to "pour letters into Congress . . . always emphasizing that we feel that the President, Defense Department, and State Department are working diligently to secure the protection of the Geneva Convention for our loved ones."

I stuffed Sybil's latest letter into my purse the morning it came and then drove the boys to baseball practice. I climbed to the top rung of the bleachers and sat there gazing out at the field. This is like a nightmare, I thought. The kind in which you're paralyzed. Something terrible is happening, and you can't stop it. I sensed that the POW families were going to be puppets for President Nixon, and I knew I had to do something—even if it was the wrong thing.

By the time I had taken the boys out for hamburgers, quieted arguments about whose hitting was wrong and why the umpire was a bum, and faked knowledge about the game I hadn't really watched, I'd come up with an idea. I would write to a columnist on the *San Francisco Chronicle*.

It was some time before I heard from anyone at the paper. The columnist had passed my letter on to the editor of the women's section, who in turn had also passed it on—and on. Finally it caught the attention of an idealistic reporter fresh from college campus journalism who called to say she thought the story might have some appeal.

I phoned Maerose to ask if some of the women would talk with the reporter. When she called back she said the others would participate only if we stuck to the *humanitarian* aspect of the cause. I was glad they would do it at all.

The day of the interview I'd had a tightness in my stomach all morning, and I felt nauseous sitting there in Maerose's living room waiting for the reporter to arrive. Maerose was out in the kitchen pouring Cokes for the other women. When she popped into the living room, she said, "Oh, there you are. You have talked to the Marine Corps, haven't you, Barbara?"

"About what?" I asked, thinking maybe they'd been trying to reach me.

"Well, you're not going to talk to a reporter without instructions, are you? We've all called our branches of service to get permission to do the interview and to find out what to cover," she said.

"No, no. I didn't think to do that," I said, trying to be tactful at such a crucial moment.

"Well, there is a Navy officer at Alameda ready to come over in case we get stuck. All we have to do is call him. I talked to him this morning," Maerose announced.

Just as that bit of news was sinking in, I saw Miss Adams, our reporter, park her car and get out. Her hair was long and straight. She wore granny glasses, purple stocking, sandals, a flowered peasant skirt, and a shawl that was draped over her shoulders. All she lacked was a "Free Huey" button, and I feared that might be under the shawl. Oh, God, I've really done it now, I thought. I gave a quick glance around the room. We were identical except for size and hair color: A-line dresses, just short enough but not mini, closed-toed shoes, and hair in various stages of teased and sprayed perfection.

The young reporter placed her shawl carefully on the back of the nearest chair, sat down, and took out a pad and paper. Two of the wives were not much older than she. I couldn't imagine that they had much else in common. She directed her first question to the youngest of our group, who, I was sure, was just about relaxed enough to tell her husband's name, rank, and serial number.

"What have you done to help end this war so your husband can return?" Miss Adams asked.

Oh, hell, I thought. This is it.

The blond Texas beauty looked as if she'd been hit in the face with ice water. For a minute I expected her to scream. I misjudged, however. Complete composure actually took a few seconds. "I have nothing to say about the war," she said. "Our efforts are humanitarian."

"I don't understand. What does that mean?" asked Miss Adams.

"It means we don't talk about the war, we only discuss the prisoners of war."

"You mean the war has nothing to do with the prisoners? The welfare of the prisoners is the only humanitarian issue of the war?"

"Of course, the war has to do with prisoners, but it isn't our business to tell men a lot smarter than we are how to run the war. The President and our generals know a lot of things that we don't."

"She's right," Maerose interrupted. "We are not going to enter into political second-guessing."

Undaunted, the young reporter continued. One by one, she circled the room asking another question. "Would you like the war to end immediately?"

Young Texas blonde: "No comment."

Past-hostess of the Kon Tiki party: "No comment."

Maerose: "No comment."

And then it was my turn. I heard Maerose say, "Don't answer that, Barbara."

"I think continuing this war is wrong," I said, trying to control my trembling voice. I avoided Maerose's glare. "I think the President should bring our troops home now and let the Vietnamese settle it for themselves." I reached into my purse and took out a mimeographed sheet of paper. "Here is a copy of a press conference that might be of interest to you. Secretary Laird gives some statistics having to do with the prisoners."

"She doesn't have permission to give you that; please return it," Maerose said.

"It says that it is a press release, which means I have a right to have it," Miss Adams said, quickly stuffing the paper into her canvas bag.

Maerose then denied responsibility for what I was doing and asked Miss Adams not to print the story at all.

The reporter gathered up her belongings and said she wished the interview had been more productive. I walked out to the car with her, apologized for the way things had gone, and returned to the house. The woman from Texas stood rigidly near the center of the room, arms folded and waiting. "Baaaaabaaara Mullen, I will never appear anywheeaa with you ever again," she said. "What you said is traysonous."

"You're supposed to be a military wife," seconded the other woman. "What do you think you're doing to your husband's career? How we act now will influence their futures in the military, don't you know that?"

"Career! You need to be alive to have a career. It's the first requirement," I said, trying to control my real anger. I grabbed my purse and headed for the door. I thought I would probably suffocate if I didn't get out of there.

On the way home, feelings of regret swept over me, but my condition improved remarkably as the distance between me and the military enclave of Alameda grew. I began to look at the afternoon's debacle realistically. Maybe I had been naïve. They said they wanted publicity, but they weren't prepared to talk about anything. Even the human problems hadn't gotten off the ground. Then suddenly I laughed to myself. Lord, I thought, if the war was off-limits, the least they could have done for me was to come up with an alcoholic, a nervous breakdown, or something. Just then, my sprawling green house came into view and I felt better. I fairly gulped the free air I breathed.

Within a few weeks I received a letter from the Marine Corps that explained how we were supposed to handle future encounters with the press. Headquarters wrote:

> I would hope that prior to a personal undertaking of your own to focus public opinion on the plight of your loved one and yourselves, you would remember . . . have confidence in your government, which is actively and perseveringly trying to bring about not only the release of our men, but an honorable resolution to the conflict . . . your personal efforts should support the overall objectives, not frustrate their realization. Your efforts should be void of reference to political or military issues, be brief and confined to the POW situation stimulated purely on *humanitarian* considerations.

I tried to get it straight. I repeated to myself. "It is *humanitarian* to protest POW treatment. It is *political* to protest the war. Therefore, to criticize continuation of the war is *nonhumanitarian* activity. The POW issue, pure and separated, must not be contaminated by *nonhumanitarian* words or deeds."

My real problem was a stubborn subconscious voice which resisted. "Bullshit," it said. "War is *killing,* and *killing* is *nonhumanitarian.*"

10. ONLY HANOI KNOWS

JULY 1969 None of us knew what to expect as we filed into an air-conditioned conference room at Hamilton Air Force Base outside of San Francisco. With the exception of the few wives I'd met, the rest of the prisoner-of-war families were strangers to me. They'd been flown in on military aircraft from several western states for our first Defense Department briefing. Some were older, and I assumed they were parents. They came in quietly and sat side by side, staying together as a couple; the man sometimes reached for the woman's hand and held it in his lap without speaking.

I hadn't met a mother and father of a missing man, except for Bill's, and I tried to imagine Sean or Terry one day simply disappearing. I could only wonder what these men and women, their real feelings hidden behind placid masks, were thinking. They had dressed befitting the occasion in suits and best dresses as if to honor the vanished son. Transported from their small towns in Utah and Nevada, they clung to one another in silence. Losing a son must be a special kind of loss, I thought.

We waited in the wood-paneled room with its tall, narrow windows. Framed insignia and emblems dotted the walls; in back of a long oak table an American flag fell in regal folds from a slim gold pole. Old Glory was holding court, and we were all her subjects. Soon the young brides, wives, and parents were all there, seated in rows of metal folding chairs—people bound together by a peculiar incident of fate. Six men were seated at the long table; four were in military uniform. One of the civilians, a tall paternal figure of a man, stood up and introduced himself as Richard Capen, Assistant Secretary of Defense. Earlier in the day he had told the press: "These girls are very courageous. We owe it to them that they know these men and their families are not forgotten." Now, in a dry, calm voice, he reassured us that this was true, that we hadn't been forgotten.

I didn't want to be remembered. I wanted to be forgotten along with the whole lousy war. My mind wandered. I'd only come to the meeting out of curiosity. Now that they had made the prisoners a cause célèbre, I wondered what they would do with us. I tried to pay attention to what this man was saying; he had traveled all the way from Washington to tell us something. "Our new effort is designed to focus world opinion on our thirteen hundred men, captured and missing," he said. "This represents a switch from the last administration policy. . . . It seems to us the time is now to express deep concern about these men."

There was stirring in the room; taut expressions relaxed. Would he now give us license to speak? As if in answer, he said, "You can be a potent force assisting the government to demand better treatment for the prisoners before the jury of the world."

Two or three other speakers repeated his promise, and then the meeting was over. On the way out, family members flocked around the secretary to shake his hand or tell him thank you. It reminded me of a high school pep rally for a team badly in need of cheerleaders.

Driving home across the Golden Gate Bridge, I looked at the spirals of San Francisco rising above the sun-streaked bay. Off in the distance tiny sailboats skimmed effortlessly through aqua-green water. Beyond the jeweled city and cloudless expanse of blue sky, I pictured another scene where young men were falling into muddy jungle swamps, being stuffed into plastic bags and laid out in wooden boxes. I imagined a ship carrying their lifeless bodies past these very bridges and on to the Port of Oakland.

I tried not to think about the war for a few days, but Hanoi announced that it would release three more prisoners and that Rennie Davis would accompany the men home. Rennie was on trial in Chicago, charged with conspiracy to incite a riot at the Democratic National Convention, but he'd been given the authority to travel to Hanoi. I dug out the old home phone number he had given me when I talked to him at the University of Chicago and dialed it. He said immediately that he remembered me and asked if I'd received any information about my husband. I explained that we'd heard nothing about the men in Laos. "I need your help, Rennie," I said. "Please try to find out who the Laotian Communists are holding prisoner. Ask the North Vietnamese to persuade them to tell us who is alive."

"I'll ask them to do that," he said, "but you know it's difficult. Our government doesn't admit that we're involved in Laos, and probably the North Vietnamese don't know much about men held by the Viet Cong or Pathet Lao. But I'll try," he said. "I'll ask them."

Three weeks after the return of the released prisoners, the northern California families were invited to meet two of them at the Officers' Club at Alameda Air Station. I was afraid of how Petty Officer Hegdahl and Navy Lieutenant Robert Frishman would look and what they would tell us. As they came through a side door at the front of the room, I suddenly had an impulse to cover my eyes with my hands the way I did as a child when a horror movie frightened me. The place where these men had been was probably worse than any of the evil castles of the cinema. A Communist prison was a place the rest of us had only conjured up in nightmares.

The men sat down at the front table, where we could see them clearly for the first time. Their uniforms hung loosely on their thin bodies, and their eyes, sunken into hollowed cheeks, created an impression of age beyond their years. I couldn't help thinking that they were a poignant reminder of what war really is—stripped of flamboyant vestments and haughty purposes—one human suffering at a time.

Lieutenant Frishman, looking unsure of himself or why he was being accorded so much attention, stood up and spoke quietly. "I have a strong obligation to blow the whistle on North Vietnam—a strong obligation to the guys who are still back there," he said. Then he told us his story: Bones were rebroken as a means of punishment. Men were being kept in solitary confinement for months, even years, deprived of sleep, and beaten. Fingernails had been ripped out, ropes tied around the arms so tight as to leave large scars. The prisoners were burned with cigarettes as a usual disciplinary practice. They were given barely enough medical care to stay alive. He said that he had two open, draining sores when released. Pieces of shrapnel had been left in his arm after the elbow had been removed, and a piece of string remained after a serum injection.

The example of Lieutenant Frishman, his elbowless arm hanging at his side, disarmed my logic. If he who had endured such suffering could "blow the whistle" on the perpetrators of cruelty, how could we refuse to do the same?

After the release of the prisoners and disclosure of their treatment, the movement on behalf of the POWs grew in magnitude. POW families sent hundreds of letters enlisting the help of the Chamber of Commerce, the Knights of Columbus, Amvets National Auxiliary, American Veterans Commission, and the American Defenders of Bataan and Corregidor. Voices silent throughout the war spoke up in defense of these thirteen hundred men.

Like a robot, I completed chores assigned by Sybil Stockdale's League of POW/MIA Families. We wrote senators and congressmen. We appealed to editors of newspapers around the world. We showered the United Nations with telegrams. MIA wives made trips to Paris to beg for information about their husbands.

Flags were hung out to designate homes and churches as centers for "writing Hanoi and Paris." O'wives clubs at bases overseas sounded the battle cry, "Write Hanoi!" The families sent telegrams to governors' conferences, city council meetings, dogcatchers' conventions.

Bumper stickers broadcast the message via the highways of our nation:

ONLY HANOI KNOWS.
POWS NEVER HAVE A NICE DAY.
REMEMBER POWS/MIAS.
THEY ARE NOT FORGOTTEN: POW/MIAS.
HANOI RELEASE THE PRISONERS!

Carole Hanson, a Marine wife at El Toro, sent me a batch of them with her confident appraisal: "Our work and our prayers will bring them home." I slapped them into envelopes and addressed them to everyone I knew on earth.

When I ran out of places to mail bumper stickers and petitions, I borrowed a card table and set it up on a street corner. The first time I tried to spread my wares in front of our local supermarket, the manager tried to chase me away. "We can't go in for this sort of thing," he said. "Everybody wants to pass out peace literature these days." I looked him squarely in the eye—as I imagined a Marine officer's wife would do—and protested, "But this is for the POWs." He told me that was different. He mumbled words of apology and offered to carry my table and chair from the car.

We were honored guests at luncheons. Our cue to pop up, smile modestly, and sit down was always the same. It came from a male voice at the speaker's table. "And today we have with us some brave and patient women who give us the incentive to go on. . . ." One day we were seated at a large round table at the front of the grand ballroom in the St. Francis Hotel. The featured speaker was Secretary of the Navy Hittle, and he was criticizing apologists for North Vietnam "who idealize a regime which brutalizes American prisoners. . . . How can we expect

Hanoi to live up to any agreement signed at current negotiations?" he asked. Applause exploded, and I knew it was time for us to go on display once more.

I sat back down and tuned out the rest of the speech.

I was running out of steam but unable to stop tending to my projects or sending my communiqués, as if doing so would tempt the devil. Each week more men were becoming POW/MIAs, grimly assuring more families for even greater success of future undertakings. The parade moved proudly on, and I believed I would be the only marcher out of step if I missed a beat. I couldn't let Bill be tortured and do nothing, could I? I tried not to think about that possibility, and I didn't all day. It was the nightmares I couldn't control. One terrifying dream repeated itself— every two or three weeks—I could depend upon it. Bill would suddenly walk into my home in California. He wore crisp green and brown fatigues. I ran to him. He opened his arms to me and wrapped them around me. We held one another until I backed away to look at him. He smiled, but his eyes were sad and he didn't speak. I told him how happy I was. I yelled, "It's over! You're free!" Then we walked together toward the bedroom; his arm was around my shoulder. I opened the door and he followed me. I turned around to take his hand and he was gone. I ran from room to room searching for him until I came to the last door. I pushed it open, and I was no longer in my own home. The details were hazy, but I could see the outline of a room in a thatched hut. In its corner was a figure in a tattered flight suit slumped on the floor. A clamp on one leg chained him to the wall. His body was thin and streaked with fresh bruises. His head hung down on his chest. I walked over to him, and when he looked up I hardly recognized the face that had been Bill's. It was drawn and thin; his eyes stared ahead without seeing me. I spoke to him, but he didn't hear me. I wanted to revive him, unchain him, and bring him home. I bent over, shook his shoulders, and screamed into his face, "Bill, come with me!" This is when I always woke up, back in my own silent bedroom.

I didn't know what he had endured in the past three years. I only knew I had to be there waiting, ready to care for him when he came back. I didn't want anyone to harm Bill. I only wanted him home, where I could treat him better than any damn Communist could.

When another of Louise's letters came, I wasn't sure I wanted to read it. I didn't want to hear that she was optimistic, in charge, and that we should keep up the good work because we were doing such a splendid job. But it turned out that was not what she wanted to tell me. "We've been getting a lot of attention," she wrote, "and have certainly been educating the public, but I *do* resent the fact that our government is now using us to support its policies." Later I wondered how those few words could have moved me to tears. I suppose I was relieved to know that someone shared my misgivings. I had never believed that the publicity and letter writing and billboards would free the prisoners or end the war, and Louise's letter was all the impetus I needed to quit working on the projects altogether.

Every now and then, while writing one of my letters protesting the barbaric behavior of Communist captors, I'd imagine doing something I believed in instead. As the date for a massive peace march in San Francisco approached, I could think of nothing else. Without my making a conscious decision, a sense of well-being came over me and I knew I would go. The night before, feeling pleased and confident, I asked the boys if they'd like to come along.

They were more excited than I was. "What if there's some rioting or something?" Sean asked between gulps of cereal the next morning.

Terry suddenly looked interested; his eyes glistened. "Hey, will the police try to knock us on the head or something?" he asked.

"Do you think your chicken mother would go somewhere to get hit over the head, Terry?" I answered.

He laughed and said, "No, I guess not."

"We're just going to ask the President to end the war. There'll be thousands of people there. And we can see ourselves on TV tonight," I said.

Sean screwed up his face. "Could Governor Reagan tear-gas that many people?"

"No, Sean, nobody is going to be tear-gassed today," I said. "Finish your breakfast."

The march started at Pier 29 on the San Francisco Wharf, but we stationed ourselves on the sidewalk about two miles down the parade route. Carefully, I examined the marchers as they passed by. I waited for the niche that would be right for us. I let groups walk past us: university students from other cities and states in clean shirts and jeans, bearded young men in ragged garments and young women in peasant skirts from Berkeley.

Terry jumped up and down and pulled on my arm. "Let's go, Mom, before I have a fit. I can't stand here anymore."

United Farm Workers in their dark shirts and pants, looking solemn and carrying boycott signs and peace flags, were now in front of us. In back of them was a red, white, and blue United Auto Workers' banner that stretched all the way across the road. Next came a mix of grandmothers, young men and women pushing babies in strollers, men in sports coats and ties. Thank goodness, I thought, grabbing each boy by the hand and melting into the sea of people.

Sean stayed by my side, but Terry wriggled in and out of the marchers, laughing and talking to everyone until he made friends with a little girl in a red-and-white jumper. By the time we reached Golden Gate Park, she was holding his American flag and he was waving a handmade peace banner she had decorated with a crayoned yellow daisy.

We wove our way through the city, along flat avenues and over the hills, past shops and parking garages and gingerbread houses. People along the route opened their houses to let marchers use their bathrooms. An old man poured glasses of Kool-Aid for small children. We thronged into the park, where thousands became united, where purpose soothed bitterness. We were held together by a simple common belief. Overwhelmed by the power of the moment, I joined hands with my children, who held hands with strangers, and we all sang song after song. "Where Have All the Flowers Gone?" "If I Had a Hammer." "The Answer Is Blowing in the Wind."

Senator John Tunney spoke for all of us that day. "They voted for Mr. Nixon because he said he had a plan to end the war. Now, after being in office ten months, 9,500 American men have been withdrawn from the war—in coffins . . . the war now has become a case of old men's pride and young men's lives."

The following week our group in the Bay Area was lessened by one. An Army wife received notice from the Defense Department that her husband had died in a Viet Cong prison camp the previous year. As I drove through the gate of the Presidio Army Base in San Francisco and then on to the chapel, I hoped this would not be the first of many memorial services.

My mind was elsewhere, and I wasn't aware that I was being followed by a military police car until the driver signaled me to pull over. In my rearview mirror I could see two men in Army MP uniforms get out of their car. One came around to the left side of my car and motioned for me to roll down the window.

"Ma'am, we are going to remove that emblem from the car," he said.

"What emblem?" I asked. "You mean my officer's ID sticker?"

"We mean that thing on the back," he said. "We don't want any trouble."

I realized then that he was referring to a sticker I'd been given at the peace march. It was an eight-inch blue square; the word "peace" was written across the outline of a white dove. Before I could protest, the other MP had ripped it off the bumper. He brought it to my side of the car and tore it to shreds. I watched in silence. When he had finished, I asked him if I could speak to his partner.

He called, "Sergeant Miller, sir, please come talk to the lady."

Sergeant Miller was still smiling when I said, "Sir, there is another sticker on the front of the car that you may have missed."

"OK, I'll get that, too," he said, and he darted around to the front. He stopped suddenly as he read, "Only Hanoi Knows."

"Not that one. That can stay," he said.

"Sergeant Miller," I asked, "how do you decide which stay and which go?"

"I only remove the un-American ones," he said, and then walked briskly back to his car.

I turned the key in the ignition, pulled out, and drove toward the chapel. Such a small word, I thought, to threaten the security of an entire Army base.

11. LAOS: THE SECRET WAR

NOVEMBER 1969 There was a covert war being waged in Laos, and I was beginning to realize that my husband was lost somewhere in its tangled growth of jungle and lies. He had risked his life flying a mission that his country now denied ever happened. The United States government still did not admit to their operations over Laos, although they had been going on for five years. Nothing of any kind was coming out of there, not even a Lieutenant Frishman with horror stories.

Senator Stuart Symington held closed-door hearings on United States activities in Laos, and I was shocked by the figures that he and Senator Fulbright disclosed. Bombing missions had been intensified to five hundred sorties a day. I could only imagine how many planes never returned from those unheralded flights, how many pilots had drifted down through those hazy skies into that never-never land.

I couldn't shake an eerie feeling I had about those missing aviators who were not being acknowledged. How could we demand information about them without owning up to them? Why should our government express righteous indignation concerning POW treatment in North Vietnam and say nothing on behalf of men held in Laos?

These worries were on my mind the morning I called Frank Sieverts, POW/MIA family liaison officer at the State Department. "Why don't we just ask the Laotian Communists who they are holding?" I asked.

"There are complicated diplomatic reasons why we can't do that," he said. "But don't worry. I assure you that all of the prisoners are our highest priority."

I felt more uneasy after the phone call than before. Though the truth about Laos was trickling out, the military remained as close-mouthed as the State Department. A colonel at Marine Corps Headquarters wrote me: "In any appeal (to the International Red Cross, Communists, etc.), the missing servicemen should be fully identified by name, rank, service number, date of birth, and country of incident. *However, if he was downed in Laos, we recommend that you do not state that he was shot down in Laos.*" Then he added: "You should be certain that you do not provide any information which would violate a confidence between you and your spouse."

With the letter still in my hand, I dialed Marine Corps Headquarters to find out which confidence between my husband and me would be violated by mentioning Laos. "Why wouldn't the Communists know they captured Bill in Laos?" I asked the colonel. I had missed the point, he said. The secrecy had to do with classified information and orders.

"Why argue with the Marines?" I asked myself later. It only made me feel guilty.

Bill loved the Corps. He always said, "The Corps takes care of its own, Barby. We're like a family." In some ways that was true. When I had asked for a withdrawal from Bill's salary account for a down payment on a car, the Marines sent it by return mail. Once my landlord came during the night and dug up all the plants in my yard and replanted them in his own yard the next day. During a conversation with a Marine captain at Alameda Air Station, I mentioned the incident. That same afternoon he visited my landlord in an official green United States Marine Corps sedan. An hour later my landlord arrived, shovel in hand, to replant the foliage.

How could I take it out on the Marines? They were just following orders—orders that had provided them the highest percentage of casualties in the war. But, damn it, I thought, someone somewhere has to take the blame for all this secrecy.

It also seemed to me that the very organization that was supposed to represent families of the missing men had become a co-conspirator in the secrecy game. The League of Families sent Sybil Stockdale to Paris to talk firsthand with the Communist peace delegation, and the North Vietnamese told her that we could write to them individually for information on specific men. It seemed to be a breakthrough for all but the families of men in Laos. To us, she wrote, "If you inquire about a man downed in Laos, use the above address but state that he was downed by North Vietnamese forces, not that he was shot down in Laos."

Though the war was all over Southeast Asia, we acknowledged one enemy, the North Vietnamese. Tough luck, Bill, I thought while mentally constructing the letter I could write to Hanoi or Paris. "Please try to find my husband, who got lost somewhere in Southeast Asia. P.S. Don't look in Laos where he got lost."

Denials of military action in Laos by the State Department, the military, and the League of Families were undermining my self-confidence. I began to doubt my own objectivity. None of our officials mentioned prisoners in Laos. Maybe Senators Symington and Fulbright had become paranoid over the years. Was I the only person who knew there were prisoners in Laos? If Bill wasn't there, where was he? The Marines said he'd been lost somewhere over Southeast Asia. Now and then I had this foggy vision of his plane still floating up there in the clouds "somewhere over Southeast Asia."

Then, when I least expected it, the news broke that there were indeed American prisoners in Laos. I was flipping hamburgers in a fry pan, and the boys were impatiently pacing around the kitchen, when the music on my portable radio was interrupted by a special news bulletin. Sot Pethrasi, spokesman for the Communist Pathet Lao, had just revealed that 158 Americans were being held captive in Laos. Pethrasi also proclaimed, "The United States and Laos have never formally declared war; therefore there will be no prisoners. They will be tried by a Laotian people's court as criminals."

Mechanically, I put the hamburgers between hot rolls, scooped French fries from a pan, and sliced some tomatoes. I poured two glasses of milk and called the boys to the table. I felt as if my head would explode. There were prisoners after all, but how long would they remain alive?

I waited anxiously for the President or the State Department to speak up for these men; to protest the terror of their possible execution. When I'd heard nothing by the next day, I called Frank Sieverts at the State Department again. He told me that these threats of trials had been made in the past but our government had no information as to whether or not they were carried out. "You mean you've known all along there were prisoners there," I screamed into the telephone. "You mean that hundreds of tennis-playing CIA officers in Laos haven't the foggiest notion if a hundred and fifty-eight American airmen, or even one, have been tried and executed?" He tried to answer, but I hung up the phone. My God, I thought, they really don't care.

A dreary day would have been more appropriate, I thought weeks later when I looked back on that bright November morning that Ginny called. I woke up before the boys, which in itself was unusual. The sun had already warmed the room. I raised the blind to let more of it in and looked out at the sky. It was pure blue. From my window, past the clusters of pastel houses, I could see mounds of hills and behind them the crest of Skyline Drive where the redwoods and eucalyptus trees had achieved a common harmony.

After three years I was used to the heaviness that hung over me. I learned to live with it as if I'd been afflicted with a chronic physical ailment. When my arms and legs were too heavy to lug around or when breathing seemed a chore, I'd just resign myself to it. But there were times when the weight was less, when I let my guard down and temporarily felt at ease with the world. This would be one of those days, I thought. I'd enjoy my breakfast before the boys got up, send them off to school, and get ready for my class at the university. I was looking forward to the day. And then the phone rang.

It was Ginny Robinson. "Barbara, the chaplain was here," she said. There was a pause and then her voice was barely audible. "And a Marine Corps officer was with him. They just left. They said they would be back in a couple of hours—eight, I think they'll be back at eight."

"Ginny, what did they say? Try to tell me if you can."

"Larry's plane was shot down. Like Bill. In Laos, they said, on a secret mission. I don't think he's hurt. He can't be. He just can't. I don't know what to do." She was crying. I waited till she was able to speak again.

"Others saw him go down, I guess. I don't know much. Just a minute. Here comes Sonja. Sonja, honey, Mother will be with you in a minute. Barbara! What can I tell the girls? I'm here by myself."

I pictured Ginny and those four little girls in that house in southern California. When Bill left for Vietnam, they had two baby girls. They visited me in Illinois, and then there was another, and now there was a fourth, three months old, whom Larry had never seen. I tried to keep her talking. "Ginny, if they don't know, don't think the worst. They rescue some, you know."

"I'll call my dad," she said. "He'll pray. His prayers will be answered. I'll call him right now. I know Larry's going to be found."

"Ginny, call me as soon as you talk to your dad," I said. "I'll stay here by the phone all day. I want to talk to you after the chaplain comes back. Promise you'll call as soon as he leaves."

"Yes. I will. I will," she said.

If only they weren't so far away, I thought after she'd hung up. Five hundred miles. It would take all day to drive there. She needs someone now.

"Pretty Ginny." That's what Larry called her. When I first met Larry in Japan, he would show me pictures of Ginny and talk about her whenever we were alone. "There's something genuine about her," he'd say. I didn't know then that Ginny and I would become close friends a few years later. Sonja and Terry had been born two weeks apart. I thought about the day Bill left and how Ginny and Larry had taken care of me, and how Larry's letters from Vietnam had sustained me through those treacherous first six months. And now, three years later, he had also been shot down during a secret mission over Laos.

It would be a long wait until the phone rang. I thought about Ginny, how her whole life centered around Larry and her children and her home. She and Larry were a part of Bill and me. The four of us were going to survive this thing. We'd said that to one another.

At ten o'clock she called back. This time I had to strain to hear her. "Barbara, they say he's dead. But I don't believe them," she said. Then she gasped. "I'm in the bedroom. The door is locked and the girls are out there. I haven't told them anything."

"Oh, Ginny. I'm sorry. I'm sorry. Can I come? I can get a baby-sitter."

"I don't know what to do," she whispered. "The chaplain's coming back with a certificate of death. Oh, my God." She was sobbing; I waited and her voice came back. "My sister Della is coming up from San Diego. She's on her way now, so she doesn't know about the death certificate. Oh, God."

"Ginny, please listen. Try not to think until Della gets there. She'll be there soon. Go out to the living room and turn on the TV and sit with the children. She'll be there soon. Call me every two minutes if you want to."

"I hope I last until she gets here," she said. Her voice trailed off.

She hung up and I threw myself on the sofa and pounded the pillow. "Damn fucking war! Poor, poor Larry. Fucking war!"

I couldn't stop thinking about Larry. Over and over I visualized him and Bill together as impulsive twenty-five-year-old pilots in Japan, as flight instructors back in the States, and then as new fathers.

The four of us had been together a few nights before Bill left. We laughed, retold stories, and talked about the future. One of my reminiscences led to another. For days I walked around with tears running down my cheeks.

*   *   *

I'd grown to dread Christmas, and this one would be all the more difficult with the loss of Larry still so fresh. Christmases became the markers of time—rip off a calendar page and another year has passed. But Christmas 1969 would be different, the wives were saying in circulated correspondence. "This is just a note from one busy worker to another," wrote Carole Hanson from southern California. "Several of us have talked of 'something big' to do this year. I think this project merits our attention and, if we all participate, can carry a tremendous impact."

The project was: We should write to a group of Veterans of Foreign Wars who would then write to a group of their friends who would send cards to a group of POWs in North Vietnam when a tiny little letter hadn't a snowball's chance in hell of being delivered. We've finally gone around the bend, I thought, picturing endless letters still finding their way out of dining rooms and church guilds and Rotary luncheons, traveling over roads, through skies and across seas, finally ending up at a destination in North Vietnam, where, piled one upon the other, the rectangular sheets of paper would grow into a tremendous white mountain, which would then be called the "Hill of Prayers."

Carole inspired me in a way she hadn't intended. With an SOS pad in hand, I went out to the car, where I released my vengeance on the ONLY HANOI KNOWS sticker until its last gummy scrap fell to the driveway. Then I plastered in its place a new one I'd had printed. I stood back and admired it from different angles. REMEMBER POWS IN LAOS, it said. I felt a little better.

Two days before Christmas, a Marine captain knocked at my door. In his arms was a huge red poinsettia. Fresh and festive, it was tied with a matching red satin bow. "It's the color of blood," I said. It was the first thing that had come to my mind.

"I beg your pardon?" the Marine stammered. The officers were uncomfortable anyway with these family liaison duties, and now he'd lost his composure entirely.

I felt responsible. "Come in. How about a cup of coffee or a glass of wine?" I said, trying to make up for it. "Thank you very much for delivering the plant personally. Two days before Christmas, you must be very busy."

He looked so young. Somewhere along the way, Bill had been promoted to major and now the lieutenants and captains treated me with a certain deference. I never knew if it was rank, age, or the circumstances. Since the liaison officers were transferred every year and a half or so, our relationship was one of polite formalities.

Between sips of coffee the captain offered advice to the boys about being young men who should take care of their mother. Terry pulled a chair up to the table, stared him in the face, and said, "I was only eight day before yesterday, you know." Sean shifted from foot to foot, examined the Marine uniform, and mumbled monosyllabic responses to the officer's questions.

As soon as the captain had left, Sean asked, "Don't the Marines want Nixon to end the war?"

"The servicemen are just doing their duty," I said. "We can't blame the soldiers. If they refuse to go to Vietnam, they have to go to prison. This war is the fault of the President and Congress and all of the American people."

"Who cares about all that?" Terry said impatiently. "What I want to know is, what good does a great big flower do us?"

"None whatever, Terry," I answered and grabbed the crimson plant from the table. "Come on, guys, follow me!" I dashed through the kitchen, living room, and out to the deck. They ran after me. When I reached the rail, I told them to each put a hand on the pot. "One, two, three," I counted out loud and we all shoved. Marvelously, it toppled from the 100-foot-high deck, crackled through the branches, bounced off a tree trunk, and shattered on the hard ground below. When the boys looked back at me, their eyes were round with disbelief. Finally Terry spoke. "Wow, shit, Mom!" I knew I could never do anything to top the admiration I had from both of them that minute.

I reached down and hugged them as tightly as I could. "Yeah, shit, Terry," I said. "Let's go back inside and finish trimming the Christmas tree.

The next day, on Christmas Eve afternoon, the mailman returned one of my letters to Bill for the first time. Once a month I
wrote a letter to him, which I copied three times. I sent one to
Paris, one to Hanoi, and one to Algiers. I never knew where they
ended up. I had no idea how one of them would ever reach Bill's
hands in the jungles of Laos. But still I sent them. A notification
in French had been stamped on the returned envelope alongside
the North Vietnam POW camp address. I was sure of what it
said, but I had to have an exact translation. I'd met a French-
speaking nun at nearby Holy Name College, and on the chance I
might find her on Christmas Eve, I shoved the letter into my
purse and drove to the campus.

"The stamp indicates that there is no such person at this address," Sister Anita said, handing the letter back to me. "I'm
sorry it had to come back on Christmas Eve."

"It's all right, Sister. He wasn't captured in North Vietnam.
We're just told to send letters there. He's in Laos," I said. She
gave me a quizzical look.

I felt particularly alone when I returned home that afternoon.
The children were outside playing. "God," I begged into the air,
"one lousy little letter. If I could only get one letter. Just two
words, 'I'm alive.'" I thought again about the letters Bill had
written during the three days before his plane was shot down.
They had arrived as usual for three days after he had become
missing. I had wanted to read them so many times.

I walked straight to the bedroom, pulled open a bureau drawer,
and reached under the hosiery and underwear. His letters had
taken on a mystical quality; for three and a half years, sealed and
tied together with a piece of string, I'd kept them hidden from
sight. I wrapped my fingers around them, slid them carefully
from the drawer, and set them on the bed. I stared at them for a
few moments and then untied the string. I ripped one blue airmail envelope open, unfolded the onion-skin paper, and began to
read. "My dearest Barbara, Only seventeen days and we'll be together. . . ."

I threw the page face down on the bed and ran from the room.
A few minutes later I returned to take one last look at the famil-

iar handwriting before folding the letter and slipping it back into the envelope. Then I carefully wrapped a silk scarf around all three letters and pushed them back into a far corner of the drawer.

This thing is never going to end, I thought. Why did he have to fly that last mission? Over Laos? Didn't he know our government would never own up to him there?

12. CAUGHT IN THE CROSSFIRE

<u>JANUARY 1970</u> Polarization, they called it. If the country was polarized, I was a free-floating iceberg, dislodged from one frigid mass and unable to attach to another.

While I didn't believe administration spokesmen, I didn't entirely trust leaders of peace groups either. Every few months a Defense Department team made a cross-country swing. I attended their briefings and listened to middle-aged men flex verbal muscles in luxurious mahogany-furnished rooms. "What we need is resumption of bombing so those people can see something of value disappear from the earth in North Vietnam. Let that crowd find out there is a new Commander-in-chief who means what he says," proclaimed one zealous member of Congress.

Another congressman declared, "All the military needs is the order. Our planes can wheel and sway and swing high in the sunlit silence. Hovering there, as the poet says, they can push those craft through those footless halls of air."

Victims of their boastful language were housed a few miles away in Oak Knoll Navy Hospital, which had grown from a cluster of Quonset huts to a modern five-story brick medical facility. Nineteen- and twenty-year-olds maneuvered new wheelchairs in and out of elevators, through its hallways, and down paths marked for their use only. Whenever I visited the hospital, I was struck by their glazed expressions and unnatural quiet. How could these young boys, so quickly turned into men, comprehend the permanent loss of use of parts of a once agile body? Silently rolling themselves across polished Formica floors, they stared ahead, facing lives changed forever.

Though I resented the cavalier attitude of administration officials, I also questioned motives of antiwar leaders who seemed to believe anything the North Vietnamese or Viet Cong told them. They returned time and again from North Vietnam, having spoken to two or three prisoners under armed guard, and stated that the prisoners were well-treated. They brought us no proof of this and little information about the men.

Women's Strike for Peace had just merged with Dave Dellinger and Rennie Davis to form the "Committee of Liaison with Families of POWs and Missing in Action." Their purpose, they said, was to act as intermediary between the Communist captors and POW families. One of their members, Madeline Duckles of Women's Strike for Peace, had just returned from Hanoi. In spite of my own uneasiness about the intentions of this newly formed liaison committee, I decided to attend a meeting at a church in Berkeley where she was to speak.

Mrs. Duckles was being introduced as I slid into a pew in the crowded Lutheran church. The wispy-haired woman would have been at home on a university campus anywhere; perhaps she was dean of a small college somewhere, I imagined. I wondered what had catapulted her from some previously serene life onto the wire services. She began by describing the "gentle people" of North Vietnam, painting a picture of childlike creatures tiptoeing around a tropical wonderland. She said they had served her tea and tangerines in flower gardens.

A North Vietnamese editor had told her, "We are not beaten. Our country is a place where strong winds blow. The water spinach will always grow in the bomb craters filled with water, and the bamboo which does not require fertile soil will always be straight, even after it burns."

"How could these warm and friendly people be capable of the kind of cruelty alleged by previously released prisoners?" she asked. "Our bombs have devastated their country, but the North Vietnamese have nevertheless treated the pilots as human beings."

Finally she talked about her visit with three American prisoners. "The once confident airmen entered the room hesitantly with their heads bent," she said. "These former war criminals were dressed in pink-and-black striped pajamas."

Subdued laughter bubbled up here and there from corners of the church, and Mrs. Duckles continued. "The prisoners stood until one of the guards motioned for them to sit down. I know they were glad to see fellow Americans." She thought that the prisoners looked well, and she said it was her impression that they were thinking for themselves for the first time in their lives.

During the question period several people asked about the morale of the North Vietnamese; many wanted more detailed description of damage from American bombs.

The meeting was about to adjourn, and I realized that no one had asked further about the prisoners' welfare. I felt myself rising up out of the pew. "My husband has been missing three and a half years," I said. "How can you say everything is fine in the POW camps if you saw just three men? Are you saying that Lieutenant Frishman lied about his treatment after he was released?"

"Lieutenant Frishman is repeating a line given him by the State Department," she said. "Perhaps in the dark of the night he reveals to his wife what lies he has been telling."

"But I attended a memorial service for a man who died of malnutrition in a Viet Cong POW camp just a few weeks ago," I said. "We know others have died."

"You mean that's what you've been told," she said.

"Did you talk to the Communists about letting the International Red Cross in?" I asked.

"No, North Vietnam has its own Red Cross," she said.

I started to ask another question, but suddenly a woman behind me shouted, "Sit down! Your husband is a murderer!" Then I heard others say the same thing, and I sank back into the pew.

Announcing that the meeting was over, Mrs. Duckles invited everyone to come downstairs for coffee and cookies. I picked up my purse and followed the crowd. I edged up to Mrs. Duckles at the refreshment table and asked her if she had brought back any specific information about any of the prisoners. "No," she said, "but I'm sure they're all well cared for."

"Well, I'm not," I said. "There are sixteen hundred men we know nothing about. Don't you think antiwar groups are losing a lot of Americans to their cause by excusing Communist mistreatment of American POWs?"

"No," she said. "We're not losing people who are really interested in peace."

They don't really care about those captured military men, I thought, and squeezed past a group of women who were clamoring around Mrs. Duckles. All I wanted at that point was to get out of there as quickly as possible. It seemed to me that everyone's concept of "humane" contained exclusion clauses.

The next morning a student reporter from *The Daily Californian,* the University of California newspaper, headed his story: "POW Wife Disputes Word of Peace Group." I shook my head and smiled to myself. At least Maerose should be proud of me, I thought.

The war continued at its grisly pace through another winter, with the President periodically stating that he was "ready to proceed at once with arrangements for the release of prisoners of war." The President acted as if the POW issue were unconnected to the end of the war, the end being nowhere in sight.

Soon it was April and the President was telling us that, if all went well, 150,000 troops would be withdrawn from Southeast Asia by this time next year, leaving 284,000 in the war zone. In three years, I calculated, there would still be 100,000. Even this rate of withdrawal, however, Richard Nixon said, was dependent on self-determination for the government of South Vietnam.

It was obvious that the war would drift lazily on unless Congress jolted itself to action. I jotted down notes about legislative plans to end the war on sheets of memo pad and tacked them to my bulletin board beneath the news clippings and casualty lists:

Senator George McGovern—Withdraw all U.S. forces immediately.

Senator Charles Goodell—Withdraw all U.S. military personnel on or before December 1.

Senators Frank Church and Mark Hatfield—Withdraw U.S. troops more rapidly.

Senator Jacob Javits—Withdraw all American combat troops by the end of 1970.

Senator Harold B. Hughes—Demand basic reforms by the government of South Vietnam or declare that the U.S. commitment is ended.

Senators Stephen M. Young and Charles Mathias—Repeal the Gulf of Tonkin Resolution.

As each bill was defeated, I ripped the slip of paper from the board and replaced it with a new one.

While I pinned my hopes and my notes on my bulletin board, the League of Families formalized, incorporated, and moved to Washington. A sense of righteousness expanded along with the organization: Disagreeing with the President was political, they claimed; agreeing with him was not. Backing legislation that paralleled the President's plans was nonpolitical; supporting legislation that opposed the President was political. The Blackburn Resolution, which would halt further troop withdrawals until there had been a resolution of the prisoner-of-war issue, for instance, was nonpolitical; the Hatfield-McGovern Amendment, which called for immediate troop withdrawals along with POW release, was political.

While the League condemned certain groups for "using" the POW issue, others such as Ross Perot's "United We Stand" were praised for "publicizing" it. Perot, a thirty-nine-year-old Dallas millionaire and computer corporation president, was traveling the country telling people that the POW cause would unite the American people, that it would heal old wounds. I had heard that he was building a life-size mock-up of a prisoner in a bleak cell which, after being viewed by millions in the Capitol Rotunda, would go on tour. He was also planning a Fourth of July Tribute in the Rose Bowl to honor the POWs.

Finally his campaign for the POWs brought him to San Francisco. As I waited for him in the upstairs ballroom of the Marine Memorial Hotel, I wondered why I'd bothered to come. Defense briefings, peace groups, and now Ross Perot. What did I expect a computer executive from Texas to tell me about my husband in a cave in Laos? My ESP man may have been a smarter move than this one, I thought. Did I want to confirm what I already believed about the man? Or did I secretly hope the rumors were true— that "through contacts" Mr. Perot had learned what no one else could about the prisoners?

In the Berkeley church they called Bill a murderer; tonight I knew Ross Perot would call him a hero. But, in truth, I felt they were both using him to gain a public forum.

After fifteen or twenty minutes I was beginning to think Mr. Perot had forgotten us; my mind drifted back to the last time I'd been in this hotel. It was pre-Vietnam, the fall of 1960. I'd met Bill when he returned from Japan. Could it be that we actually made love in a room above where I now sat? I smiled, remembering our rides on the cable cars, eggs Benedict in Pacific Heights, the walks along the Marina. Sometimes the past seemed close enough to touch. I felt that he might be standing there in his cable-knit sweater and gray slacks waiting for me if I ran down to the street.

My memories vanished suddenly as two double doors swung open and four men marched through them into the ballroom. They were all in their early thirties and dressed alike in dark suits, white shirts, and blue ties. One moved to the center of the room and announced that Mr. Perot would be along soon. Two others reclosed the double doors. The demonstration gave truth to a rumor I'd heard that Ross Perot hired only ex-military officers.

The men stayed anxiously near the entrance. Suddenly the doors burst open again and two additional dark-suited men hurried in. "He's coming!" they announced. As if rehearsed, three more stood at attention on either side of the doors. A man nearest each side of the entrance reached for a door handle, pulling forward in unison. As the doors parted, we got our first glimpse of H. Ross Perot. He was an amazing copy of his orderlies, or they of him, more likely. He was smaller, but he made up for that with an air of authority. He rushed past us, and I knew I hadn't seen anything like this precision since a Marine dress drill at Camp Pendleton.

There was a lot of hustling around before Mr. Perot reached the front of the room. One of his men pulled a chair out for him, and some of the women who had stood when he entered sat down.

"Sorry I'm late," he said, "but certainly you know what a hectic day I've had—press conference, meetings, speech, et cetera. Well, I'm very glad to meet all of you."

If he says "brave" or "courageous," I'll vomit, I decided. I had taken to imagining a huge raffle bin, full of words. Officials would reach into it every week or so. "OK, Army, you get 'honorable' this week, Navy 'patience,' Marine Corps 'duty,' State Department 'sacrifice,' White House 'highest priority.'"

Almost preoccupied, Ross Perot continued, "I want to commend you on your loyalty and patience all these years, remaining united to your cause. As soon as these people we are fighting realize how important these prisoners are to the American people, I'm sure they'll send them home.

"Now just ask me questions," he said. "That's the best way to do this." I couldn't think of a blessed question any of us could ask this Texan for which he'd have an answer. Just as a woman raised her hand to speak, one of the attendants rushed up to Mr. Perot and whispered something which seemed of an urgent nature. The man hurried out of the room. A few moments later he reentered with a white bag, which he handed to Mr. Perot. Ross Perot then removed a Big Mac, French fries, and a milkshake from the sack and placed them on the desk before him.

"Sorry, but this is the only chance I'm going to have to eat," he said. "Just go ahead with the questions."

A woman asked if we could expect any more information from the prison camps than we had received in the past. "Prison guards can be bought," he said. "In fact, I expect information from that source in the future."

As far as I knew, Mr. Perot had never acquired specific information on any of the prisoners, and I suddenly resented that he should dangle such hopes.

"Where do you think the men taken prisoner in Laos are being held?" I asked next, mentioning the forbidden place just to put him on the spot.

"China. In China," he answered immediately.

"What proof do you have of that?" I asked incredulously.

"Well, let's just say we have informants. And that's what they tell us."

"Do we have any more details—where or who or anything?"

"No, that's all we can talk about now. You understand."

No, I didn't understand. Those rumors had flown around every year or so, and there was never a shred of fact to back them up. And so it went. I suppose the women wanted to believe. Someone somewhere had to know something, and Ross Perot had been chosen.

At the end of the meeting he said he would see us in Washington the following week. Then he left the way he entered, surrounded by his entourage, and we left with whatever we wanted to swallow.

A few days later League women from the Bay Area flew to Washington to attend a national convocation to honor the POWs. On the same day, the United States invaded Cambodia. Reaction to Richard Nixon's "incursion" into Cambodia was immediate. Dormant antiwar sentiment was revived, exploding into renewed protest, but in Washington the speeches, dedications, and formal dinners for the prisoners went on, oblivious to the commotion in the rest of the country. I gave no thought at all to the gala events; I only knew that I should be doing something to demonstrate my personal indignation at the war's enlargement.

When I heard that students at the University of California wanted to participate in open dialogue with people in the Bay Area, I decided to call them. The young woman who answered told me to gather my neighbors together, and they would do the rest. "We'll bring students to exchange views," she said. "We'll even set up a baby-sitting operation for you if you want."

After promising to do it, I had second thoughts. Would my neighbors come? Noel diBortelli, a foreman at the telephone company, lived across the street. I'd heard him state more than once, "I support Nixon because he is our President." His wife, Rosi, had never expressed herself on the war in front of me, but I supposed she felt as he did. Most of the nearby homes belonged to families like the diBortellis with small children, but some housed an assortment of part-time students and hippies. Perhaps the bearded, barefoot man who gave Terry a notebook full of handwritten Timothy Leary poems would come and I could count on the Chicano family which had pasted a peace emblem next to a "boycott grapes" sign in their living room window. But what about retired people who had lived on the block for more than fifty years?

The invitation would have to be phrased just right. I wrote it two or three times, had it mimeographed, and handed a stack of two hundred to Sean and Terry to deliver throughout the neighborhood.

The notice read:

Question:
1. Why is there so much violent controversy about the U.S. presence in Vietnam?
2. Why are so many of us—young and old, men and women, rich and poor—screaming at one another about this issue like no other in the last hundred years?

Answer:
We really don't know, but we think it has something to do with people not talking to each other about it or about their feelings toward it.

A number of us living in the El Centro–Dolores Avenue–Benevides area are meeting at the home of Barbara Mullen to talk about the war and how we do feel about it. We would like you and your neighbors to come and be with us. Baby-sitting provided. Wednesday, May 27, 1970.

Rosi diBortelli arrived before anyone else, and I wondered if her husband knew she had come. "I thought I'd come and listen," she said, offering me a plateful of fresh chocolate chip cookies. She sat down in one of my rented folding chairs in the backyard just as the first women students drove up. I was relieved to see that they had brushed their long straight hair; they all wore shoes and their clothing appeared to be clean. They came in groups of three or four, served themselves coffee or fruit punch from a picnic table, and wandered around the yard. One at a time, my neighbors were showing up, and the students were introducing themselves.

I was congratulating myself on how well things were going when suddenly one of the students stood in the center of the yard and announced, "My name is Charity—that's what I call myself. Someone has to start the dialogue, so I will." She swung herself around in a circle to be sure she had everyone's attention, and said, "In my opinion, the masses should dump that Nazi government in Washington." She paused. "The police pigs in our cities and fascists in the Defense Department, too."

She directed her next remark to me. "Our nation is pervaded by a Marine Corps mentality," she said. "I don't know how any woman could sleep with a military killer."

I was stunned. Immediately I looked toward Rosi. I wouldn't have been as embarrassed if she weren't there. Rosi got up from her chair, and I was sure she was going to leave, but instead she addressed the young woman. "Don't insult Barbara," she said. Charity threw her hands in the air as a gesture of hopelessness and muttered something about others taking over. She shuffled across the grass and leaned against the fence.

Another student had taken her place and was speaking. "Rather than speeches," she said, "why don't we just talk with one another, one to one? It might work out better." Slowly conversations resumed.

Mrs. Andrews, my neighbor from across the street, a thin, white-haired lady, walked over to where Charity was now stretched out on the grass staring up at the sky. The older woman wore a silk print dress, pearl earrings and necklace. Though the afternoon was warm, she seemed unruffled and cool. Her face had been finely powdered and a delicate dab of rouge had been carefully applied to each cheek. She reached down to tap the girl's bare shoulder. The young woman leaped to her feet, pulled at her halter top, and twisted her peasant skirt into place before accepting the older woman's extended hand. "My real name is Susan," she said.

I approached them just as my elderly neighbor was introducing herself. "I've always been a Republican," she was saying, "but still I don't see why we should be spending our taxes in a foreign country when we have so many problems at home. I never told anyone that, but I'm almost mad enough to write a letter to the President."

"Right on," Susan said, flashing her first smile, "and I'm mad enough to overthrow the whole damn government."

After a second or two of uneasy silence, the old lady smiled back. "Why don't we have some fruit punch first," she said.

After the students had driven away and my neighbors had left, some of them carrying "peace" buttons and bumper stickers, I tried to sort it all out. I wasn't sure anything had been accomplished; I only knew that I felt better than if I had been in Washington waving flags for Richard Nixon under the guise of a POW convocation.

13. ON MY OWN

SUMMER 1970 The uproar over Cambodia quieted and the country returned to its preoccupation with other matters: inflation, mini-skirts, communes, rap sessions, baseball, topless nightclub dancers, *Hair,* LSD. And I fell into another slump. I would no longer try, I decided, to fit in where I felt uncomfortable or unwanted, which it seemed to me was just about everywhere. I borrowed a philosophy from Alcoholics Anonymous: "Change what you can, accept what you can't, and learn to know the difference."

I have my children and my studies, I thought, and flipped another page. I was lost in my books when Terry came up and tugged on my arm. "Come on, Mom. Stop reading. We have to finish drying our race cars. We have to be at Cub Scouts in an hour."

His face, full of urgency, reminded me of the evening ahead. It was the night that the Cub Scouts were to race cars they had designed and carved themselves.

Sean came in from the garage. "The knife marks still show, and we sanded and sanded," he complained, plopping the result in front of me on the table.

"Geez, Sean, don't worry," Terry said. "Nobody will notice."

They'd come straight home from school to put the finishing touches on the paint job. Sean sat on the end of the sofa and swirled a hair dryer around the surface of a silver-and-red object. He'd managed to round it slightly at the front and back ends and had dug a hole out for the imaginary driver. Now and then he held it up in front of him to admire it. "I don't know," he said. "It looks good, but I hope it's dry enough."

I gawked in disbelief when I walked into the gym and saw the slick, perfectly designed models displayed on eight-foot-long tables. Had they really sprung from the same hunks of wood Sean and Terry had brought home? Finer, sleeker lines never streaked around an Indianapolis track. One father proudly unveiled a prize miniature before the envious eyes of a fellow dad while his son tried without success to wrench it from his hand. I overheard two fathers discussing the amount of lead each had inserted in an exact strategic spot to cause calculated precision downward momentum on a roller-coaster track in the center of the gym. My heart sank. Sean and Terry hadn't taken their cars out of the brown paper bag, and we'd been there twenty minutes.

When Sean's turn came, he placed his wooden creation, which now seemed barely to resemble the race car he'd envisioned it to be at home, behind the starting gate at the top. It began its roll, but to my disbelief, and against all the rules of physics, came to a complete stop partway down the first slope.

He stared at it blankly for a moment, then picked it up and struggled to turn the wheels, which had become glued by a glob of paint to the axle. When it was obvious the wheels were permanently sealed, he shoved the car into his pants pocket, tossed his head in the air, and marched back to our table.

Terry had slid down in his chair as far as he could; his eyes barely peeked over the table top. Sean sat down and Terry kicked him under the table. "Wow, am I glad you went first," he said. "I'm not entering mine."

"At least you two learned to carve on a piece of wood," I said later at an ice cream parlor, where they had agreed to go only because it was blocks away from the school gym. "That's more than most kids learned."

Terry darted a look at Sean and then dropped his head on his arms on the table and burst into a fit of laughter. I knew he'd been holding it in ever since we left the gym. Between hoots, he squealed, "Did you see Jerry's father? He almost cried when they lost!"

"When I walked into that gym and saw those works of art on the table," I said, "I almost fainted."

Sean finally grinned and poked Terry's arm. "You wouldn't think it was so stinkin' funny if you were the one looking stupid," he said.

"I wouldn't want my father to build a race car for me, even if I had a father," Terry said.

"Me either," Sean agreed.

"Do you think we're ever going to see our dad, Sean?" Terry asked.

"Sure," Sean said, scraping the last spoonful of ice cream from the bottom of his dish. "We will."

"For now, the three of us will manage just fine," I said.

At nine and seven and a half I wanted Sean and Terry to have an ordinary childhood. I hoped their father's disappearance wouldn't deprive them of that, but I couldn't let them forget him either, and it was a contradiction I dealt with on a daily basis.

One afternoon I overheard Sean talking with a schoolmate. He had asked Sean where his dad was, and Sean answered without hesitating. "Oh, my mom and dad are divorced."

It came out so easily I knew it wasn't the first time he'd said it. I waited for his friend to leave; then I asked Sean why he hadn't told the truth. Before answering, he gave me a long, slow glance, as if assessing how much he should reveal. "Geez, Mom, I want to seem normal, you know," he said. "I just hate when people look at me with big sad eyes. Like they feel sorry for me. Especially the other guys."

It took me a moment to come to grips with what he'd said. By then I realized I'd often felt the same way myself. I'd never lied about my situation, but often it was easier to let people assume I was divorced than to relate my dreary tale. "I know what you mean, Sean," I said. "I hate that, too. I don't want anyone to think I'm a pitiful character."

He swiveled around on his kitchen stool and waited for me to go on. "Try looking people straight in the eye, so they'll know that," I said.

"I don't know," he said. "That might work for you, but not me. I'd just look stupid. I should tell them, though, 'cause they usually find out anyway."

"Come on, Sean," I said, putting an arm around his shoulder. "A kid as smart as you could never look stupid."

"Well, you're right about that, I guess," he said, a grin creeping over his face.

The children were growing up to the point where I could be more honest with them, and I felt less controlled by forces outside myself. But this same sense of self was stirring impatience on another level. I felt lonely a lot of the time. Bill had been gone five years. It was a long time, but I certainly had to tolerate that, I told myself, considering that he was merely trying to survive somewhere.

Believing that, however, didn't stop the loneliness, which rolled over me in waves. When I felt particularly anxious, I forced myself to picture Bill in a dark cave, a straw hut, a cell, anywhere, as long as I could visualize him. I concentrated until the features sharpened in my mind, though a fraction of a second later the vision was gone.

At night I'd wake up, turn on the bedroom light, and run my fingertips over the smooth surface of the headboard, where two Kahlua glasses had left tiny rings on long-ago evenings. Sometimes these delicate circles imprinted on the walnut wood reassured me; I'd turn out the light and go back to sleep.

On other evenings I'd get out of bed, slip into an old pair of jeans and sweater, and drive my car up through the old canyon roads. I often thought about heading in the other direction, down the hills to places where people met one another, talked and laughed. I yearned to do that, but instead I kept driving up to the top of Skyline Drive. From there, I could see the flickering lights of Berkeley, Oakland, and San Francisco across the bay. The hills and trees separated me from the human activity below, and this comforted me. When I felt calm again, I returned home.

In the morning I was usually more philosophical, able to think about Bill's absence in a detached way. The boys and I had become such an intact family, it was difficult to imagine Bill there with us. I often wondered what kind of father he would have been. Surely he would have given the children something that I couldn't, but I wasn't sure what that was or how to make up for the lack of it.

Sean climbed into the car after Little League practice one morning and announced, "Tomorrow the coach is going to pick his team. He's going to call the ones at home who made it."

After that he stared out the car window and didn't speak. When I reminded him that it was just a game, he glared at me. I quickly added that I hoped he would make the team, but he kept his eyes fixed on the trees and hills and didn't answer me.

Just as we were leaving for the swimming pool the following morning, Sean decided not to go with us. "I think I'll stay home today—watch television or something," he said. I knew there was no use trying to budge him.

When we came home at five o'clock, he didn't need to say he hadn't heard from the coach. One look at his face gave me the answer.

He picked at his dinner. Later when I asked him to go for a ride with Terry and me, he said, "No thanks, I'm going to stay here and work on my model airplane tonight."

About eleven-thirty that night, I heard a knock at my bedroom door. When it opened a crack, I saw him standing there in the dark hall in jeans and T-shirt. His hand clasped the doorknob tightly, and somehow he looked smaller to me. He tried to sound matter-of-fact as he asked, "Do you think the coach has called everyone by now?"

I hated to answer. "I guess he probably has, Sean," I said.

He looked down at the floor and brushed a bare foot back and forth on the carpet. I wished it were possible to take him back to bed with me, where I could hold him in my arms and protect him. Instead, I got up and walked over to him. "Maybe there were so many good ones he just couldn't choose them all," I said, placing a hand on his shoulder.

"And maybe I just stink, too," he answered. Shaking my hand loose, he turned and ran back to his room. When I opened his door a few minutes later, he had already flopped onto the bed, rolled himself in blankets, and covered his head. "Get out of here now, Mom," he said.

"OK, I'll see you in the morning," I answered. I stood in the hall, feeling helpless. What would a father do now? I wondered. Oh, hell, I thought, maybe he'd feel just as inadequate. I just didn't know.

We went on coping, the three of us. I tried to be mother and father. Once I had a terrible battle with the school principal because I wasn't allowed to attend a father-and-son banquet. "But I am their father," I said, "and they want to see those Oakland Raider highlight films with the other boys!"

The principal didn't see it that way, and it angered me, but I suspected that on balance there were compensations to being a single parent. The three of us were pitted against the world— sharing the good and the bad. I cracked a rib wrestling on the floor with Terry, took them dirt-bike riding on hot dusty tracks at seven on Sunday mornings, helped them care for a raccoon family under our front deck, along with a dog and two cats. The cats were refugees smuggled home under blankets in the back of our car at the end of a vacation trip.

All the while, I felt as if the three of us huddled together for security, with the war always looming on the horizon like a hurricane ready to change course, head landward, and strike. My only shelter had become an elusive attitude that allowed me to track potential storm patterns from a distance.

Getting my B.A. degree suddenly seemed very important to me. I signed up for extra classes. There, alone with my books and assignments, I felt more in charge. That summer I finished my last course and breathed a sigh of accomplishment.

My diploma arrived, unceremoniously, in the mail. I'd snuck down to the mailbox tugging at the belt of an old terry-cloth robe.

When my hand touched the stiff envelope, I left the rest of the mail where it was and ran back up the stairs, tearing the envelope open on the way.

I slid the diploma out and ran my fingers over the leather binding. It opened like a book—the lettering was gold and engraved: The University of Northern Michigan has conferred the degree of Bachelor of Arts . . . leather, gold, and legal. How many credits had I transferred back to Northern Michigan University over the years?

Smiling with satisfaction, I kept holding it up to view it from different angles. I could almost hear the chords of *Pomp and Circumstance* in the distance. It's about time, I thought, laughing to myself and remembering a recent conversation between Terry and a friend.

Terry had said, "Be quiet. My mom's trying to study."

The friend asked, "Why does your mom go to school? Moms have more important things to do."

Terry scowled at his friend. "Not my mom," he said. "She's always been going to school, and when she grows up, she's going to be a social worker."

This occasion had to be celebrated, I decided. I dashed to the bedroom, grabbed a pair of jeans from a hook in the closet, and yanked a sweat shirt over my head. Pulling a brush quickly through my hair, I realized how much it had grown—to three or four inches below my shoulders. Imagine that—still dark brown, though. I sighed while giving a sidelong glance toward the full-length mirror on the door. I may be ravaged on the inside, but the exterior is holding up fairly well—a little skinny, but not bad. In fact, I could be arrested for looking like this in the officers' club, I laughed. I threw the strap of my purse over my shoulder and bounced down the stairs.

Good old California. The best champagne, cooled to perfection and sold alongside groceries in the supermarket. At home I poured the bubbly liquid into three long-stemmed crystal glasses and then called to the boys from the front porch.

Terry's baseball cap was on backwards, and his frizzy hair fringed out from under it over his ears. He was at bat and pretended not to hear me. Sean shrugged and motioned for Terry to follow him. Together they trudged up the street in dirty jeans and scuffed sneakers. "What's up, Mom?" Sean hollered.

"Come in and sit down, boys," I said. "Congratulate your mother. She just graduated from college." I dangled the diploma before their eyes, displaying the proof.

Terry reached for it, opening and closing it and opening it again. He'd never looked so solemn. I waited patiently for his proper recognition. "Wow," he said. "Is that all you got for all that work?"

"You don't get it, Terry," Sean said, pulling it from Terry's hand. "Mom is smarter now, so she'll make a lot of money. Probably we'll be very rich before we know it."

"OK, you two. This is an honor. Someday you'll appreciate it. Never mind, just raise your glasses and toast me. We all click glasses, and then you say something nice."

"Here's to you, Mom," Terry said, clunking the side of my glass. He gulped a mouthful and then let out a loud "Yuk!" He leaped up from his chair, coughed, and held a hand over his mouth. "You can have the rest of mine, Mom." He swished his baseball cap through the air in front of him and bowed from the waist. "Please excuse me, madame," he said, and then disappeared from the room. The front door slammed behind him.

"I'm glad you made it, Mom," Sean said, trying to smooth Terry's abrupt exit. "I never thought you'd do it," he added. "Can I go back to the game now?"

I poured myself another glass of champagne. Well, Bill would be proud of me, I thought. Suddenly I was feeling better, more in control and wanting to use my new sense of independence. I set my champagne glass on the table and went straight to the telephone.

I'd thought for some time that Congressman Pete McCloskey was one person who might understand me. I'd simply been too lethargic to contact him. McCloskey was a highly decorated Marine Corps veteran of the Korean War who doggedly hammered away at Nixon's war policies. As far back as 1967 he had questioned our involvement in the war when he first ran for Congress and beat Shirley Temple Black in the Republican primary.

John Wilson, McCloskey's staff assistant, answered my call and said McCloskey would indeed be glad to meet with me the following Sunday, when he would be in California. I looked forward to the meeting all week.

His office was an old white house in San Mateo. In the shade of tall, lazy trees I sat on the steps of its long porch and waited for McCloskey to arrive. No one was around on a Sunday afternoon, and I was glad it was quiet. I'd come early so I'd have time to unwind before meeting him.

His car drove up and he waved. "Hi, Barbara Mullen?" I nodded.

"Let's go inside," he said, bounding up the steps. He reached in his suit coat pocket for the office key and then patted his other pockets. "I know it's here somewhere," he said, "but I can't seem to find it."

"Is there anything I can do to help?" I asked. I'd never been locked out of an office with a congressman before, but I assumed I should be doing something.

"Let's try to jar a window loose," he said.

We both pushed and shoved, but the old repainted windows refused to budge. Finally he gave up and started to laugh, and then I laughed too. "Why don't we go next door and have a drink?" he suggested.

Next door was a restaurant with a cocktail lounge. He ordered drinks for us, smiled, and asked, "How can I help?"

It was the first chance I'd had to have a good look at him. Up close, he was more handsome than he was in pictures. His dark hair was the right length, not too short; a few unruly strands flopped forward onto his forehead. He had a wonderfully modulated voice; he sounded like a newscaster.

I almost forgot why I was there. I was wishing I'd worn something more attractive when I realized he was waiting for me to say something intelligent. I was thankful my mouth finally opened. "I thought that with your military background, your motives and patriotism—silly as that sounds—wouldn't be questioned by the families of the prisoners. Maybe they would listen to you. I really think as a group we could have an effect on the President."

"I'll be glad to try," he said. Then he looked puzzled. "Don't they know their husbands won't be home until this war is over?"

"These families, you have to understand, have been stroked with flattering words by Nixon's people," I said. "And the guilt is laid on all of us. This business of being disloyal to the military and to our Commander-in-chief can be overwhelming."

I could tell by the look on his face that I had struck a sensitive chord. "It is difficult to speak out," he said. "But none of your husbands created this policy. You don't have to agree with actions that are going to get a lot more servicemen killed. You're all citizens. You have a right to express your opinions."

"Did you have to tell yourself that in the beginning—when you first spoke out?" I asked.

"Over and over," he said. "And yet it's the basic foundation of our democracy. I don't know why it scares people so."

"You don't know how many times I've wanted to call you," I said.

"You should have," he said. "I'll be glad to talk with the wives and families if it can be arranged. There surely must be others who feel as you do, not knowing where to turn."

He asked about the boys and the Marine Corps. It turned out we'd been at Camp Pendleton once at the same time. As we talked, I was beginning to feel comfortable for the first time with my Marine Corps connection and my opposition to the Vietnam War.

Before leaving, he said, "Don't be afraid. It sounds corny, but it's really what our country is about. Freedom to say what you think. Why claim we're fighting for someone else's freedom and then not use your own?"

From my rearview mirror I watched Pete McCloskey walk toward his car, and I thought, Maybe there is still a place for words like "honorable." It seemed a long time since I'd genuinely respected and trusted someone, and it felt good.

Right then I'd have followed him anywhere—certainly out of the parking lot. But he was married and so was I, I supposed, and besides, he hadn't asked me. So I'd have to settle for merely being uplifted. He'd risked everything for his principles, and it suddenly occurred to me that all I really had to lose was a heavy burden. I felt airy, lighter, ten years younger, and I wanted to chase after him just to shout, "Thank you, Pete McCloskey, thank you!"

14. THE FAMILIES DIVIDE

<u>MARCH 1971</u> Ever since meeting Congressman McCloskey, I'd felt more at ease. When I wrote to a congressman or attended a peace rally, I did it alone, true to myself and my own beliefs. I refused to participate in League projects, and I felt that leaders of the peace movement showed little compassion for the serviceman or his family. I almost felt I should apologize to them for the fact that my husband had worn a uniform, as though he in some way bore guilt for this doomed war.

But things might be different after tonight. Sally and Delia Alvarez were driving down from San Jose. I'd been peering out the window every few minutes and listening for the sound of their car. Since I first read about the family in the *Oakland Tribune*, I'd wanted to know them. Commander Everett Alvarez, Jr., was believed to be the longest-held prisoner in United States history, having been captured during the Tonkin Gulf episode in 1964. I wouldn't have had this opportunity to meet them if it weren't for an article that had appeared in the *San Francisco Chronicle* back in January.

Louise and seven other POW wives had publicly backed an end-the-war bill, introduced by California Congressman Robert

Leggett. As soon as I read the UPI story, I called Leggett's office in Washington. I told his aide, Bob Sherman, that I knew Louise, that I would also back the plan, and that I was disillusioned by the League. When I stopped talking for an instant, Bob Sherman informed me that they'd already heard from several other families in California. He offered to have the Alvarez family in San Jose contact me and I agreed readily.

I had seen Delia once on television when she appeared on a Dick Cavett show with Jane Fonda. Jane had done most of the talking, indicating that she didn't believe the horror stories about the POWs and hinting that the Communists had been provoked into doing whatever they were doing. Jane seemed to believe that the North Vietnamese had given our government the names of all the prisoners they could. She also dodged Dick Cavett's questions about lack of Red Cross inspection of all the POW camps. Most of the POW families resented Fonda's willingness to believe the North Vietnamese, and I sometimes wondered if she'd have accepted their word so easily if her brother or husband were hidden behind those barricaded walls. It was a shame, I thought, that such a principled woman didn't use her antiwar credentials to better advantage. She just might have been able to get some real information about the prisoners from the Communists.

I had watched the Cavett program, anxiously waiting and hoping that Delia would challenge some of Fonda's assertions about POW treatment, but she hardly had an opportunity, sandwiched as she was between the two superstars. I wouldn't bring up the topic of the Fonda show unless Delia did, I decided; we would have so much else to share.

We talked for hours that night in my living room. Delia and Sally Alvarez were as excited about our first meeting as I was. We related common personal experiences and damned the war that had caused them.

Delia was nothing like the subdued woman I'd seen on TV. Rather, her dark short hair and amber skin conveyed a notion of strength. She talked with pride about her job as coordinator of

Chicano projects at a community center, and reminisced about her older brother, whom she idolized and missed.

Sally, her mother, was a small wiry woman; she shifted from topic to topic quickly and her slight accent became more pronounced with enthusiasm. She leveled her dark eyes at me and asked, "What do you think of all these Statue of Liberty women, these wives who will let the war go on and on as long as they don't have to cross the President?"

"I can't worry about them," I said. "They aren't going to say anything unless it has a Defense Department stamp of approval." It seemed to be the right answer, because Sally laughed and agreed.

Delia said she wanted to tell everyone in the country how she felt about Richard Nixon. "If Congress would cut off the money," she said, "the war would be over."

As the evening progressed, our plans solidified. They were so sure of themselves; I envied that. Government and patriotism had always been inseparable concepts for me. The nation of my ideals had been good, just, and right. The Alvarezes seemed to have less difficulty than I did admitting that our country had made a mistake. They talked about their country as having promise and potential, but they weren't shocked by its ability to err.

Our plans were whirling around in my head after they left. Maybe they were right. Together we could put pressure on the President. He was becoming more vulnerable all the time as the Communist offers to release prisoners along with our withdrawal were repeated.

I bounded out of bed the next morning feeling like a potent force. I would send telegrams to the White House, I decided, until someone answered my question: "Is the President willing to offer a withdrawal date for release of prisoners?"

A few weeks later Delia got her chance to tell the world what she thought of Richard Nixon. She was invited to speak at a massive peace rally in San Francisco.

Again I packed lunches and drove to the pier area where the march would begin. As we walked past the same Victorian homes and stores and restaurants, however, I realized that this march was different from the last. Bystanders seemed less spirited and the marchers more serious. Vietnam veterans, concerned military officers, and clergymen added a sober element that affected everyone. The boys felt it, too. They stayed by my side this time all the way to the park. It was not a day for optimism or celebration. The picnic atmosphere was gone.

Delia's voice echoed from loudspeakers. "My brother was sent to Vietnam by Kennedy, captured during Johnson's administration, and has been imprisoned indefinitely by Nixon." A hush came over Golden Gate Park, and Pete McCloskey, who stood by her side, took the microphone when she finished. He issued his own emotional appeal for peace. He was followed by Dick Gregory, who vowed to fast until peace came. The cast of *Hair* sang "Let the Sunshine In," but in spite of the songs and speeches and nature's own sunshine, a chilling sadness seemed to cling to the crowd.

Following the march, James Reston wrote in his *New York Times* column: "The administration has brushed the Communist offers off as old stuff and propaganda, but since the President has been emphasizing the security of his troops and release of the POWs, their propositions are at least worth discussing, but probably won't be without pressure from the public and the families of the POWs."

One by one, outside the League, parents and wives were contacting one another. On April 30, 123 members of families of prisoners and men missing in action placed an ad in the *Washington Post.* In the form of a letter, we asked the President to set a timetable for withdrawal after a Communist agreement to release the prisoners.

Soon after the letter appeared in the *Washington Post,* our Bay Area families were invited to a luncheon in honor of Admiral Zumwalt, Secretary of the Navy. I had decided, along with the Alvarezes, not to attend, but changed my mind when Pete McCloskey asked us to meet with him afterward at his office in San Mateo. It was the only reason I'd ended up in the Grand Ballroom of the Fairmont Hotel listening to Admiral Zumwalt deliver a speech that could have been lifted from a 1967 file folder. The difference, I thought, half listening and glancing about the banquet room, was that I would have believed him then.

My reverie was interrupted at the halfway point in his speech when, according to tradition, we were introduced to the audience. I hadn't planned it, but when the applause began and Admiral Zumwalt asked us to stand, I remained seated. Why should I be his visual aid? I cupped my fingers under the seat of my chair so my body wouldn't betray me by rising. Two women at my table who had bobbed up were glaring at me, but I looked past them and scooped a spoonful of sweet refreshing sherbet from my fruit cup.

"They and their husbands stand today in the front ranks of those whose sacrifice and suffering in defense of freedom can never be fully known," Zumwalt said, and then more applause broke out.

He ended his dreary speech by defending what he termed the successful Vietnamization program and "the stable democratic government which exists in South Vietnam today."

I hurried out of the hotel to my car, glad to be on my way to San Mateo and Congressman McCloskey's first real meeting with the families.

Nearly half of the family members who had been at the Zumwalt luncheon showed up at McCloskey's old white house. Also there, much to everyone's surprise, was a *Newsweek* reporter snapping pictures and taking notes. Representative McCloskey, in shirt sleeves, was leaning against a desk, casually explaining his position when I walked in.

"Ending the war is the best way of getting your husbands back," he said. "The President is perpetrating a cruel hoax when he says we will keep fighting until the prisoners are released. If he does what I think he's going to do—get all the troops out before election time, but continue the bombing for two or three years—I don't think you can have an expectation of any prisoners coming home. If I were President, I would have only one condition for getting out—the release of the prisoners.

"So," he continued, "let me ask you the crunch question. If you had to choose between Mr. Nixon's policy of long-term bombing while negotiations continue and mine of making the release of prisoners the only condition of withdrawal, which would you choose?"

Slowly the hands went up in support of McCloskey's proposal, six out of the eight. With two simple choices, even Maerose's hand had risen with a certain uneasiness.

After most of the others had left, I talked with McCloskey out on the porch. He seemed satisfied with the way the meeting had gone. "I think more of the women are coming around to your way of thinking," he said.

Maerose and others expressed resentment the following week, however, when the whole session, along with a photo, was recorded in *Newsweek*. The women grumbled that they'd been trapped by a question they didn't want to answer, especially in front of a newsman. I received a letter from Maerose, and I knew McCloskey's temporary victory had backfired. Her note was hand-written on small sheets of white paper:

Dear Barbara,

Marines are noted for their esprit de corps. I know that means nothing to you because you hate the military, but I am hoping you still do not hate your country. . . .

You are in pretty fast company with Delia Alvarez. I heard what she said at the peace march. Think carefully of what you align yourself with.

I'm trying to tell you some things I had learned in D.C. It is nice to think you can use some of these congressmen and senators, but they are "pros." Just four hours after we saw McCloskey, he told an audience that six of eight family members voted to oppose the Administration. . . .

All that flag-waving about the Marine Corps by McCloskey is pathetic. You probably have more regard and respect for it than he does, and you know that is not much.

I am not the star-spangled girl, and I have lived in a foreign country, and I'll take this country over all, anytime.

I consider myself a friend to you, Barbara, and I hope you do the same.

Your friend,
Maerose

Stuffed into the same envelope was a copy of a letter she had written Louise Mulligan earlier. She had told Louise, "You are falling into a pattern of what the North Vietnamese and their allies and Communist friends in this country want. We have to stand united on this issue for the men's sake and for our country's sake."

Maerose's letter was only the first of many encounters with indignant members of the League. I tried to avoid face-to-face confrontation whenever possible. One morning at the PX I swung my cart 360 degrees and headed up a different aisle to avert contact with one of the women, but she was waiting for me when I came around the corner, in front of the lipsticks and mascara. "If you were in Russia, you couldn't disagree with your government the way you're doing," she bellowed.

"Yes," I said, catching my breath, "aren't we lucky we don't live there?"

Nothing I could say, however, would pacify them. Anonymous notes were delivered by my mailman every few weeks. Typewritten and unsigned, one asked, "What would your husband think of your un-American activities?"

Bill loved the Marine Corps, and he thought the cause was just when he was ordered to go. But in 1965 we all thought it was just. What would he be thinking now? That the world had forgotten him? That a memorial service had been held for him years ago? He probably didn't know that Martin Luther King, Jr., and Bobby Kennedy had died along with 45,000 servicemen. He'd never heard of My Lai or President Thieu or Vietnamization. I could only guess what Bill would be thinking now, but I was sure he would have expected me to fight for his life, one way or the other. It was what I hadn't done, what I could have done, or had forgotten to do—not what I had done—that ate away at me.

Carole Hanson, League coordinator in southern California, ran a half-page ad in the *Washington Post*. In large block letters she pleaded:

HELP KEEP THE POWS/MIAS OUT OF POLITICS. WE HAVE ONLY ONE PRESIDENT AT A TIME. HE IS COMMANDER-IN-CHIEF. IT IS HIS RESPONSIBILITY TO GET THE POWS BACK. SUPPORT HIM IN HIS EFFORTS.

Soon after that, Carole appeared with Mitch Jones on "The Advocates," a public television program. Both of their husbands had been shot down in Laos, but Mitch had signed the letter to the President in the *Washington Post* asking for an end to the war.

I looked forward to seeing the program and settled comfortably in front of the TV to watch. Carole's smile seemed frozen above a stiff white collar. Below the hem of her semi-mini-skirt were a pair of shiny white boots. Her hair, a perfect beehive, was relieved by one corkscrew curl which appeared plastered to each of her cheekbones just in front of each ear.

Her smile prevailed through questions of life and death from the moderator. Whenever cornered, she explained quietly but patiently, "We have only one Commander-in-chief at a time. Who are we to doubt his word?" Carole seemed confused that this didn't end the discussion.

Mitch Jones was a different sort of woman, handsome by anyone's standards and sure of herself. She was an engineer by profession and didn't mince her words. "We're sacrificing good men for a corrupt government," she said. "There will be no victory. We have to get out and end it. That's the only thing that will bring the men back who are still alive."

The interrogator tried one final question on Carole. "If every provision is made in writing, and in public, by the Communists, for positive release of our men everywhere in Indochina and a full accounting of the missing with neutral verification, will you then feel that President Nixon should name our withdrawal date?"

"No," said Carole. "The President has a right to fulfill the purpose for which the men were fighting, *before* negotiating for the prisoners' release."

I wasn't surprised by her answer. I was sure what she said was true—that many of these women would sacrifice their own husbands if Richard Nixon or Henry Kissinger asked them to. It reminded me of junior high school, where our principal, Miss Deasy, a tall thin woman with wavy gray hair, reigned supreme. Every day she stood at the bottom of the stairs and clapped her long slender hands together as she directed her "pupils" to pass from class to class or to proceed to the auditorium. We moved quickly in single rows, never missing a step, as over and over again she repeated, "Follow your leader. Follow your leader." And through those halls we marched off to become the silent generation.

The split between the families was deepening fast; I knew we had to organize ourselves or lose an opportunity for good. I'd been tossing the theory around for a couple of days when Bob Sherman, Congressman Leggett's aide, called from Washington to tell me he'd come to the same conclusion. I didn't expect him to lay the responsibility at my doorstep, however. "Why me, Bob?" I asked, and then ran through a list of other women who I was sure could do a better job.

"What about Mitch Jones or Louise? I hear Valerie Kushner, the Army doctor's wife, is getting in touch with everyone who signed the letter in the *Washington Post*. Come to think of it, Valerie is the best bet, Bob," I said, relieved to have come up with someone.

"I don't think any of them will take the initiative. They're all still trying to get the League to change its ways. You know that's hopeless," he said. "If you don't form a separate group quickly, the media won't treat you seriously."

"Are you sure Louise won't do it?" I asked, seeing the options shrink before my mind's eye.

"No, she's worn out," he said.

"I'm tired, too," I said, more to myself than to Bob.

"We can help with numbers," Bob said. "We can write to every family in the country who've written us in favor of withdrawal. We'll explain what you're trying to do and tell them how to contact you."

The more Bob perked up, the more trapped I felt. "I don't know," I said. "Maybe I'd look stupid. Maybe no one would join us." I listened to my own voice, and out of nowhere I seemed to hear Pete McCloskey asking me what I was afraid of. "What the hell, Bob," I said. "Send out the letters."

After hanging up, I walked in a daze into the living room and plopped onto my sofa. I lay down and gazed out at the canyon. The sun was beginning to cut through the morning fog, and the hills were a hazy yellow. Something in me said, "Phone him back. Say you've changed your mind," but I burrowed deeper into the corner of the cushions, closed my eyes, and hoped for the best.

A letter or a phone call materialized every two or three days from families wanting to join our group. They came from a large city in Michigan, a farm in Iowa, an apartment in Florida, a town in Iowa.

A mother in North Dakota wrote:

Under the present policy, our government is writing off our POW/MIAs. They cannot last much longer. We must act now. I am pleased to learn you believe the solution is peace. I'll do anything to help. God bless you. Let's get the American people to back us.

The day finally came for us to announce formation of our new family organization. Though we'd heard from thirty-five families spread across the country, our initial meeting would consist of the Alvarezes and me. I was waiting for them to arrive when the doorbell rang. I saw the Western Union car, and hoped it would be a message of congratulations. Instead it was a warning from a member of the Bay Area League:

. . . URGE YOU ALL TO VOCALLY TAKE STAND YOU HOLD
NO POLITICAL POLICY. THE ONLY HOPE FOR OUR MEN IS
TO SUPPORT THE GENEVA CONVENTION.

I'd been having panicky thoughts all morning, and the telegram
certainly didn't help matters. What if Delia and Sally didn't make
it, I worried. My mind created terrible scenarios: An ambitious
young reporter would rush over in pursuit of a POW family re-
bellion, and there I'd be sitting by myself at the kitchen table,
gazing out the window; or members of the League, dressed in
Green Beret uniforms, would conduct a search-and-destroy operation on my house. Slithering from tree to tree, they'd get closer
with each slither. Eventually one would turn into Betsy Ross and
beat me to death with a flag.

Suddenly I could see myself grabbing the flagpole from the
hands of my attacker. Waving stars and stripes like a magic
wand, I sent the trespassers fleeing back through the woods—
because in the driveway I heard the Alvarezes' car come to a stop.
Relieved, I ran up the stairs and threw my arms around them.

We admitted we were not off to an auspicious start. Sean and
Terry made jokes about our "fantastic meeting." They offered to
direct people where to park their cars and asked if they should
borrow chairs from neighbors for the crowd.

I was warning them to stop pestering us—weren't things bad
enough as it was?—when I looked up and saw Julie Butler, who
was Maerose's right-hand woman, coming down the front stairs.
At the same moment the phone rang and I picked it up. A man
from Channel 4, the NBC-TV station in San Francisco, said, "I
understand that today is the official beginning of the new POW/
MIA family group. I wonder if I could come out with cameras in
about an hour to do an interview?"

I stammered out something about how I appreciated his interest, as Julie peeked through the front window. Weakly, I hailed
her to come in and asked the reporter if he could wait a couple of
hours to come out since we had a lot of planning to do. "How
about three o'clock?" he asked.

"Yes, yes, that will be great," I said. Julie was giving me a look. "When does the meeting begin?" she asked, peering past me into the empty living room.

"It has," I said, pointing to Sally and Delia and some half-eaten plates of spaghetti on the table. "Have you had lunch?" I asked. Why pretend, I thought; at least I can be polite.

Delia kept giving me sullen glances. She'd made it clear often enough that she wanted nothing to do with military wives. I could see she was already beginning to seethe. It wasn't long before she was poking away at everything Julie said.

I kept sneaking peeks at the kitchen clock. At last Julie got around to the reason she'd come. "Above all," she said, "we shouldn't destroy the public's conception that the POW families are united."

"Well, they're not united," I said, "not any longer."

Julie left, looking more distressed than when she'd come. Minutes later the television reporter arrived. "Yes, this is the right house," I said. "Come in." I sounded like I was leading a repairman to a leaky drain. I was just beginning to get hold of myself when I spotted a huge camera being carried down the outside steps, and I figured I had two choices: one, sneak out the side door; and two, slip into the kitchen for a quick slug of brandy. Neither was any good. The man near the car would see me run through the woods. The second was worse. I could see the headlines: "Drunken housewife makes statement on foreign policy." Too late, anyway, for by now the camera was in the living room and the handsome man was telling us where to sit. I cranked myself into a seated position, bent at the knees, straight-backed, and perched at the edge of the sofa like a Barbie doll.

"My name is Steve Huss," the handsome man said, flashing a TV smile. He asked if the others at the meeting had left. We said yes, that only the leaders were still there. He glanced around the room and said he would start with Delia.

Why not, I thought. He certainly can see she has more wits about her than I do.

The camera was rolling, and he asked Delia, "What is the name of your group?"

Name. We hadn't even discussed that, but Delia didn't blink an eye. "We are called Families of POWs and MIA's for Indochina Peace." I was sure now that she was a genius. It had been smart to start with Delia.

Next he turned to Sally. Though Sally had been quiet, she at least looked dignified, not comatose, as I was sure I did. Her voice was trembling, but still the words poured out. "My son has been captured for seven years. If the South Vietnamese don't want to fight for themselves by now, it's too bad. Too many people have been killed already. We have to say it. End this war now."

I knew I couldn't top that. He asked me why we needed a separate group since there already was a group for POW families. After two or three tries my words began to form sentences. I told him that we'd lost patience with the President's policies and couldn't express that within the pro-administration League of Families.

The reporter and photographer packed up and left; we fidgeted and waited for the five-thirty news. Sean turned the dial to Channel 4, and the announcer who had been in our house earlier appeared on our TV screen. Delia, Sally, and I huddled together on the sofa. The boys flopped on the floor in front of us, stretched out and leaning on their elbows. We were the lead story: "POW families nationwide have organized a new group that will oppose President Nixon's Vietnamization. Their first meeting was held in Oakland today. Three of the leaders were interviewed this afternoon. . . ." Our faces came onto the screen. At first I was dissociated from the person speaking. Then I became so enthralled, watching myself, that I didn't hear what the reporter was saying. I could tell, though, that my stumbling phrases had been edited. We seemed to be making sense.

When it was over, no one spoke for a moment; then suddenly Delia screeched, "Damn it, they believed us!"

"Of course they did," Sally said with a sweet smile.

"Even though you looked scared stiff, Mom, you weren't too bad," Terry commented.

Sean leaped up from the floor and threw a hand out. "Congratulations, Mom," he said. "You all did good."

I grabbed my car keys. "Let's celebrate!" I said. The boys promised to stay home, in the house, and behave themselves.

At a wharf restaurant Sally lifted her wineglass. "We toast ourselves and an end to the war," she said.

"Here's to our success, whatever we can do." I clinked Sally's glass.

Delia made our wineglasses into a triangle. "And to hell with Nixon!" she said.

15. SOUNDING TOUGH

<u>JUNE 1971</u> My telephone started ringing early the morning after we announced our split with the League. By nine o'clock I had taped three radio interviews. I heard that CBS Radio had played our segment on its ten o'clock news, but I'd been too busy to listen. When I called the Alvarezes, they said the same thing was happening at their house. "We're news," Delia said. "We're saying what people want to hear, and the media knows it."

An *Oakland Tribune* reporter came to our house that afternoon with a photographer. "Ughhh, no way. No way, Mom!" the boys grumbled as I shoved them into the bathroom for showers. Their hair was sopping wet when they begrudgingly sat next to me on the sofa, where the flash of the camera captured their sulking faces. By the next morning, however, they fought over which one of them would stuff the newspaper into his lunchbox in order to show it off at school.

I was stirring my coffee after they had hopped onto their school bus, and I was wondering if maybe the excitement was over, if we were a twenty-four-hour blip, when the phone rang again. Leif Ericson of Associated Press and our first wire service story were at the other end of the line. The next day, sprinkled across the country, headlines read:

POW WIFE SEEKS ACTION BY U.S. ON RED PROPOSAL
FAMILY OF FIRST POW ACCUSES NIXON

It was all happening fast. We were beginning to look like a
bona fide protest group. Pete McCloskey was now able to obtain
travel funds for us from Business Executives' Move for Peace.
Suddenly there were nine or ten family members in the capitol
lobbying, and McCloskey and Bob Sherman thought we should
get some publicity from it. First Bob Sherman, and then Mitch
Jones, the woman who had presented our case so well on the
"Advocates" program, called me. They both suggested that we call
a Washington press conference immediately.

"I know McCloskey and Leggett will help organize it," Mitch
said. Mitch had a lot at stake, and you could hear it in her voice.
She told me she'd lost a brother in Korea and now had a husband
missing in Laos. "We'll just state our views on this friggin' war
and say we disagree with those Nixonettes over at the League,"
she said.

One day was not enough time for me to get a baby-sitter and fly
to Washington, but Delia was packed and on her way within
hours. Her plane had no sooner taken off, however, when Bob
Sherman was on the phone with me, fretting and saying that the
event was going to be too loose. The participants were all meeting
for the first time, he said, and we hadn't even agreed on a press
release.

The next morning Delia gave credence to Bob's concerns. She
called before noon to report that the press conference was over
and it had been an "asinine tragedy." "It went terribly, Barbara.
You wouldn't believe how bad. I told you we couldn't trust those
'military wives, even if they do want the war to end. Hell, they're
all crazy, sex-starved neurotics." She was almost incoherent.

"Louise dropped out the day before the conference for fear the
left wing was about to take over our activities against the administration. I guess I'm the radical left," Delia said. "A few minutes
before the reporters were due, Mitch said she had changed her
mind about a new group—she thought we should just speak for
ourselves as individuals. Then Valerie Kushner, the Army doc-

tor's wife, was badgering me about the program I did with Jane Fonda, as the cameramen were setting up their equipment."

I asked Delia to wait and see how the coverage turned out, but she wasn't very hopeful. That evening I turned on the news and waited for doomsday. Switching from channel to channel, I saw none of the chaos Delia had described. A petite Valerie Kushner looked too innocent to badger anyone. She was the pretty young girl who'd married her college sweetheart, whose budding medical career had been interrupted by Vietnam and the VC guerrillas who captured him. All she wanted, she said, was for President Nixon to put her husband's welfare above that of President Thieu. Delia, again subdued, this time by her treatment prior to the conference, told about her brother's long confinement. Mitch Jones, at her feisty best, said, "We feel that President Nixon is bartering these men, using them as an excuse to continue the war. If this war goes on another two or three years, the prisoner issue will solve itself because the prisoners will all be dead."

I held my breath when she was asked about our group. "We are Families for Immediate Release," she said, "and that says it all."

I didn't mind what she called us; at least she hadn't denied our existence. There seemed no explanation for the variance between Delia's account of what had happened behind the scenes and what I'd just seen on television. Then a remark I'd heard earlier in the week began to make sense. A reporter had told me, "You'll have no trouble getting coverage; the press will be kind to you."

It didn't take long for Delia to regain her spunk after reading accounts of the press conference. She left Washington on a goodwill tour, beginning with a drive to Virginia Beach to swear to Louise that she didn't carry Mao's Red Book and had never burned a flag. Louise laughed and said she believed her, but she was just too weary to help with the new group. Delia went on to Massachusetts, Florida, and Michigan, where she found people no angrier than Louise but less fatigued. She got firm commitments from other families who were sick of the war and excuses.

The Washington publicity and Delia's travels generated fifty more offers of support from families. Our count was now up to seventy-five. The only reservation came from some who hoped we wouldn't align ourselves closely with peace groups. Valerie had taken to calling me evenings to emphasize the point. She wanted no publicity in connection with John Gardner's Common Cause, Bess Myerson's Another Mother for Peace, or Business Executives' Move for Peace, she said.

Since these were the most mainstream antiwar groups around, I asked her where we could go for help. Looking over our collective shoulders, we might be afraid to place trust in anyone. "We've all gotten paranoid, Valerie," I said. "General Shoup is a past Commandant of the Marine Corps, and he belongs to Business Executives' Move for Peace. You don't think he's suspect, do you?"

She wasn't sure, she said, but conceded that we weren't going to get help from the Defense Department or the American Legion.

About all we agreed on—Delia, Sally, Bob Sherman, Valerie, Mitch, and I—was that we wanted the war to end.

Delia laughed. "We'll do just fine," she said, "if we can get support from saints, money from angels, and have a little bit of luck."

"Barbara Mullen," a voice said. "This is Congressman Leggett. We just returned from Paris." I had one hand on the receiver, and I groped with the other for the light switch. I held the clock up to the light—5:30 A.M.

"I want to alert you to some of what happened at our meetings with the North Vietnamese and NLF," he said. "I thought I would give your name out to the press this morning after I reveal my report." These last words pierced my sleepy state. I whipped open the nightstand drawer, grabbed some notepaper and a pencil, and began to scribble.

"We saw representatives of both," he went on, "and they agreed to certain basics. If we set our withdrawal date, they will cease fire, give information on POWs, and release all of them by completion of our withdrawal. They also agreed to no shelling or bombing from the time the agreement is signed."

He was about to hang up, and he hadn't mentioned the Laotians. "What about the Pathet Lao?" I asked.

"Yes, both the North Vietnamese and the NLF said that the Pathet Lao would adhere to an agreement if we signed it now."

I stumbled out to the kitchen to fix myself a good strong cup of coffee. What did he mean—he'd give my name to the press? I'd have to call Bob Sherman. He was at the bottom of this, I was sure. What had he gotten me into now?

"He's not in yet," a woman in Congressman Leggett's office said. "He returned from Paris late last night." I froze for an instant and then remembered that Bob had given me his home phone number.

His wife, Carolyn, said he was there, and I relaxed. Bob would take care of me. "I'm surprised the congressman called you already," he said. "Honestly, I didn't know he was going to give your name to the press. Now that it's done, I'd better brief you quickly. Take notes.

"We met with Nguyen Minh Vy, deputy chief of the negotiating delegation from North Vietnam, on May twenty-ninth. Vy said he was concerned that Nixon would not withdraw until, number one, the North Vietnamese troops were withdrawn and, number two, the stability of the South Vietnamese government was assured.

"It was Vy's position that the South Vietnamese government could never be described as stable, since there is no objective criterion for stability, and therefore our troops probably could be in Vietnam more or less indefinitely. Mr. Vy said, 'We're insisting on a date of withdrawal, and we can assure you there will be no problem in solving the POW problem if the date is set. But if Nixon does not do his part in setting the date, we *cannot do ours* in releasing the POWs.'

"What they said, Barbara, agrees with legislation we're proposing in Congress.

"The meeting with the Provisional Revolutionary Government—the Viet Cong—also went well. Carolyn and Mrs. Leggett were invited to the first hour or so of the meeting, which was very cordial. After that, we talked seriously with Nguyen Van

Tien, the second man on the PRG negotiating team. I asked him outright, 'If the President were to announce withdrawal of all troops by Christmas of this year, 1971, could the prisoners be released earlier than that date?' Mr. Tien smiled and said that this was possible. He also added, 'When President Nixon sets a day, the prisoners can be released without attacks on withdrawing troops.'"

"In other words, it could be done now?" I asked Bob. "How much longer do you think Nixon and Kissinger can go on being so stubborn?"

"I don't know," he said. "Ambassador Bruce and our own negotiating team were most cooperative. They helped Congressman Leggett in every way they could. Leggett said it was regrettable they're burdened by our government's refusal to set a date. They deserve to represent a more workable policy."

Then Bob hesitated. "I'm sorry, Barbara, we weren't able to get specific information on Bill. Congressman Leggett asked the North Vietnamese and the NLF for a list of the prisoners, and they both said that the list would be given out as soon as we set a date. We left all the facts about Bill with them, and they said they would let us know if there were any details available."

Intellectually, I knew it was unrealistic to expect information about Bill before the war ended. The Pathet Lao weren't represented at the peace table in Paris; officially, we weren't at war with them. Identifications gleaned from Communist propaganda films or photos placed in the hands of French, Japanese, or East European correspondents were always of men captured in North Vietnam. Even the intelligence photo that resembled Bill was of unknown origin. None of the downed pilots in Laos referred to by the Pathet Lao themselves had ever been identified by name. But I still imagined, against all odds, that a Laotian villager would wander out of the jungle with a description of Bill and drop it in the lap of a North Vietnamese or Viet Cong or an American intelligence officer.

I wasn't dressed yet when the first call came from a local radio station; the next was from CBS. "Are you Barbara Mullen, a national coordinator for the new POW group?" the reporter asked.

"Yes, I am," I said. I felt as if I were playing a game. Leaning on an elbow, robe half unbuttoned, hair uncombed, I explained peace negotiating positions to the press all morning. Bill used to change our light bulbs, I thought. How I wished he could see me. Someday, I'll tell him, I decided, and we'll both laugh like hell.

Bill Kurtis of CBS News in Los Angeles called later in the day. He said he'd been assigned to interview leaders of "our group" for an upcoming CBS special, if we were willing.

"Wasn't that program filmed weeks ago?" I asked him.

"It was," he said, "but the dissent within the families in the last few weeks has practically made the thing obsolete."

Sally was stunned. "You mean we're going to get equal time with the Pentagon princesses? I can't believe it," she said. "Wait until I tell Delia. She's going to shriek out loud."

"They know we'll spice it up, Sally," I laughed. "Can you imagine how dull the thing is now? 'We also serve, who sit on our duffs and wait'?"

The filming was only a week off, but that didn't bother Delia or Sally. They didn't make lists the way I did and practice answers to pretend questions. I memorized by the hour until I could tick off various versions of peace offers on cue. When I was stuck on a minor point, I called Bob Sherman for clarification. By the night of the TV shooting, I could point out any and all inconsistencies in administration statements; I could recite figures on casualties or the bombing war. I was ready for a one-woman interview on "Meet the Press," not a spot on a special. Facts were my only security.

I had changed my clothes three times before Sally and Delia arrived. Don't look like a '62 version of an officer's wife, I told myself. Don't look like a peace hippy or a flower child. Don't look personally glamorized for the occasion. And for God's sake, don't look depressed beyond professional help. Finally I got bored with the whole thing and put the skirt and sweater back on that I'd worn all day—a brown turtleneck, tan skirt, and beads. My only compromise was to tuck my long hair behind my ears. Then I dug out some ladylike pearl earrings I hadn't seen in years. Ready or not!

The Alvarezes had come early, giving us a chance, I thought, to rehearse the points we wanted to make, but Delia shrugged off the suggestion. "We're psyched, Barbara," she assured me with a pat on the shoulder. I smiled and poured each of us a glass of wine. As Sally and Delia chattered away, I realized they were looking forward to the taping. It hadn't occurred to me until then that we should enjoy this occasion. But why not, I thought. Think of all the mornings of grumbling over newspapers, the nights of arguing with TV sets. And here we were waiting for Cronkite's crew to arrive.

By the time the CBS van drove up and they were carrying equipment down the stairs, I had relaxed. In fact, I felt like an observer, as though I were outside of my own body, taking it all in. It was a trick I had been practicing in the past few weeks to get me through the interviews. Self-hypnosis, a friend called it when I described it to her. But I said it was nothing that clinical. I just listened to the words coming out of my mouth and pretended someone else was speaking them.

Bill Kurtis, cameras, and lights paraded through the front hall and into the living room. "OK, everybody," he said, "let's see if we can do this right. If it doesn't work one way, we'll do it another."

Kurtis swept his glance past Sally and me to Delia. "How would you like to go first?" he asked.

After Delia had blamed President Nixon for her brother's suffering, for breaking promises, and for prolonging the war, he asked me to sit in a chair opposite him. The camera passed back and forth from his face to mine. For a moment I was distracted by the bright glare, but I quickly began to reel off my facts and figures. Suddenly Kurtis lifted his hand and the cameras stopped. When he motioned to the cameraman to continue, he asked how I felt about the war and the President and my country. My answers became more real and human after that.

At the end he asked, "Why do you need another POW group for action?"

"Because the League of Families takes no stand on the war and we do," I said. "It's time that the President listened to our views, too."

The Alvarezes invited us to a backyard barbecue the night the CBS special was to air. We ate hamburgers, corn on the cob, and salad. The boys asked for extra dessert. When it was time, we all gathered around the TV set in the living room. Terry scooched his way into a big stuffed chair alongside Delia's father, Everett Alvarez, Sr. He was a quiet man who didn't take part in political activities himself, but he said he was proud of his women. He waited nervously with the rest of us for the program to begin.

Walter Cronkite's dramatic narration began: "POWs—Pawns of War—that is what they've become. . . ." Administration officials were questioned. They all expressed concern but acted as if nothing they had done or could do would change the plight of these men. It was out of their hands, they implied, a complicated problem beyond solution.

Wives were interviewed in their homes. Children ran about. The women clutched a picture of a uniformed man or a year-old letter in tight fingers and stared into the camera. They didn't understand why the Communists had not given in. "We've told everyone about the Geneva Convention and prisoner treatment," they said with lowered eyes, as though they knew they'd been duped, but not sure by whom.

Women who were League officials said they believed their Commander-in-chief was doing all he could, but the words sounded tired and worn from wear. "Great," Delia said after they'd finished. "We'll pep it up. Our words will be last in all those millions of minds out there watching."

"There's only one person watching I care about," Sally said, and we all nodded.

When our segment was over, Terry looked up into Mr. Alvarez's face. "They sure told everyone," he said. "You wait and see. The war will end now."

Sean tilted his head slightly and grinned. "You sure sounded tough, Mom. I bet Nixon is scared to death tonight."

"You're right, Sean," Delia said. "He won't sleep a blessed minute all night." And we all laughed.

But I remembered the years of words tossed in bottles to the sea, blown into the clouds in the sky, and I felt moist tears well up in my eyes. I enjoyed winning for a change.

16. LOUD AND CLEAR

<u>JULY 1971</u> On July 1 the Communists made a formal proposal at the Paris peace talks, repeating what they had said publicly in the past. The National Liberation Front offer, endorsed by the North Vietnamese, agreed to the withdrawal in safety of U.S. troops and the release of the totality of military men of all parties and of all civilians captured in the war if the U.S. would set a terminal date for withdrawal of all U.S. forces in 1971.

The offer included the two things the administration claimed it wanted. Back in January, Secretary of Defense Melvin Laird told a reporter, "I expect us to maintain a presence in Vietnam until the prisoner-of-war issue is settled. So you can't project the reduction in our forces without keeping in mind that one factor. We are willing to take every American out of Vietnam, providing that question is settled."

Then on March 16 Secretary of State Rogers had been asked by a newsman, "Are the prisoners the only reason we would be leaving the troops there?"

Secretary Rogers answered, "Yes."

The reporter clarified, "So if the prisoners are released or if the North Vietnamese agree to release them, we will get out?"

Secretary Rogers repeated, "Yes."

At a more recent press conference, President Nixon was asked if his only condition for a residual force was that it would be there until the prisoners were released. "You have also stated that it will be there until the South Vietnamese have a chance to defend themselves," the reporter added. "Are both of these conditions for the residual force, one of them, or the other? Could you clarify that for us?"

"The residual force, I think, first, with regard to POWs, will be indefinite . . . and second, however, with regard to the ability of the South Vietnamese to defend themselves is concerned, we have a very good idea when that will occur. And as soon as that eventually occurs, we will be able to move. . . . So one will occur before the other . . . ," the President answered.

It was clear now that the President didn't intend to withdraw from Southeast Asia to gain release of the prisoners, yet he and other members of his administration had been promising to do just that for months. The very issue the President had used to gain public backing for his policies was turning on him, and I waited to see how he would dismiss this latest offer.

The NLF proposal had been made public in the morning, and by afternoon Maerose Evans and Julie Butler had called a press conference in San Francisco. They said they were very suspicious of the offer by the Communists. They also attacked certain politicians for being "Johnny-come-latelys" who were using the POWs as political footballs. Maerose condemned Senator Kennedy, Congressman McCloskey, and others for "their willingness to abandon the POWs to reach a political settlement."

"I'd like to be optimistic," Julie said, "but I'm not. We can't tie the President's hands. We must leave him every option, every card to play."

The front page of the *San Francisco Chronicle* headlined:

REDS OFFER TO FREE POWS IF U.S. PULLS OUT COMPLETELY

On another page an account of Julie and Maerose's conference began: ". . . the women spoke at a press conference set up by Pacific Gas and Electric Company public relations men who said they had been asked to do so by a high administration official."

On July 2, the day after the peace offer, northern California families were invited to attend a meeting at Travis Air Force Base outside Sacramento. I sat next to Sally in a packed formal meeting room in the officers' club where representatives of the national security affairs staff, the State Department, and military services sat in a row at a long front table. These briefings were indistinguishable, one from the other, in my mind; there was almost a religious ritual about them. "Are you ready for this traveling road show?" Sally asked.

Dr. Roger Shields, a Defense Department representative, took charge of the presentation. His round young face peered out at us through shell-rimmed glasses; his hands shifted through pieces of paper. I guessed that everything he'd ever learned had been gleaned from file folders. His monotone voice recited human statistics as if they were Dow Jones averages. The missing POW total was now nearly 1,600; they had no recent information on men held by the Viet Cong in South Vietnam or those missing in Laos.

Up to this point there had been nothing different about this meeting; it was during the question period that a change in family attitude revealed itself. When the speakers finished, men and women stood up. The same parents who'd been flown in for meetings in the past now asked about the Hatfield-McGovern end-the-war bill and the Mansfield Resolution. When Dr. Shields told them that legislation would hinder progress at the peace talks, a father of a POW in the back of the room stood up and asked, "Excuse me, sir, aren't we going to talk about the Communist offer yesterday to release our men?"

Dr. Shields answered that the offer to release the men for a set date was nothing new. He said the administration had tried to get better treatment for the men; it was also winding down the war. He then cited troop withdrawal figures. I jotted them down on a note pad. According to his figures, we would not reach President Nixon's 50,000 residual force for another year and eight months.

As soon as Dr. Shields finished, I asked him if the President would be willing to trade complete withdrawal in a year and eight months to get the POWs back.

"That will be contingent on whether or not the South Vietnamese can get along without our air support," he answered.

"The prisoners won't be released while we're still bombing," I said. "Why not offer the date now, get the prisoners back, and withdraw all the troops?"

Dr. Shields leaned down toward me from his standing position in the aisle; he looked directly at me. "Do you want to have it on your conscience that South Vietnam went Communist?" he asked.

A thin gray-haired man a few rows ahead of me got up from his chair. "You can't sell us on that any longer!" he shouted, and then stormed out of the room.

Sally Alvarez was now on her feet; her voice was shaking with anger. "Dr. Shields, you are just a little boy," she said. "You weren't in college yet when my son was captured, and now you are telling us we haven't given enough. What have you sacrificed for South Vietnam?"

"The President doesn't want a coalition government forced on him," Dr. Shields answered.

"Coalition government," Sally said. "He'd be lucky to get that."

The Marine guard issued us a snappy salute as our car left the Air Force base an hour later. "They have no intention of accepting any offers, you know," I said.

"I know," Sally said. She reached over and patted my hand on the steering wheel. "We'll just have to change that," she said.

From my window at the Hotel Congressional, I looked out at the Capitol. The streets were empty; massive concrete structures appeared formidable at the end of a long Fourth of July weekend. I'm glad I decided to come, I thought, closing the drapes. Actually, the peace offer and Dr. Shields's "briefing" had made the decision for me.

I went into the bathroom, rinsed my panty hose and slip in the sink, and hung them neatly over thick white towels. Then I climbed into bed. The next day Bob Sherman and Shirley

Culbertson, sister of a POW, would give me my first lessons in congressional lobbying.

Shirley Culbertson met me in the hotel lobby the next morning. When I saw her I wandered how this pretty suburban wife had become a Joan Baez in white gloves. I couldn't imagine her cajoling politicians. The dignified brunette would have seemed more at home at a benefit for the arts, I thought, but she immediately began to tick off the day's schedule. "Don't worry," she said, noticing my stricken expression, "I was the perfect executive wife—my husband is an official over at NASA. In a month's time I've turned into a lobbying expert. If I can do it, you can."

Our first stop was at Congressman Leggett's office, where Bob Sherman was waiting. Bob and I had talked many times on the telephone, yet I was nervous meeting him. I always felt he expected more of me than I could give. At the same time I didn't want to let him down.

The slight young man who greeted us was much as I'd pictured him: warm and sincere, but anxious to get down to business. Speaking rapidly and fidgeting with his glasses, he commented on our scheduled appointments. His being seemed propelled by intelligence. It was like a fusion of two live wires when he and Shirley converged; their sparks transmitted a raw energy, and I hoped I could absorb some of it. They really seemed to believe that one person could make a difference.

The Democratic Study Group and Common Cause had come up with a list of senators and congressmen for us to see. They'd divided them into three categories: those who would definitely support us, others who never would, and those we might possibly convince to vote for end-the-war legislation.

Shirley read the names out loud. Now and then Bob grimaced, adding comments such as "Impossible," "Well, maybe he is wavering," or "Pulling that off would be a miracle."

Our first appointment was with Representative Rarick of Louisiana, whom Bob had dubbed "impossible." We soon understood why. Shirley barely had the words "prisoner of war" out of her mouth when Rarick started to fume about how we should have dropped the big one on those Commies to begin with. He went on slapping the desk and talking to the air even as we backed out the door and closed it behind us. I leaned on a wall outside. "What a beginning," I moaned.

Shirley tapped me on the shoulder. "Keep moving and don't despair. We'll have at least one of those a day."

Bob had warned us not to spend too much time with friends, reassuring as it was. But I was glad our last meeting that day was with Senator McGovern. John Holum, his legislative aide, spent half an hour with us, outlining the next legislation that McGovern would introduce. After that the senator joined us. When George McGovern wandered in, he greeted us with a broad smile. He seemed genuinely excited that we were there and thanked us for our help. As he explained his agenda for peace, I marveled at his optimism in the face of so many defeats. When we were leaving, he said, "Don't give up. We'll pass something and end this terrible tragedy."

My recollection of the next two weeks was of hallways streaming by me on either side of Shirley's departing form. Our feet carried us through endless corridors to connecting buildings; miniature trolleys whisked us through underground tunnels; elevators transported us to the tops of buildings.

As the chase continued, I picked up information by bits and pieces. Somewhere in the middle of the first week I learned what "rubber-stamping" meant and why it had been so hard to pass antiwar legislation over President Nixon's objections. It happened the morning I clip-clopped after Shirley down another hallway. A door opened and we were facing Congressman Bob Wilson from southern California. With the mention of Wilson's name earlier, Bob had said, "You've got to be kidding."

The congressman brought us to a sofa and gestured with a sweep of his arm for us to sit down. Prancing in front of us, he boasted how he had seen other POW families and told them what he was about to tell us. "I promise you," he said, "I will never let the President down." Then he fished into a file and displayed "before and after" letters from Richard Nixon. One had been received before each end-the-war legislative vote, and one after.

The first of each set told him he was the kind of congressman who could be counted on to vote against such legislation and the second congratulated him for having done so.

"Congressman Wilson, do you think we are against ending the war?" I asked.

At first he seemed confused by the question, then astonished. "You don't want to end it now if the President doesn't think he's ready, do you?"

"Yes," I said.

It was obvious he hadn't understood our views before agreeing to see us. He seemed embarrassed and said we could be sure he would go on supporting "our boys." He then ushered us to the door.

By the time Shirley tossed a "Never mind" at me over her shoulder, she had nearly reached the elevator. "Just another little boy showing off his Brownie points," she said. "The House is full of them."

We'd finished our appointments another afternoon, and Shirley and I went back to my hotel room and kicked off our shoes. That morning Senator John Tunney of California had made a suggestion we'd been thinking about all day. We should write a letter to the President, he had said, and present it in a way the press couldn't ignore.

We stretched out on the beds, stared at the ceiling, and drafted versions of a letter out loud, then spent another hour trying to think of a way to publicize it. On her way out the door, Shirley said, "Don't worry about it. I know we'll come up with something fantastic by morning."

After Shirley left, I gave Louise a call. "I'm depleted," Louise confessed. "For the first time I'm really letting myself think they may never come back. I see no hope at all right now. The people who count don't really care. By the time Nixon decides to do anything, it will be too late. I'm tired, and I can't think of any more avenues to pursue. The thought of helping all of you to start a new group is just beyond me."

I felt lousy when I hung up the phone. I knew I wouldn't sleep well that night. How sure Louise had been when we first met in

Massachusetts in the summer of '66! Her new words haunted me: "They may never come back." Every human being has a finishing point. I knew that. I just didn't want Louise to be human.

The next morning when Shirley and I met, we decided to tell Pete McCloskey about our plans to write the President a letter and then make it public. When we finished, he jumped to his feet. "Write it today," he said. "I'm flying to Los Angeles this afternoon. Tammy Bloodworth, an Air Force wife, lives near L.A. See if she's willing to meet me at the airport and hand-deliver the letter to the President at the San Clemente White House tomorrow."

Shirley's eyes widened. "I know it will work," she said.

"We need help!" she announced a few minutes later as we streamed through Congressman Leggett's suite of offices in search of Bob. "We have to call at least six people for permission to use their signatures on a letter to the President and get it to Pete McCloskey by one o'clock."

Bob eased our letter outline from my hand. "Sounds like a good idea," he said, but he was already scratching out words and scribbling across the draft of the letter.

I dialed Louise, then Mitch. Neither answered. "This is no time to panic," Shirley said. "I've got Tammy Bloodworth on the phone and she says she'll do it."

We'd heard that Bernard Talley, a POW father who had been active in the League, was wavering in our direction. "Worth a try," Shirley said. I called him and he agreed to sign. We reached another Air Force wife in southern California who said she was with us. We had our signatures—three wives, two sisters, and a father.

Our letter began:

Dear Mr. President:

We are immediate family members of American military men who are prisoners of war and missing in action in Indochina. . . . We fear that we will spend years chasing the light at the end of the tunnel which always remains just around the next bend, while for our men in the prison camps, one by one, the light will go out forever. . . . We feel our Government's obligation to the American prisoners now should take precedence over its obligation to the Government of South Vietnam. . . .

We shoved the letter into McCloskey's hands just as he was leaving for the airport. I was out of breath and famished. "I'll faint if I don't eat," I groaned.

"Come on, Barbara. We don't have time," Shirley said. "How can you complain? Think of those men in their cells getting two bowls of pumpkin soup a day."

My grumbling was silenced. We stuck some quarters in a vending machine and stuffed a package of crackers and cheese into our mouths on the run.

Shirley checked her watch. "Just Alan Cranston and two more congressmen and we're finished today," she said.

Back in my room, I peeled off sticky clothes and soaked in a hot bath. There'd been a message to call Joan Vinson, national coordinator for the League of Families. My goodness, I thought, what does the mother superior want with the wayward sister? Then I submerged myself farther into the steamy water and sighed. It doesn't matter what they want—we're on our way.

The next day, on the spur of the moment, I stopped off at the League's new and larger offices in the American Legion Building on K Street just to find out what they'd dreamed up this time. Joan Vinson leaned back in an executive chair behind an oversized desk. I could hardly keep the women or their newly acquired titles straight anymore. "We all want the same goal," she said. "We just have different methods of achieving it. Besides, things are happening secretly that we don't know anything about. I feel sure there's going to be a break soon."

So that was the new tack, secret things about which we knew nothing. Would the women wait for these secret seeds to bear fruit, or would they invent chores to occupy themselves with, I wondered. Surely there wasn't a person left willing to write another letter to Hanoi.

"Would you like to serve on a committee we're forming to deal with psychological needs of the men and their families when they're repatriated?" she asked. A lot of study was required, and there would be reports to be written. The need was there because surely there would be psychological problems.

Enough to keep a lot of fingers and minds busy another year or two, I thought. I begged off.

I hailed a cab and returned to the Capitol. Tammy Bloodworth had called from California while I was gone. She said she had met Pete McCloskey's plane and driven to the San Clemente White House early that morning. A Secret Service man had accepted our letter, and she was sure the President would read it, considering the fuss reporters on the grounds had made, asking her questions.

It was Friday afternoon. If the media were to show interest in our letter, it would be over the weekend. I was glad Shirley had invited me to spend a few days with her family in Virginia, because we'd be together if the media broke the story, and Bob Sherman would be nearby if we needed him.

Shirley stirred tall gin and tonics for the two of us and laughed when I asked how she could move after the week we'd just put in. "It only takes getting used to," she said. "One day I got sick of looking at myself in the mirror. I saw a woman whose brother was incarcerated in North Vietnam, and I realized I was doing nothing to help him. It was hard to extract myself from this cushy suburban existence, but I'm glad I did. At least I can live with myself now. So I suppose psychic energy keeps me going."

"How about if we psych up on Monday then," I said, "and just slouch around in our jeans and be lazy in the meantime."

When we came home from a ride on Sunday morning and rounded the corner, Shirley gasped, "My Lord, I think it's CBS-TV!" A panel truck was parked in front of her house.

Shirley's husband, Phil, met us at the front door. "They've been here about twenty minutes," he whispered. "They said they would just wait for you to return."

Shirley put an index finger in front of her mouth and tiptoed up the stairs. I followed her into the bedroom. Still not speaking,

172

we stopped in front of the nearest mirror. She picked up a lipstick from the bureau, and I reached into my purse for a brush. Our eyes met in the reflection, and we both burst into a nervous giggle. "Eventually we'll have to go down there," Shirley said, "unless you want to leap out the window instead."

We crept back downstairs and into the family room, where the news team was waiting. Surprised that cameras and equipment were already set up, I asked, "Did you call before coming?"

One of the men stepped forward. "We'd miss a lot of stories that way," he said. Then he smiled. "Here's your chance. We'll ask questions and you can say whatever you want."

While Shirley was spouting her piece, I mentally constructed a strong, dignified statement. When the interviewer turned to me, however, I said something entirely different. "If the President doesn't end this war now, he'll hear from us loud and clear before the election next year." I was embarrassed once the words were out and the threat had been made, but I could see that the crew loved it.

After they'd packed up and left, Shirley was feeling elated, but I was fighting a sinking spell and wondering how long could we go on boasting with no real means of fulfilling our promises. The doubts clung to me until I saw our interview on the evening news and the telephone started to ring. Local radio stations asked to tape something; Associated Press wanted to do its own story. Shirley and I took turns answering the calls until after midnight.

I woke up in the morning to Shirley's frantic knocking at my door. "Barbara, come on down. We made the *Washington Star,*" she said. Half awake, I reached for a robe on a chair by the bed and tripped over my belt as I ran down the stairs.

The newspaper was spread over the kitchen counter. Shirley was quoted as saying that our group represented 335 families. "Listen to this." She read: "'In an interview with UPI, Mrs. Mullen pointed to stories last week attributed to unidentified sources that the Central Intelligence Agency had told Nixon the Communist offer was made only to embarrass the United States. "How often do CIA reports come out in the press?" she asked.

She suggested the story was planted to stir up opposition to the proposal.'"

"Well, that's it," I said, lowering myself into a chair. "Nixon and the CIA in one swoop. I'm going to be hearing beeps on my telephone before the week is out."

Shirley had a satisfied smile on her face. She poured coffee into two cups, and I complimented her on the 335-family figure. "Well, I'm sure we have that many," she said, grinning sheepishly. "So many have lobbied here in Washington, and you and Delia have a lot of names now."

Before we left the house, Henry Niles, National Director for Business Executives' Move for Peace, called. He offered us more financial assistance and apologized for the fact that it was no match for the huge amounts donated to the League by pro-administration forces. He could promise, however, that it would be enough to pay for travel around the country and newspaper ads.

We stopped at my hotel on the way to the Capitol, and there were a fistful of messages waiting. One was from Joseph Lelyveld of *The New York Times;* one from Lee Ewing of *Army, Navy, Air Force Times,* and another from Herman Nickel at *Time* magazine. I went straight to the room and dialed *The New York Times.* Mr. Lelyveld wanted an interview that afternoon. *The New York Times Magazine* was doing a story on POW families, he said.

"My, my, you sounded cool," Shirley said when I'd hung up. "You'd think *The New York Times* called every day."

That afternoon Karen Butler, a POW wife from southern California, joined us for the first time. We'd just come from an unsatisfactory meeting with Senator Griffin, Republican whip of the Senate, and faced another disappointment when we reached Gerald Ford's office. The congressman had canceled our meeting and handed us over to an aide. The assistant was a middle-aged man, who, we learned, had been with the congressman a long time. In the same room was a much younger man who swiveled around in his chair and listened intently to our conversation.

The older man was trying to be tactful, but his answers were evasive, and I kept pressing him to be more specific. "Why can't

Congressman Ford vote his own conscience rather than as the President wants him to vote?" I asked.

"It is his own conscience," he said. "He believes we must stop the Communists in Vietnam."

"But we haven't been able to do that, and the government we support in the South is not worth any more lives or years of captivity. President Thieu has never thanked any of us for our sacrifices," I said.

At that point the young man across the room got out of his chair. In a tight voice he said, "We all know we have to stand up to the Communists over there rather than here." He paused for a few seconds. I thought he was finished, but then he said, "I think this discussion has gone far enough. I'm afraid you're all going to have to leave now."

The other man said, "They're POW families." His face had paled.

The young one didn't notice. "The interview is over," he said. "You will have to leave now."

I couldn't believe what was happening. "Why don't you kick us out?" I said. "If you do, I'll call UPI to cover it. Go ahead and kick us out!" Then I asked him, "How old are you anyway?"

"I'm twenty-three," he answered. "What has that to do with anything?"

"If you're twenty-three and think it is so important to stop Communists, why aren't you over in the swamps and jungles? Why aren't you in uniform? Why aren't you offering your fanny to President Thieu?" I asked.

His face reddened. "Leave now," he insisted.

"I'm sorry," the older man said, trying to intercede. "Please sit down again. Let's talk this over."

"No, thank you," I said.

Shirley and Karen were wide-eyed; they followed me out the door. Outside, Shirley was finally able to squeak out a few words. "I've never seen you let go that way," she said.

Karen covered a gaping mouth with her hand. "Is this what happens every day?" she asked.

Shirley started to laugh, and then we were all doubled over, holding onto our sides. "I thought that poor young baby was going to hit you, Barbara," Shirley managed. "He should have. What a story! For a minute I thought you might smack him, though. Did you see the look on his face when you asked him to offer up his fanny?"

I wished Delia had been there. "Reserved, in-control Barbara." That's what she called me.

I was still hyped up from the afternoon's confrontation when Mr. Lelyveld of *The New York Times* came to my room. I told him how we'd been muzzled by the government and used by the President and manipulated by everyone. I said that the President didn't really care when the prisoners came home; he was determined to go on propping up that dictator Thieu. I told him that the military wouldn't tell families how to contact our group as it had done for the League when it began. I described our grandiose plans, all the more inflated and bolstered by our successful weekend caper. He wrote furiously.

I was still floating when I closed the door on him. Why did I get the feeling that the press was cheering for us? Maybe they believed we were right. Then again, maybe we were just a better story than military families who backed their Commander-in-chief.

I hoped it wasn't too late to reach Lee Ewing at the *Army, Navy, Air Force Times*. I was still high and in the mood to talk with someone else. "I really want to include the viewpoint of you and your group in an article I'm doing for the magazine," Ewing said. "It's called 'How Long Would You Wait?'"

"What does that mean?" I asked him.

"Answer it as you like," he said.

"In that case, 'Not another minute' is the answer for the President," I said.

On my last evening in town Bob Sherman, his wife, Carolyn, Shirley and her husband, Phil, and I met at a restaurant in Georgetown to celebrate and also to plan future conspiracies. The fact that we were underdogs compared with the League created a kind of bond among us; we vowed not to give up. Carolyn laughed and said we looked like a strange little band of patriots shaking a slender fist at a fierce ruler.

At the airport the next morning, Shirley and I were still making plans when suddenly she said, "Look over there. It's John Gardner—head of Common Cause!" She darted across the terminal, and I chased after her, as was my habit, nearly ramming into her when she stopped in front of a tall statesmanlike figure.

"Mr. Gardner," she said, "I'm Shirley Culbertson. This is Barbara Mullen." She sucked in a quick breath and said, "We've organized a new POW family group and would appreciate any help you can give us at Common Cause."

If he was surprised by the intrusion, he didn't show it. "I know about your activities," he said. "Call. We'll be glad to help."

When we'd left him, I said, "Can you imagine running into John Gardner like that!"

"It doesn't surprise me," Shirley announced in a matter-of-fact way. "Luck is with us. You'll see."

My taxi maneuvered the last curve in the road and stopped at our house. The front door flew open and Terry ran up the steps, skipping every other one until he reached the top.

"Mom, Mom," he shouted. "I told you not to go away. You missed something important. A guy dropped out and Sean made Little League."

"Wow, that's terrific," I said, handing him a suitcase. I ran down the stairs after him.

The air was cool this time of evening. There was a slight rustling of leaves at the top of the eucalyptus trees, and the sun was dropping behind the hills. I breathed the sweet odor of the trees and thought how the splendor of my canyon seemed to match my own feelings of hopefulness.

17. NIXON'S DILEMMA

JULY 1971

Mary McGrory, *Washington Star,* July 1971.

The President is pacing the floor at San Clemente. . . . The new Hanoi proposal is forcing him to choose between President Thieu and the prisoners . . . and there is reason to believe that the wives and mothers . . . are beginning to burn over the President's silence.

I'd been back from Washington a few days when I drove over to see the Alvarezes in San Jose. Delia met me at the door, waving a handful of newspaper clippings in the air. "People are sending these to us from all over the country," she said, spreading them out on their kitchen table. Choosing one with bold headlines, she read out loud, "The families of some of the men being held prisoner fear the President is putting the safety of the Saigon regime ahead of rescue of the POWs. The POW families have a point. . . ."

"The press isn't going to forget us," Sally said as we sifted through the rest of the clippings.

We had good reason to believe that. Jack Kramer of *The Wall Street Journal* had called that afternoon wanting to interview all three of us, and Delia was leaving the next day for Washington to appear at a press conference with John Kerry of Vietnam Veterans Against the War. The extent and smoothness with which our media events had been covered, however, had left us unprepared for the confrontation that occurred at the Kerry press conference in Washington.

Sheila Cronin, sister of a POW from the Washington area, and Valerie Kushner, the Army doctor's wife, along with Shirley Culbertson and Delia, sat at a front table with John Kerry. About twenty-five members of the press had arrived at the meeting room in the Old Senate Building. Some were already seated; others were busy setting up cameras.

As soon as John Kerry stood up and tried to introduce our women to the media people, a voice from the back of the room shouted, "What office are you running for anyway, Kerry?"

It was immediately apparent that a group of women from the League had come to disrupt the proceedings. From then on, flanked by members of the Veterans of Foreign Wars, the women stood by the rear door and heckled anyone who tried to speak.

Kerry, hair grown long but dressed today in a suit and tie, tried to remain calm. He attempted time and again to answer charges leveled by the irate women and veterans of another era. "I only want Mr. Nixon to set a date for withdrawal of troops so that the prisoners can come home," he said.

"You're getting support from POW families for political purposes. You're trying to give the impression that all the relatives of POWs want a quick withdrawal," a woman screamed. When she finished, a VFW member patted the shoulder of her ruffled blouse, and she smiled up at him.

Another woman then turned her assault on our people. "He's using you—don't you know that?" she hollered.

When Sheila Cronin tried to speak, one of the officers' wives cried out, "This is a humane issue and should remain so."

Another shouted, "Rather than putting pressure on our government, why not put pressure on Madame Binh and the Viet Cong?"

"The first point of the latest Viet Cong peace proposal guarantees the return of American prisoners when the date is fixed," Kerry answered.

At that, the four women stalked out of the news conference with the Veterans of Foreign Wars who had brought them.

Reporters seemed surprised by the women's behavior. Some of them jumped up and chased down the hall after the League women; others ran up to the front of the room to get a response from Kerry and our people.

Delia told the group who were still there, "It's too bad they can't be tolerant. They've had their say for years and we've never interfered with their press conferences."

"I know those League women," Valerie said. "We've all been through the same kind of hell together, and we don't need it from each other. If they want better treatment for the men for the next seven years, the present course is all right. If they want the men home, it's time for us to enter the political arena."

The President concentrated on his upcoming trip to China during the weeks that followed our disrupted press conference. The families I was hearing from sensed an eeriness about the sudden lack of interest in Vietnam and the POWs. "It's as if the prisoners were being groomed for martyrdom," some said. "Has the President written our men off? He doesn't talk about them anymore," one woman asked. She was calling from Nebraska at eleven o'clock at night.

I found a letter from a mother in my mailbox one morning. On legal-size lined paper, she related the gruesome account of her son's disappearance and expressed doubts about our government's concern:

The Army informed us that our son disappeared when his helicopter was shot down. Four days later he was declared dead. We finally went to a base in Alabama to talk to the only surviving eyewitness to the crash. He told us that our boy was last seen on a landing zone miles from where the Army told us he had taken off. He told us that the copter went down and did not explode. It began burning slowly and

was surrounded by enemy troops. There were only two men
in the copter. The Army buried the remains of three men—
or so they say. He also told us that our son was the only man
on board who carried an MI6, and his gun was found eleven
days later leaning against a tree away from the crash site.
When the Army sent us the three skeleton charts showing
the remains of supposedly each of the three men, our family
doctor said none of them fitted our son's description. Do you
think they care anymore who is alive or dead?

How could I respond to her concerns? I was asking the same
questions myself. Did our government really know who had been
sent home for burial or who was still missing? In fact, now that
the prisoners were a liability, had it all but buried them too?

Bob Sherman called one afternoon to ask if I was in the mood
for some black humor. He told me about an organization called
American POW Memorial Committee that had proposed putting
a flag on the moon, when the astronauts landed, as a memorial to
the POWs. Congressman Leggett wrote them that the name of
their group and their proposal were appalling; they were treating
the POWs as if they were already dead.

Clayton Fritchey titled one of his syndicated columns "POW
Issue Vanishes." "What has become of the American prisoners of
war. . . . Or, more precisely, what has become of our interest in
their fate?" he wrote. "It seems to have vanished into the summer
air. . . . The administration's only concern at the moment is that
the impatient wives and other relatives of the POWs will start
pressuring the government for action. . . ."

Though the prisoners had disappeared from administration
statements, a twenty-five-million-dollar White House–backed
campaign announced earlier by the Advertising Council to protest
their treatment was about to be launched. The spots would not
be controversial, according to the Council and the administration.
The POWs would be presented as victims of Communist cruelty;
the ads would not allude to recent peace proposals, and the war
would not be on trial.

Our decision to challenge the campaign came quickly. It was an opportunity to put the prisoner issue back in the news. PKL Advertising in New York offered to assist us in producing counterads, and we took them up on it. Sheila Cronin, Shirley Culbertson, and Valerie Kushner flew from Washington to New York to tape our own messages, which were screened at a press conference at the Plaza Hotel.

After reporters had seen the tapes, Orville Schell, our legal spokesman, announced that Families for Immediate Release was prepared to seek a Federal Communications ruling demanding equal free time for our counter-position.

The event served its purpose; all three women were on the network news that evening. Valerie Kushner claimed that the White House–backed ads were only designed to improve conditions in the camps, to get the men better meals. Sheila asserted that Nixon was trying to resign the American people to the POWs' being there a long time. "We don't want to clean up the cells, we want to empty them," Shirley said.

A week later a Western Union messenger pulled into my driveway and handed me a telegram from the San Clemente White House. I left Terry in the car, grumbling that he was late for soccer practice, while I ran back into the house. I ripped open the yellow envelope and read:

AUGUST 20

YOU ARE INVITED TO ATTEND A MEETING WITH DR. KISSINGER FOR A DISCUSSION ON POW/MIA MATTERS AT TEN O'CLOCK AM, THURS. AUGUST 26, THE WESTERN WHITE HOUSE. PRESENT THIS WIRE AT THE MAIN GATE, WESTERN WHITE HOUSE, SAN CLEMENTE, FOR ENTRANCE. RSVP BY COLLECT CALL TO SALLY NEUBAUER. 714-492-9900.

BRIGADIER GENERAL JAMES D. HUGHES
MILITARY ASSISTANT TO THE PRESIDENT

As soon as I dropped Terry off, I found a public telephone and called Sally Alvarez. She had received the same telegram; she thought three or four others from our group had also been invited. "This is our chance," she said. "Only League ladies have been asked to these meetings in the past." I moaned that I didn't have enough time to prepare, but Sally said she wasn't worried, she'd been ready for Henry for years.

I spent the next five days pawing through thick folders full of clippings. I flipped the pages of old magazines, studied statements, and memorized quotations.

I gleaned the essentials of the seven-point Communist peace proposal from a State Department document Bob had sent me. Number one promised POW release for a set withdrawal date. "These two operations will begin on the same date and end on the same date," it stated. Point two dealt with power in Vietnam, a provisional government, and the armed forces; point three with reunification; point four, no military alliances; point five, foreign policy of neutrality; point six, reparations for damages, and point seven guaranteed that the accords would be concluded. I could recite them backward and forward in my sleep. When I couldn't stuff another fact into my head, I packed the overflow into a briefcase, and Sally and I started the drive down the coast.

Sally Alvarez loved California. We took detours. She showed me places where she and her family had stopped on their way from Mexico when she was a child. We visited missions and a series of cousins along the way. Her wealth of knowledge reached backward through U.S. history and Spanish domination to Indian California. There's a reassuring sense of order about the past, I thought as I listened, transported in time, soaking up her conversation with the sun and the sound of the ocean. We arrived in San Clemente about eleven that night. Sally dozed off immediately. It had been a long, relaxing day, and it felt good to stretch out. I was soon asleep, too.

The next morning we showed our telegrams to guards at the gate of the San Clemente White House. We parked our car and walked across the estate grounds. Blue-green grass formed a velvet carpet which sloped gently down to the edge of the Pacific Ocean. A Secret Service man directed us into one of the white

Spanish-style buildings and on to a long formal room where rows of chairs had been set up.

I was disappointed to see that twenty-five or thirty people were already there and seated. I'd hoped that the group would be smaller. The women who had heckled our press conference with John Kerry were sitting together. I also recognized several League of Families officials. Sally and I slid into two chairs near the back of the room and waited.

Someone closed the doors, and six or seven men at the front table stood up. Dr. Kissinger came in through a side entrance and went directly to the podium. "Welcome, ladies and men," he said. "Let me start by saying that everything stated here today is off the record—that is, not to be repeated to the press."

Dr. Kissinger's heavily accented bass voice seemed to convey simultaneously a strength of character and worldly knowledge. We waited anxiously for his next words. "It would only be cruel to pretend that something was going to happen soon," he said.

"I want to explain that conditions in the world are improving," he continued. "These conditions will back the North Vietnamese and Viet Cong into a softening position. Russia is thawing, and China wants relations with us enough not to jeopardize this opportunity by continuing a hard line in support of the North Vietnamese. South Vietnam is becoming more and more secure in a military sense.

"The Communists in Paris are going to realize that the time is now to negotiate. Then they will be ready to present some realistic proposals. This will become more apparent to them as we get closer to the next U.S. election and they realize that Mr. Nixon is going to be our President for another four years."

I didn't dare look at Sally; she would be seething at that prediction.

"Since I have nothing specific to tell you," he said, "I will open it up to your questions. I see some familiar faces. I'll begin with them." He smiled and motioned for Maerose to begin.

"Since the situation in Laos is so different from that in Vietnam and possibly can't be settled for some time, please don't try to include it in your plans for settlement in Vietnam," she said.

Maerose's husband had been shot down in Laos; I couldn't believe she had said a thing like that, and I wondered why she had done it.

The next woman to stand up was Carole Hanson, the Marine wife who had appeared opposite Mitch Jones on the "Advocates" program. "Are we planning on the elections in South Vietnam to prove that South Vietnam is politically secure?" she asked.

"Yes," Kissinger said. "Some people have expressed too much concern about those elections in the South. After all, they've never had anything resembling a free election in the North. And when has anyone ever heard of an election being held in the middle of a civil war? The elections shouldn't affect the security of South Vietnam." I thought it was strange that he referred to the Vietnam conflict as civil war since they had always claimed it was an outside invasion by North Vietnam.

Next Alice Stratton asked if we had any other plan to get our men back if we couldn't find acceptable agreement in Paris, to which Kissinger answered: "No, the only way we'll ever get them back is through agreement with the people who hold them."

A man in the front row stood up suddenly as if he'd just heard something startling. "Then are we talking with them about the latest peace proposal in Paris?" he asked.

"All the Communists have really said is that they will talk about the modalities of release of the prisoners," Kissinger said. "Nothing more."

"What does that mean?" the man persevered. "I understood they would release the men for a withdrawal date."

His eyes narrowing, Kissinger spoke slowly. "No, the other conditions are the same old demands of a year and a half ago," he said. "Some of the people you hear flippantly saying, 'Set the date and all will be well,' do not have the diplomatic responsibility for the future of the peoples of South Vietnam. Diplomacy, contrary to what *The New York Times* advises, is not conducted on editorial pages."

Laughter broke out here and there. Dr. Kissinger smiled and continued. "Also, most of those now screaming at us to set a date are those who got us into this war in the first place."

When the room quieted, a sturdy, matronly woman Dr. Kissinger seemed to know rose from her seat. "Don't you think this would be a good time to declare a moratorium on public discussion of the POW issue by the families?" she asked.

I was beginning to think some of the questions had been rehearsed in the Oval Office. I realized my suspicions could be getting the best of me, but it did seem inconceivable that the wife of a POW would advise that we stop talking about the prisoners.

Kissinger said he agreed with her suggestion. "The Communists gauge their hardening position according to the domestic discord in our own country," he said. "Our President has pressures on him to withdraw more rapidly and to set a date. However, he is pursuing his own course. We must realize, though, that the situation in the United States has deteriorated to the point where some legislation detrimental to our President's policies might pass. We would be able to conduct diplomacy much more effectively if individual citizens, congressmen, and newspapers didn't try to do it for us."

I had been trying to get his attention since the meeting began. At last he pointed a finger in my direction, and I leaped to my feet. "Dr. Kissinger," I said, "since the Communists have stated publicly that they would settle this point of withdrawal date and prisoner release separately, is our government willing to treat it as an issue separate from the other six points? Or will we insist that the political future of South Vietnam be settled first?"

"I do not intend to discuss what we would or would not do in the course of negotiations in Paris," he said.

I remained standing and ready to press further, but he looked away from me and called on Joan Vinson, the woman I'd met at the League offices in Washington. "Did our new ambassador to the Paris peace talks take any new initiatives with him?" she asked.

"Nothing specific," he said, "but I can assure you that we will not let any opportunity to negotiate be lost."

Then he turned to Maerose again. "According to *Time* magazine, this week Vice-President Ky gave you a four-point program which he would follow if we would back him in this election in South Vietnam. Is this true?" she asked.

"I have not read the *Time* story, but I must say that each candidate has pressured us and would want us to let him win—that is, of course, in case we would let any of them win," he said. "What I really mean is that they wanted us to rig it for them. This business about the candidates needs explaining. Outside forces have influenced the other two candidates to resign from the race to embarrass the United States and create instability in the South. However, it may work in the reverse. The North Vietnamese may assume that what appears less than a free election in the South may provide them the perfect time to negotiate more earnestly in Paris."

I was trying to make sense of this last statement when he called on Darthy Hughes, a member of our group from New Mexico. "If Vietnam is, as you say, more militarily secure than ever, why do the North Vietnamese and V.C. continue to have such high morale and willingness to fight compared with the South Vietnamese?" she asked.

"Don't confuse fanaticism with high morale," he said, and then he embarked on a lecture in which he compared free-spirited people to those under Communist rule.

An elderly man waited for Kissinger to finish and then asked: "Why do we just hear from our government about those still unaccounted for in North Vietnam and not those held by the V.C. in the South or those captured in Laos?"

"We are mentioning those in the South more now in our statements and will begin to talk more about those in Laos also," Kissinger said.

Karen Butler, whom I hadn't seen since our foray in Gerald Ford's office, asked, "Since the North Vietnamese have regained strength in the demilitarized zone and are now attacking our bases along the DMZ in a renewed effort, will this mean we will be reescalating?"

Kissinger first turned to one of the generals and then to a Defense Department official. "Oh, a few of our fire bases have been reactivated," the Defense Department man said.

"I have time for two more questions," Kissinger said.

I stood up quickly. "Will our government continue to oppose setting a withdrawal date if that's what it takes to gain the release of our prisoners?" I asked.

"I will not comment on that point," he said. Then he added, "It is all tied up with other demands which are unreasonable. We cannot and will not agree to the installing of a government, coalition or otherwise, in South Vietnam. Free government is developing very well on its own in South Vietnam."

"But the Communists have already stated that they would settle the prisoner issue for a set withdrawal date separate from other considerations," I said. "Will we be willing to do that?"

"I will not talk about negotiations," he said.

I wanted to scream, "Wasn't this supposed to be a discussion?" but I gave up and sat down.

In the meantime Sally Alvarez had risen from her seat. "Dr. Kissinger," she said, "I have more seniority than anyone here, and I'm sick of the whole thing. Sick to death of it and finished being patient."

Sally was still standing, but Dr. Kissinger announced that the meeting was over. "Thank you, everyone. Please have some coffee, tea, and Danish now," he said.

On his way out Dr. Kissinger stopped to chat next to a dazzling silver tea and coffee service and doilied plates of frosted rolls. Sally and I nudged our way through a group of people surrounding him. I had barely introduced myself when he grasped my hand and said, "I know, Mrs. Mullen, and I understand your impatience. You've been under a terrific emotional strain."

"That's not the point," I said. "Of course, I'm impatient. My husband has been missing in action five and a half years! We have to end this thing."

Before he could respond, Sally added, "Dr. Kissinger, I have been making a lot of noise and I am going to be making a lot more noise."

"I understand you, Mrs. Alvarez, and I know how you feel," he said. But he was already holding someone else's hand.

Sally whispered over the top of her coffee cup, "The hell he knows how I feel."

In the next instant he was gone. But not really, I thought, gazing at the back of his pin-stripe suit disappearing through a doorway. He's left us with his plans to end the war. We can wait for Russia to thaw, China to forsake all other Asian Communists in return for a visit from Richard Nixon and for the Pathet Lao to release U.S. pilots while our bombs scorch 80 percent of their land. "Well, Sally," I said, "I guess we can go home now and give up all this nit-picking about death and destruction."

I swallowed the last drop of my coffee as we were herded out the door. "We will now take you on a tour of the residence, everyone," a young aide announced.

I caught Darthy Hughes's eye on the way out. "Terrible," she whispered in disbelief. "Awful."

"Mrs. Nixon has just redecorated all the rooms," our young guide was telling us. We wandered through one airy room after the other. The colors were springtime: lime green, yellow, and pink.

No hospital green, khaki brown, or blood red here, I noted. "This is Tricia's room," the aide was saying. "She's staying here with her mother and father for a few days."

On her nightstand was a copy of *The Sun Also Rises*. How could she understand that and not Kent State, I thought, then suddenly realized I was standing in the President's bathroom. Rise shaving cream and yellow john paper—somehow it didn't fit. I would have figured him for white. I almost laughed out loud. It was the biggest revelation of the morning!

Our car was hailed down by newsmen as we drove through a gate on the way out. A CBS camera pointed at me through our front window, and a voice asked, "Did you hear anything hopeful in there?"

"Absolutely not," I said before making a thumbs-down signal I'd seen used on the streets of Berkeley. "God, Sally," I stammered, "I'm going to look like a revolutionary—I don't know what's happening to me."

Just in back of us another car was being stopped by the same newsman. I saw Carole Hanson's head pop out of the window and heard her cheery voice. "Yes," she was saying, "these meetings are so encouraging to the families—a real morale boost."

I looked over at Sally. A grin was creeping across her face. "Well, I suppose there's nothing left to do but get rid of those two—Nixon and Kissinger," she said.

I smiled back.

Mary McGrory, *Washington Star,* end of summer, 1971.

Nothing can hide for much longer the fact that the prisoners of war campaign, his proudest propaganda initiative, is about to blow up in President Nixon's face. The National League of Families, an organization sponsored to tell it to Hanoi, is breaking up with a rapidity that alarms the members. . . . A new organization has sprung up which calls itself "Families for Immediate Release," and its members have "gone public" with their demands.

18. KEEP YOUR CORSAGES

SEPTEMBER 1971 Shirley Culbertson looked like a determined sea captain who'd just brought her ship about and was now heading into the wind. I'd arrived at Dulles International on a late Saturday afternoon flight, and she'd already taken command. "It's time to separate the girls from the women," she said, laughing, but only half kidding.

It was the week of the Annual League Convention in Washington; sixty or seventy of us would be there to present "the other side," and none of us knew how it would turn out. Louise had come back to life, and in the process she'd found the Beechers. Margaret and Sam Beecher were parents of a son listed as missing by the Army. Sam was an Indiana attorney, and they had spent the past few weeks formulating elaborate means by which to challenge the League on many things—foremost was its claim to rightful ownership of the term "humanitarian."

"We should shout and holler to be heard if necessary," Louise said. "If we're forced to leave the room, at least one of the group should remain to take notes. I feel like an underground agent, I swear."

Minnie Gartley, the mother of Mark Gartley, a POW in North Vietnam, was coming up from Florida with a group which was also ready to stand by us. Minnie, a history teacher who saw events in a larger context, had arranged a strategy session for the first evening of the convention. We couldn't operate helter skelter, she said. We needed a planned agenda.

Mrs. Curtis Glenn, another mother of a POW, was flying from Oklahoma, though she could hardly afford it, she told us. She wouldn't stay at the Statler Hilton, where the convention would be held—she had found a room at a less expensive hotel a few blocks away. "I'll be there," she said. "Nothing could stop me. It should be a rip-roaring meeting; there's bound to be a split in the League."

This was the atmosphere as we landed one by one in the capital that weekend. Besides adding to our numbers, something else had happened that gave us reason for confidence. It had to do with Alice Cronin, who was married to Sheila Cronin's brother. Alice had gotten the list of names and addresses of family members from the Liaison Committee. Dave Dellinger, Rennie Davis, Cora Weiss, and Madeline Duckles, the woman I had tangled with in a Berkeley church, all belonged to the Committee, which had been set up to receive information on POWs from North Vietnam. Since it was the only channel through which meager bits of information or a handful of letters might pass, most of the families had sent them their addresses.

After Alice Cronin received one letter from her husband, Mike, through the Committee, the idea had come to her. Our problem had always been one of reaching other families, and the military had refused to disseminate information about our group in its monthly newsletters as it did for the League. Since we had no way of contacting families who wanted to join us, the Committee list would give us that opportunity. Cora Weiss had encouraged Alice to take the list, promising to keep the transaction a secret. It was to their benefit as well as ours, she said, to keep it quiet.

Alice had called me from New York. "Barbara, it's done," she said.

"Good," I answered. "See you in Washington."

Soon I would meet Alice in Washington, away from abbreviated telephone messages. I would find out that she'd been a student at the University of California when her husband's plane was shot down five and a half years earlier. They'd been married just six months. "We've been separated almost a year for each of those months," she would tell me with a far-off gaze. The next three years at the university had passed by in a fog, she said. As she spoke, her eyes tilted slightly upward at the edges, and she smiled easily, as if she'd really been talking about someone else.

Our group of planners had already congregated in Shirley's family room when we arrived from the airport. Bob Sherman and his wife, Carolyn, were there, as well as Fred Wertheimer, a legislative councilor from Common Cause. Alice and Sheila Cronin were bending over a stack of pamphlets when we walked in. Sheila glanced up and flipped loose shag-cut curls back from her face. She wore a red flight suit nipped in at the waist and looked more like eighteen than twenty-two years old. She was the youngest of our group, only sixteen when her brother's plane was shot down. I imagined she had matured quickly in the past few months, though, having come through the disrupted Kerry press conference and TV video tapings in New York.

Our display at the hotel was ready, Sheila reported. She had gotten hundreds of photo prints of our spot commercials from the advertising people in New York, and Business Executives' Move for Peace had contributed five hundred pamphlets. Alice laughed and told us that the League had stuck our booth in the most obscure spot in the hotel—down at the far end of the mezzanine. "What they didn't realize," she said, "was that everyone would have to pass by us on their way to all the meetings and press conferences in order to get to the auditorium."

We spent the rest of the evening planning strategies—whom could we depend on? Whom not? Fred Wertheimer promised that Common Cause would be on hand all week to help us. Ready or not, we would all meet at the Statler Hilton the next morning.

Our booth was indeed located at the intersection of traffic on the mezzanine. A picture of a mother and father, about three by two feet, taken from our ad agency film, was in clear view on a three-legged stand next to our table. A Common Cause poster designating which congressmen had voted for, which had voted against end-the-war legislation hung on the wall at our back.

Alice and I had just begun unpacking crates and Sheila was slapping pamphlets on the table when a young woman breezed in, her arms full of handouts and boxes.

"Hi, there," she said. "Who wants one of my dandy little pins—'POWs No. 1—Not Thieu'?"

We each grabbed one, and then Valerie Kushner bounced off in another direction.

"So that's Valerie, the Army doctor's wife," I said. "She makes quite an entrance, doesn't she?"

Other tables were going up around us. "Back our POWs," the red, white, and blue posters commanded. Seven hundred families were being registered at a desk on the mezzanine. They strolled by our booth in groups, stopping to read the material we'd laid out. Some smiled approval, but others looked confused as the sense of its message sank in. They shook their heads, wandered away, and sent friends down to verify what they'd seen and read. Our four-foot-long FAMILIES FOR IMMEDIATE RELEASE sign was tacked to the front of our table, and we had a pen and pad out for signatures in case anyone wanted to join our ranks.

The place was filling up; uniformed men, some of high rank, were welcoming the families; mothers and fathers milled about as if waiting to be rescued and led somewhere. I began to feel exposed and unprotected. It wasn't like being in the center of Golden Gate Park surrounded by thousands of kindred souls.

A small group was gathering at a table near us, three or four booths away. A red banner stretching the length of their table nearly reached the floor. Across its front, VIVA was spelled out in large white letters. The VIVA now stood for Voices in a Vital America, but it had formerly been called the Victory in Vietnam Association. One of the men abruptly left his circle of conferees and headed toward us.

"What are you doing here at our POW convention with this antiwar literature?" he said, shuffling through our neat piles of leaflets and spreading them out on our table.

"Are you a relative of a POW?" I asked him.

"No, we're VIVA—we sell the POW bracelets," he announced without looking up. "I'm going to see about this," he said, still not meeting me eye to eye. He squared his shoulders and tramped off.

I took a closer look around us. Displays had already been constructed by the VFW and the American Legion, and a half dozen more were being assembled. Ours was the only one I could see that represented POW family members. "We belong here more than they do," I said. "Let them try to expel us." We restacked our printed material and explained our position with new assurance.

Disapproving passersby argued with us. Some told us we had no legal right to be there. Every so often someone dashed off, indignant, threatening again to report us to officials in charge. It didn't take long for individual press representatives straggling in to find their way down to our little nook. They were already curious.

Some of Louise's Virginia Beach group had shown up; with peeks over their shoulders, they had been sneaking down to our table to cheer us on. Minnie Gartley and her following from Florida were there, as well as the Beechers from Indiana, who carried a fat briefcase around with them which they said was loaded with legal ammunition. Sally Alvarez would be arriving that afternoon on a military aircraft. Tiny Mrs. Glenn had come by herself from Oklahoma. She was already at our booth handing out leaflets and pins. Other voices on the telephone and signatures on letters had transformed themselves into living people.

Minnie's strategy session for the convention was to be held that evening. We'd tried to keep it secret, but discussion in the coffee shop and cocktail lounge had made that difficult. As the four of us—Shirley, Sheila, Alice, and I—headed toward the room Minnie had reserved, a few League officers rushed ahead of us. In fact, we realized that several people were hurrying in our direction. We suspected now that our meeting was being infiltrated, and we were sure of it when we opened the door. Sprinkled throughout the room were military uniforms and familiar League women. Then I spotted Lieutenant Frishman, the released POW, across the room.

Margaret Beecher would describe the affair later as a "disaster." It started when Minnie Gartley attempted to take charge. She tried several times to deliver her prepared speech, but we couldn't hear her above the voices of the intruders. I was sure if they refused to listen to this middle-aged schoolteacher, the rest of us wouldn't stand a chance. Finally Minnie came to the end of her statement and relinquished the microphone to Lieutenant Frishman, who was waiting by her side.

From then on, we sat helplessly by as he and others took over our meeting. This released prisoner deserved our respect, but he had expressed his view often at Defense Department briefings. Besides, he was already scheduled to speak at formal League meetings throughout the week, and this, our only planning session, was going up in smoke.

Suddenly a man's voice bellowed out, "Sit down, Lieutenant Frishman. This was supposed to be our night!"

Sheila stood up and tried to speak, but a League coordinator from Boston began shouting her down. "What do they all think they're doing here?" Shirley whispered to me.

A short muscular man stood up and told us he was a Church of God preacher from South Carolina and father of a POW. Jesus would forgive those of us who were against this war if we prayed, he said. "Because God is on our side against the Oriental Communists."

The four of us scrambled from the room hastily. He was still delivering his sermon when we closed the door. We looked at one another and burst out laughing. Even though they had sabotaged our session, we couldn't take the affair seriously.

"They sure went to a lot of trouble to screw up our plans, didn't they?" Alice said.

We'd chosen Congressman Leggett to present our view at the opening session of the convention the following morning. In a speech Bob Sherman had helped him write, Leggett told a crowded auditorium that victory was "beyond the rooftops"; that there was never a better chance to negotiate than today, when a trade could be made from strength.

Then Senator Dole spoke. He claimed that George McGovern had misled the American people into believing that the POW issue could be settled separately from political demands. "We shouldn't let them dupe us that way," he said, "using the prisoners as pawns." The auditorium went wild with applause.

At the next meeting that morning we positioned ourselves throughout the room in order to spread the effect of our own presence. A video tape by Al Seamans, president of the ad agency handling the League's Ad Council campaign, was shown. He said their advertisements had not been distributed to television networks because a "certain group" had obstructed progress of the Ad Council's campaign. "The networks are reluctant to schedule them," he explained, "because of demands for equal time from a protesting group." Everyone knew who the "protesting group" was; I felt uncomfortable and suddenly wished we'd huddled ourselves together in a corner of the room instead.

In the auditorium that same afternoon I was waiting for Sheila to speak at a meeting to which the press had been invited for the first time. I was thinking about the day, which so far had been unproductive, when I felt a tap on my shoulder. Fred Wertheimer was crouched behind me and whispering, "Barbara, come out to the hall, please."

Minnie Gartley waited outside. "We've decided to go through with the demonstration," she said. I knew what she meant. We had talked under our breaths about the possibility of picketing the White House the day before.

During the past two days, every time a few of us had tried to conduct a private discussion, we had been followed by Lieutenant Frishman and a brother of another POW. Materializing out of nowhere, they would step forward to criticize our ideas. League meetings were producing resolutions that Nixon's staff could have written. Most members of our group were running out of patience because the rules of the convention had been stacked against us. Picketing, however, was to be used as a last resort.

"All right, Minnie, let's do it," I said.

Fred Wertheimer and I drove to the offices of Arnold and Porter, a law firm that had volunteered to assist us. Stuart Land, one of their attorneys, prepared a waiver of advance notice to picket the White House, and we were scheduled to appear in court the next morning.

By the time I returned to the Statler Hilton, the press conference was breaking up. Reporters from assorted magazines and newspapers had stopped at our display. While I was gone, one of our mothers had unknowingly gotten herself interviewed by *The Daily World*, and a mysterious Eastern Orthodox priest had attached himself to one of our chairs.

Valerie was making periodic out-of-breath appearances, but Louise hadn't shown up yet. There had been a message from her stating that she wouldn't participate in the League convention. She would arrive the next morning, however, for a nine o'clock coffee with Senator Ted Kennedy. I considered that to be real style. Louise was always so queenly but effective. I smiled and wondered why I couldn't be classy enough to stroll in with Senator Kennedy on my arm rather than tearing around signing papers to picket the President of the United States.

By the time Shirley and I headed for MacLean that evening, the reality of what we were about to do was setting in. I opened the car window for a little air. Shirley didn't seem as enthusiastic about the next day's demonstration as I'd hoped. She went straight to the kitchen, whipped up a snack and mixed us a drink, then set them down on the coffee table. "Just remember to keep your white gloves clean, Barbara, and for God's sake find some pearls to wear," she said firmly. "That's very important."

I smiled gratefully and picked up the drink.

What the hell, I thought after I was in bed. So we're going to picket the Commander-in-chief tomorrow. I pulled the quilt up to my chin and fell into a sound sleep.

I had difficulty dragging anyone out of the hotel and over to the courthouse with me the next morning. They all wanted to witness Louise's debut with Senator Kennedy. In the end, some of our more determined mothers agreed to sacrifice the enjoyment of the moment and come along.

198

As it turned out, Fred Wertheimer, Shirley, and I sat on a bench near the front of the courtroom with four gray-haired ladies lined up next to us. None of them weighed more than 105 pounds, I was sure.

Judge Jones, U.S. District Court for the District of Columbia, examined our documents which lay before him. He lifted his head slowly and stared down at us. His gaze moved from one end of our row to the other, then back again. I could see by his expression that mothers of servicemen didn't request permission to picket the White House every day. He picked the papers up one more time and unconsciously shook his head as he read them again. He swept one final look across the earnest faces before him and read aloud:

ORDER

"This case having come before the court on Motion made on behalf of certain Families of Prisoners of War and Missing in Action in Indochina . . . to conduct a demonstration and other public gathering activities on the south sidewalk of Pennsylvania Avenue in front of the White House with estimated number of participants being not more than twenty-five at any one time on Tuesday, September 28, 1971, between the hours of 12:00 noon and 7:00 P.M. . . . Motion made on behalf of this particular group . . . is granted, and they are authorized to hold a demonstration. . . ."

Back at the hotel, the League women were lying in wait for Senator Kennedy and Louise. Sheila and Alice and four or five others from our group stationed themselves in the room set aside for his visit. As it turned out, however, they could do little to protect him from the women who swarmed over him as soon as he walked in. Screaming and attacking his position, they accused him of exploiting the prisoner issue. They allowed him no time to respond. Sheila had to push her way through what had nearly become a mob to get close enough to thank him for his concern and for coming. She thought he was handling himself well, but saw that his hands were trembling.

What was supposed to have been a coffee discussion evolved into a quasi-press conference. Reporters fired questions at Senator Kennedy, who seized the opportunity to speak. "American servicemen are rotting in POW camps because the Nixon administration failed to respond to a peace proposal," he said. "This view was expressed to me this morning by Louise Mulligan, wife of James A. Mulligan, who was captured in North Vietnam on March 20, 1966. Mrs. Mulligan would like to make a statement."

Up to this point, Louise had been standing by his side, looking somewhat stunned by the turn of events. "There is not one family member who does not want to see this war ended," she said. "I am firmly convinced that if the membership of the League were to say to our Congress, our President, and indeed to our country, 'We want a negotiated end to this conflict immediately with provisions made for an accounting of the missing,' the Congress would end this holocaust."

Before leaving, Kennedy declared, "The administration is suffering from excessive pride in its approach to the peace talks. If I were running the talks, I would crawl into the room if it meant winning freedom for the POWs."

Sheila told me later that she was embarrassed by the behavior of the women and felt sorry for Kennedy. The irony was that one of the resolutions passed by the League the day before had asked that Congress take a more active role in settling the POW question.

I came to a conclusion after hearing about the Kennedy visit. We needed a show of force in front of the White House, and a few of us were not going to do the dirty work for everyone else. Alice, Shirley, Sheila, and, of course, our faithful mothers would be there, but who else?

The demonstration was only an hour away when I found Louise and her group from Virginia. I said I'd been asked to set this thing in motion with the understanding that we would all be there. Then I asked them to spread word of the picketing to everyone who had had enough of luncheons, speeches, and folded napkins.

Sheila and Alice had already left. I ran the four blocks to the

White House, cursing myself all the way for wearing sling-back high-heeled shoes. Suddenly I caught my breath. There it was—that perfectly rectangular white building, wings on either side, a mansion in the center of a green rolling lawn speckled with manicured foliage and trees, surrounded by its iron grille fence. Our symbol of leadership, as familiar as an old friend. My heart sank. Could we really go through with this?

Sheila, Bob and Carolyn, and Alice were standing in a group; Fred Wertheimer was instructing them on the legal guidelines for White House picketing. When I walked up, he stopped long enough to call out, "We're going to have Ron Nessen, NBC-TV News, here shortly."

Just then I saw Valerie coming down Pennsylvania Avenue. Mrs. Glenn and Sally Alvarez were tramping toward us from another direction. In a few minutes the Beechers arrived, and then Minnie Gartley and the Florida group. A taxi drove up. Louise and her ten-year-old son got out. And then others came: Sharon Walsh, a Marine wife from Minnesota; the Virginia Beach group; many whose names I didn't know yet. But they had come, and I was grateful. For these military wives trained in obedience, the parents reared in the tradition of pre-World War II, a lifetime of rules would be forsaken in this single act.

Sheila was passing out handmade cardboard signs—MY SON IS WORTH MORE THAN PRESIDENT THIEU; POWS: BRING THEM HOME; END IT NOW. We were allowed only twenty-five picketers at a time, and since we had far more than that already, we were taking turns, some walking in a circle, others leaning on the cement wall in front of the iron fence. An NBC truck drove up and parked. Ron Nessen got out and looked over the group. Addressing Fred Wertheimer, he said, "I'll take the volatile one over there."

I looked over my shoulder to see whom he meant, and realized it was me. He called me aside and then directed his crew to arrange the camera so the picketing and the White House were behind us. Then he asked me, "Why are you and your group here today?" and the camera pointed straight into the center of my face.

"We wanted to trust our President and our government, but they've let the American people down," I said. "President Nixon could end the war today and bring our men home if he wanted to. He hasn't listened to the American people, and he hasn't listened to us. This is the only avenue we have left to try to get his attention. . . ."

Nessen asked a few more questions, thanked everyone, and left. Other news people were beginning to arrive: the Washington newspapers, AP, UPI. I heard a man ask Bob, "Which one is Barbara Mullen?" and Bob brought him over to me. The man said that he was White House Security, which surprised me because he was dressed in a dark conservative suit rather than a guard's uniform.

"I need to ask you a few questions because your name appeared on the order to demonstrate," he said. He took my name, address, Bill's name and rank, and then walked quickly back to the gate. I supposed my name would now be added to some sort of list, but it was too late to be concerned.

By now radio reporters were showing up with tape recorders. I noticed a man in jeans and a turtleneck sweater hanging onto the iron fence and watching us as though we were invading his territory. His END THE WAR sign was upside down, and he was resting his elbow on the end of the stick. After a while he dragged it behind him and approached me. "Ma'am," he said, "I don't know what it's all about. I'm a Quaker, and I've been walking up and down here off and on for months. I have never been asked a question by a newsman or anybody else. I'm just going to stand back and enjoy this. You don't mind, do you?"

I laughed and asked him to join us.

News people were mingling around, interviewing everyone. One question kept popping up. "What would your husband or son or brother think of you doing this?" I was asked the same thing, and things suddenly came to mind—especially the way Bill celebrated the night Kennedy beat Nixon in 1960. He probably wouldn't even believe that Richard Nixon was in the White House after all these years. Bill didn't know how the war had escalated under Lyndon Johnson and dragged on under Nixon.

Once more I thought—how can I speak for Bill? He doesn't know what the years have wrought.

I looked at the hand mike stuck in front of me. "My husband would expect me to do whatever I could to save his life," I said. "But what that is is my decision and a matter for my own conscience. I believe what we're doing today will call attention to this unending war." The newsman strolled away, and I thought of myself in 1962. Would Miss July, prancing across the Pensacola Officers' Club stage in a scant red, white, and blue costume, have understood that answer?

Bob sat on the sidelines, looking like a proud papa at a dance recital. Shirley had gone home and come back with sandwiches and a large thermos of orange juice.

Near the end of the afternoon one of the reporters became concerned about tiny Mrs. Glenn, who looked very frail in her black dress. He said, "Mrs. Glenn, why don't you sit down for minute to rest? You look awfully tired."

"No," she answered stubbornly, "my son Danny is tired, too. I can't stop."

Valerie was giving an extensive interview to a woman from the *Washington Star*. Don McLeod, the AP man, kept asking me questions about the meeting with Dr. Kissinger in San Clemente. "Straws in the wind again," I said, "phony promises, secret happenings they can't discuss." *Time* had just taken some pictures.

By five o'clock we were hot, dirty, and tired. Alice had been walking in stocking feet for about an hour, and two runs were creeping up the sides of her legs. It was time to leave. We packed up and trudged back to the hotel. After a block or so I whipped my own shoes off and stuffed them into my bag. Then, almost unconsciously, I reached for the pearls at my neck and ran my fingers carefully over each bead.

Sheila, Alice, and I limped into the hotel. We had no room of our own to use since none of us was staying at the hotel, so we plopped into plush chairs in the lobby. The place was already coming to life, with people spruced up for the evening's activities, and we looked like a trio of refugees in comparison. We were in the process of pushing swollen feet back into what seemed

shrunken shoes when a friendly face bent over us. "Congratulations, women, I just heard about your afternoon's work. Good
job!" It was Senator Cranston sporting a big grin.

"Thank you," Shirley said.

Sheila's face lit up. "God, we did it!" she said, thrusting her
arms up in the air. We all smiled.

Clutching ham sandwiches and coffee in brown paper bags, we
followed Minnie Gartley up to her room. Other people were soon
filtering in. The room filled up; we curled up on the beds or
crouched on the floor. A few of the Concerned Officers Association members and Vets Against the War came in, and we all
waited for the evening news on NBC. Chet Huntley switched to
David Brinkley, who began his lead-in story "Families of Prisoners of War and Missing in Action picketed the White House
this afternoon to protest President Nixon's lack of progress in
ending the war." In the film behind Ron Nessen our people were
marching around, carrying their signs in front of Nixon's White
House. My speech was carried in total. I sounded like a real
officer's wife, which somehow surprised me.

We had stolen the evening news from everyone at the convention. When our piece was finished, a loud "Yahoo!" went up
in the room. We had done it. Someone poured wine into plastic
cups, and we toasted one another.

Alice and I combed our hair a little, brushed off our skirts, and
pulled our panty hose up tighter. It was time to relieve the other
women at our booth. Sheila moaned as she got up from the bed.
"Here it is the evening of the semi-formal League dinner and look
at us. If only we had some perfume."

"Believe me," Shirley said, as we sauntered up to the table, "no
one will notice how we look tonight. They're too impressed with
themselves." The women at our booth said there had been a message asking us to report to the front desk.

Early arrivals for the dinner were beginning to fill the
mezzanine. Just as the four of us were settling in at our booth, a
door opened off to the right. Inside, military men and wives of
POWs were dressed to the teeth, chatting, laughing, and sipping
cocktails. It was too much for Sheila. She said she didn't think

she could bear to hang around any longer, and left to phone a friend who belonged to the Concerned Officers' Association to come pick her up.

By the time she returned, the cocktail party was breaking up. They would be parading by us on their way to dinner in a few minutes. Melvin Laird, the Joint Chiefs of Staff, and General Westmoreland came out of the room together. They were laughing and joking. As they moved toward us, Sheila propped one of our signs up on the table. Westmoreland stopped for an instant to read it, and his smile vanished. He caught Sheila's eye, and they stared at one another until he turned away and walked toward the ballroom. The afternoon's triumph had left Sheila's face. "Michael is struggling to survive," she said, "and the very men who trained him are making a party of it."

The extravaganza was beginning to affect me, too. There was a terrible disparity between our declared purpose and what was happening here. The women swished by in their long gowns, perhaps formerly worn to dances or receptions at an officers' club. Long-legged younger ones darted past in perky mini-dresses. Their hair had been freshly styled in the beauty salon that afternoon. And there were the parents: mothers in church, Saturday night, bridge-club dresses adorned by special jewelry; fathers in good suits, out of the closets and pressed for the occasion.

Sheila had a stricken look on her face. "This is profane," she said. "Look at these military leaders. They're just flattering the women. The brass is playing on their weaknesses. That's all they're doing."

For every two or three family members there was a military officer in dress uniform. Had the call gone out, "Duty for handsome officers only—tall, with charming personalities"? The uniformed men seemed to know just what to do. They trekked by with a woman on each arm. It had been a long time since these women had had such attention. Others, the mothers, had perhaps never been to such a grand affair. They passed by us as if we were invisible.

"My God, they look a lot prettier than we do," I said. We gazed numbly at the fairy tale as it unfolded. Even Shirley could think of nothing to say.

Sheila finally stirred. "Let's go see why they want us at the desk."

A League woman behind the counter reached for two small white boxes from a shelf behind her. She said they were from the Defense Department for the formal dinner and set them on the counter. I untied a pink ribbon on one of the boxes and opened it. Cradled protectively in crunched tissue paper was a fresh white carnation corsage.

Sheila backed away from the boxes. Neither of us touched them. Instead, I ripped a sheet of paper from a memo pad on the desk and wrote:

To the United States Defense Department:
Keep Your Corsages!

19. AFTER THE BALL

SEPTEMBER 1971 The last of the families and military brass had just disappeared behind the doors of the ballroom, a stone's throw away from us. No sooner had things quieted down, however, than the place began to stir again. Two at a time, well-dressed gentlemen began wandering in. They were positioning themselves here and there about the mezzanine, and several more of them came running up the stairs. "Secret Service, I'm sure," Alice said.

One of the Vietnam Vets rushed over to our booth. "We just heard that the President decided about half an hour ago to make a surprise visit at the banquet tonight." The vet laughed. "After the evening news, no doubt."

All the doorways to the ballroom were now blocked by the men. An entourage entered through one of them, and a round of applause broke out, and the orchestra burst into "Hail to the Chief." I could picture the women on their feet, cheering and clapping their hands as the music stirred them on. "And this is their annual 'nonpolitical' dinner," Alice said. "What a joke."

Within minutes the President was speaking. From our table on the mezzanine we heard his voice resounding with sympathy and promise. He was telling them that he was totally committed to the release of our men. Though there was still no firm timetable, all channels were being explored, he said.

"I think I hate him," Sheila said, wrenching her hands together. "I didn't think I could really hate anyone."

The ballroom was quieter now, and we could hear him more clearly. "People sometimes feel that all the great burdens of the world are on the shoulders of the President and that the responsibilities are heavy," he said. "But let me tell you something: Any day that I sometimes feel that it has been a rather hard day and that I have had to make some real tough decisions, and I haven't had much support, and anytime I begin to feel a bit sorry for myself, I think back . . . I think of the airports where children have come up and said, 'My daddy is missing in action.' I think of the wives I have seen and the mothers and the rest. I think of their courage and what they have done and what they have given for their country, and then I realize my job isn't all that hard."

The applause was more prolonged this time. Sheila said, "I can't just sit here. Maybe if I stand by the entrance one of the press will notice and realize we're not all in there cheering."

She got up and walked over to the banquet room doors. She had been standing there just a moment when to our disbelief we watched one of the Secret Service men approach her from behind. Without warning, he grabbed her under the arms, lifted her up, and turned her around. He then shoved her against a wall. Suddenly she was looking up into the face of a man who was twice her size. As he held her to the wall, Alice and I got up and ran over to her.

"Let me go," Sheila said. "You have no right to do this! You could have asked me to leave."

Still holding her, he said, "Now, Miss Cronin, that sign isn't very polite. It's not courteous to the President."

He removed his hands from her and she repeated, "You had no right. This is our convention. I have a right to be here. What is your name? I know you're Secret Service. I'm going to the press with this."

"Now, now, Miss Cronin," he said, "you and your friends had your day in front of the White House. Now it's the President's turn."

"I'm not stopping him," she said, demanding again, "What's your name?"

Finally he answered, "Richard Kaiser."

By now, she was shaking. "I will go to the press!" she said.

Mr. Kaiser said calmly, "Remember, Miss Cronin, what just happened to you will continue to be *your* interpretation."

"That's a threat," she said, her voice quivering. Just then, a League woman came out of the banquet room. "Let her go back to her table," she said. "Her brother is a POW."

Alice and I took Sheila back to the booth and sat her in a chair. We were afraid she was in shock; she had a dazed look and we couldn't get her to speak. A few minutes later Steve Gilbertson, the Concerned Officer she had called earlier, came up the stairs. Before we could tell him what had happened, two other Secret Service men made a dash for our table and told him he had to leave that instant.

"I'm an Army captain stationed at Fort Detrick," the young officer protested. "What's going on here?"

The Secret Service men didn't answer; instead they stood on either side of him and escorted him out of the hotel. We heard later that they followed him to his car and stood there until he drove off.

We still couldn't get Sheila to talk to us. She was tapping the table with her fingers and staring at the floor. "I don't understand it," Shirley said. "Who was Sheila bothering? Listen to them in there. They're still applauding that man for offering nothing."

We sat there listening. Finally Alice said, almost in a whisper, "They're so thrilled the President showed up they don't know what he's saying. It wouldn't matter, they'd be cheering anyway."

"Maybe so, but remember, we're the ones who got him off his bottom and over here," I said.

Shirley heaved a deep sigh. "OK, everybody, let's go home and get some rest. They've got Laird and Westmoreland coming up next. I can't take that. Come on, Sheila, we'll put you in a taxi."

"All right," Sheila said, and followed us down the stairs.

In the morning the papers were full of the previous day's activities. We were doing a good job of competing with the President for publicity. "If the purpose was to focus attention on the war and the prisoners, we did that," Shirley said.

We were getting ready to go back to the hotel and pack up our table when a reporter from the *Washington Post* called regarding a story filed by Don McLeod, the AP reporter who had interviewed me in front of the White House. McLeod had called Kissinger to verify some of my quotes, and Kissinger had denied my version of the San Clemente meeting. "These are terribly emotional meetings for these women, and they cling to every straw," Kissinger said. "I could not under any circumstances have said our meetings with Peking would help our negotiations with Hanoi. . . . I could have said that if there is a general relaxation of tension it would contribute to peace."

"Tell Dr. Kissinger not to worry," I told the *Post* reporter. "We no longer cling to any of these straws. Over the past five years 'the straws' have changed from military victory, to pacification, to Paris peace talks, to President Nixon's secret plan, to Vietnamization, to a thaw in U.S.–Russian relations, and now to this upcoming China trip. Who knows what will be next?"

Sheila called a few minutes later. "Les Whitten in Jack Anderson's office phoned me a little while ago," she said. "He had heard what happened last night with the Secret Service. He had most of the facts and wanted to print the story. I should have let him, but I asked him not to. Somehow I'd come off sounding guilty, I was sure. Damn it. That's why they get away with this dirt. How I'd love to nail them for doing that to me! But they're not going to trap me. I won't be labeled some kind of radical—which is just what they want. From now on, good-bye jeans, hello Tricia Nixon dresses. I mean it."

By the time we got to the hotel, League women were turning

up for a chicken à la king luncheon sponsored by the Red Cross.
A featured speaker was going to discuss the articles of the Geneva
Convention pertaining to prisoners of war. As we packed up the
rest of our leaflets and took down our signs and posters, old and
newly acquired members of our group came by to say farewell.
Leaving them wasn't going to be easy—especially the mothers
who'd stuck by us so loyally. We all promised to keep up the
fight.

Alice, Shirley, Sheila, and I met at Shirley's home that afternoon, and Alice brought "the list" she had gotten from the Liaison Committee in New York. She untied the ribbon on a brown
legal folder and lifted a thick stack of yellow legal-size sheets of
paper from it. On each line was the name and address of a
mother, father, wife, sister, or brother who had written Cora
Weiss and Dave Dellinger on the odd chance that a letter from
their loved one might find its way from Southeast Asia to their
Liaison Committee in New York.

Even though the Defense Department had refused to put us in
touch with other POW/MIA families, I had some reservations
about using names that had been acquired by the Liaison Committee. As much as I hated the war, I never understood why
these antiwar activists traveled all the way to Hanoi to criticize
U.S. policy when they could have done it in Washington, D.C.
Also, they should have known that the two or three prisoners
they interviewed on each trip had been coerced into talking with
them. What did they expect the prisoners to say about their treatment with a gun at their back? The POW/MIA families, having
no choice, had written to the Liaison Committee, but most of
them felt that in doing so they had been forced to deal with the
devil.

Now, ironically, this same list of addresses would allow us to
communicate with these families, I was of two minds about it,
but I hoped some good would come of it. We spent the afternoon
planning the large mailing we would send out at once.

Alice and I stayed in Washington an extra day in order to
talk with John Holum in Senator McGovern's office. Senator

McGovern had just returned from talks with Communist leaders in Paris, and John brought us up to date on their discussions. He said we would never get a better treaty than we could now, that McGovern was convinced peace could be negotiated immediately.

John thought we had done a good job of embarrassing Nixon. How much longer the President could hold out was anybody's guess, he said. "Surely as the political campaign heats up he will become more sensitive to criticism. I realize that's not much comfort," he added, "the election being a year off."

We left McGovern's office, and Alice and I walked across the street to the cocktail lounge in the Hotel Congressional. I'd grown close to Alice that week; it seemed I'd known her longer than that. As soon as we'd settled into a sofa in the corner of the lounge, a weariness crept over me. I didn't want to talk war or politics; I wondered if Alice was in the same mood.

Seething just beneath her prim clothing and quiet manners, Alice had a sensuous quality about her and I suddenly wondered how she was handling her personal life back in southern California. We ordered drinks, and I found myself wishing we were just two women out for the evening. I rarely let myself imagine being that free again, but that night I thought it would be wonderful. I asked Alice how she coped with the loneliness, and she answered, "Not very well. You try to do the right thing, but if you tell people you've been faithful, they look at you as though you're either lying or abnormal."

"Let me tell you about one of my neighbors," I said. "She informed me that she could never have waited as long as I have. 'Of course I've always been turned on as far as sex goes,' she added. The same woman gave me a real lecture when I told her about a professor at the university who asked me to have dinner with him. She seemed shocked and asked how I could think of betraying Bill that way. I tell you, Alice, it's a no winner."

"Living the double life is the hardest part," Alice said. "When we're doing the work, I feel totally involved, whole and honest. But then I have to return to a daily existence where I have to pretend that my life is normal. That's when it falls apart. I never discuss the war or this political work with my new friends in San Diego."

"We're social freaks, Alice. That's the truth. People can't empathize; they can't understand our grief over a husband they've never met. So for the most part I just keep it to myself, too."

"It's all such a pretense," Alice said. "We can't even have a friendly cup of coffee with someone of the opposite sex. It isn't fair, is it?"

"Sometimes I just don't feel like a woman anymore," I said. "If I talk to a man under the most innocent circumstances, I think of Bill over there in some kind of cubicle, dying maybe, and I feel guilty. But still, I'm dreading those nights alone, more all the time."

Our morale was slipping fast. "Well, maybe this thing will end someday," I said, but my voice lacked conviction. "Right now I just feel like I'm dangling in the breeze."

"Me too," Alice said. "I wish something would happen." She rolled her glass back and forth between both hands and stared into it as if it were a crystal ball. Tears were forming in the corners of her eyes, and the next I knew the two of us were sitting there crying quietly at the table.

Finally Alice shoved a Kleenex back into her purse and said, "Come on, let's go out to Sheila's. We can go out for a good steak and a salad and listen to some music. Surely that's not immoral."

The house was quiet when I got home the following evening. Sean and Terry had gone out to eat with the baby-sitter. Sally Alvarez had returned the day before, and I found myself dialing her number before bringing my bags in from the car. She said her military aircraft had put down at an airfield in Utah. The League women on the plane had bought newspapers, and everyone had read the A.P. Kissinger story.

"You should have heard Maerose and Julie Butler and the rest of the northern California contingent," she said. "Your ears must have been burning. If they had their way, we'd all be charred at the stake. The picketing was enough for them, but they really blew their stacks at the idea of criticizing the god, Kissinger. They also said you weren't a good officer's wife and that you hated the Marine Corps, just for starters."

"We only did what they were too chicken to do," I said. "I'd be crazy if I'd been closeted in that military plane for twelve hours with all of them. I told you not to do it."

"I wish I'd taken your advice. You should have heard the names they were calling us. I was practically in isolation the whole trip back. Guess what, Barbara? When they weren't horrified at our actions, they were planning the next annual meeting. Next May! Next May—eight months away!"

"I'm beginning to just feel sorry for all of them," I said. "I don't care what they call us. We're the ones who put the war back on page one."

"That's right," Sally said. "I guess I'm just tired. I'm glad to be away from them and home."

Thoughts and emotions were jumping around inside me when I finished talking with Sally. I paced around the house for a while and then wandered into the kitchen. When I flipped the light on, I saw that Sean had left a note for me on the table. I dropped into a chair and read it:

Mom,
Here is a thing I had to write about my father for school tomorrow. Look for wrong spelling please. Be home about 8:30. I hope you had fun.

Love,
Sean

HOW I FEEL ABOUT HAVING A MARINE FOR A FATHER

Well, I feel proud because I'm probably the only kid in the school with a father who is a Major in the Marines who flies a jet and has been captured for about five years. I'd like to see some kid try and top that. Or when we go to the Navy Base or Navy Hospital the guard gives us a salute because my dad is a Major. And when we're at the Navy Base sometimes we get toured through my dad's plane or some other planes. Boy, am I glad my dad is a Marine and nothing else.

Sean Mullen

20. OPEN CHALLENGE

OCTOBER 1971 That fall, divisions within the prisoner-of-war families became more pronounced and bitter. We aired our differences openly before congressional committees, in court, and on network news. This once tightly controlled constituency was as polarized as the rest of the country.

Mrs. Glenn returned to Oklahoma ready to conquer her state. Louise worked with Senator Kennedy. Minnie Gartley made a film for Another Mother for Peace. Back in Indiana, Margaret and Sam Beecher appeared on radio talk shows. Shirley assisted at Common Cause. Alice and Sheila lobbied Congress. We all made statements whenever the President was questioned about the war. And along the way the League became more militant than ever.

A League national coordinator in Washington sent a letter to Congress expressing opposition to legislation to cut off funds for the war. "We are not in agreement with Congressman Boland or Senator Mansfield . . . for we have faith in our government . . . ," she wrote. A memo uncovered by a POW father who had resigned from the League revealed that the Republicans were directing fund-raising for the organization. The memo had been sent to League board members with an explanation: ". . . no one will know that we are using the lists owned by the Republican National Committee . . . the mailing will be done in such a way that the Republican donors will not know that their names have been supplied by the Republican National Committee."

We countered their activities by doubling our own lobbying efforts, using the media more effectively, and pursuing our legal case asking the FCC to stop the League's ad council campaign. We also asked the Defense Department and the administration for the kind of assistance it was providing the League—military transportation, dissemination of information, and fund-raising. Again, our request for assistance was turned down by Roger Shields, an assistant to Defense Secretary Laird. "While your objective—the release of prisoners—is humanitarian," he wrote, "the efforts of your group are political. As stated in your own correspondence, you believe that the issue is a 'two-sided question,' and you believe a date should be set for withdrawal of all American forces." Our attorneys in Washington advised us that it was illegal for the U.S. government to give aid to a separate organization such as the League, which propagandized the policy of the administration in power, and we talked of pursuing a class-action suit.

The articles we'd been interviewed for earlier were appearing in print. *The Wall Street Journal,* Jack Anderson, and the *Army, Navy, Air Force Times* all took note of our group, giving us credit for making the connection between the war and the prisoners. All the columnists agreed that the POW issue was becoming political dynamite.

Joseph Lelyveld of *The New York Times Magazine* wrote:

> Since President Nixon took to decrying the mistreatment of prisoners, the list of imprisoned and missing men has lengthened by more than 300. . . . It has been the distinguishing characteristic of the outcry in this country over the prisoners of war and their suffering families that it has gone on in nearly perfect abstraction from other facts about the

war and even as an escape from them—My Lai, the free-fire zones, bombing, napalm, defoliation, relocation programs, the toll among the Vietnamese. Much has legitimately been said about the Geneva Convention on the Treatment of Prisoners of War, little about the Geneva Convention on the Protection of Civilians. Schooled as they have been in the theological position that the question of war and the question of prisoners are wholly unrelated, most relatives have been unable to work up even an opinion on the Viet Cong proposal to release the prisoners in exchange for a firm withdrawal date. . . .

Our battle over the Advertising Council campaign came to a head in October when we officially requested equal time under Section 315 of the Communications Act. ABC and CBS objected to the White House-backed ads' use of the networks to "talk to Hanoi," and all three networks asked for a Federal Communications Commission ruling on whether they would be required to also run tapes from our group under the "fairness doctrine."

The Ad Council claimed that there had not been a counter-campaign to anything it had prepared in more than a quarter of a century, and Joan Vinson called me from the League offices in Washington to say that the League was aghast that the ads had been stopped.

"We haven't asked that they stop anything," I said. "We've only requested equal time on the networks for our tapes. Without the Geneva Convention to sidetrack the issue, the administration might have to address the real issue of ending the war."

In the meantime PKL Advertising, which had produced our films, sent letters to 500 TV stations, 1,300 radio stations, and 1,200 periodicals. Within two weeks half the stations had answered, saying that they would run our tapes. Many of them were also willing to do live interviews with members of Families for Immediate Release.

We spread ourselves thin, for the most part doing single interviews. Then about the middle of October Business Executives'

Move for Peace offered to send a group of us to St. Louis in order to reach a large area of the Midwest. Delia and I were to fly out from San Francisco and meet Alice and Shirley there.

I'd been excited all week about the four of us being together again. As it turned out, however, our schedule allowed little time for more than screeching delight and throwing our arms around one another. At 6:30 A.M. we were fluttering around the hotel room trying to freshen up from our all-night flights. Delia sat on the bed and read the day's agenda to us; Alice dialed room service to order Ramos fizzes for breakfast.

By 9:30 we were in the throes of a press conference in the formal lounge room of the St. Louis Media Club. We slipped in and out of camera range, mixing and matching our statements, hoping all the while that the wave of an editor's magic splicer would turn each little packet of film or tape into words of wisdom by the six o'clock news.

A young lawyer representing Business Executives' Move for Peace sidled up to me as the conference was breaking up; he informed me I was to do a live interview on the NBC-TV noon news program. "Why not her?" I asked, motioning toward Delia, but my voice was lost in the commotion, and he was already heading toward the exit. I chased after him for four blocks through crowded downtown traffic in order to arrive at the studio in time for the broadcast. The interview was over before I had a chance to be nervous and we were on our way back to the Media Club for a luncheon.

I tried to think of something appropriate to say while I was eating my chicken over rice and peas. When my turn came, I started to give a rundown on the President's change of position regarding the prisoners. "I'd like to cite four examples of his statements before and after the peace offers," I said—then suddenly my mind went blank.

I felt frozen in time, for how long I wasn't sure, gazing out at oblong tables of people facing me, waiting for me to continue. At last I found my voice, but still I couldn't recall the specific quotes I'd so carefully memorized. "There isn't time to recite all of them," I said, "but he used to say the prisoners were the reason he wouldn't withdraw. Now, with the Communist offers staring him in the face, he has to admit that President Thieu is the real reason we are staying."

I looked quickly around the room after I'd sat down. I was embarrassed by my lapse of memory and a little frightened. I began to wonder if the interviews and travel of the past few weeks were affecting my mental processes.

Shirley had already stood up and was speaking. The audience was listening intently and acting as if nothing unusual had happened, so I decided to take a deep breath and collect myself.

After lunch we trooped into the lounge room where the press conference had been held that morning to meet Dickson Terry of the *St. Louis Dispatch*. By then I'd regained my composure. When Terry came through the door, all four of us were seated in a row on a long sofa as if lying in wait. I wouldn't have been surprised if he'd swung around and exited immediately. It must have taken courage on his part to seat himself squarely in a high-backed chair and ask his first question. "How does your view differ from that of the League of Families?"

Four voices responded; while writing rapidly on a pad on his knee, he said, "One at a time, please."

"Do you know what they were doing at that League convention in Washington?" Shirley asked him. "They were planning next year's banquet—as if it were a national Kiwanis meeting, I tell you. Can you believe that?"

"I understand you're opposed to President Nixon's handling of a solution to the war?" he asked. Alice and Shirley both started to answer. "One at a time," Terry repeated. He later described us in his story as "flushed with indignation and burning with zeal for their cause."

"We want an end to this horror," Alice said.

"What is this mysterious thing that is keeping us in Vietnam? Everyone wants out," Shirley asked.

"Kissinger tells us to cool it, world conditions are getting better and we can expect a development in two or three months. More lies. We've been hearing that forever," Alice complained.

"I don't see how anyone can still trust President Nixon," I said.

"We are fed up, fed up, and fed up; how can we be anything but cynical?" Delia exclaimed.

Then Shirley pulled her shoulders back and made a final statement. "We all believe that Nixon holds the keys to the jail cells in Hanoi," she said, "and he will hold them as long as it's politically expedient."

By then it was three-thirty, and Delia and Alice were scheduled as guests on a local TV conversation program. "The Dick Ford Show" was already in progress with the host seated at a desk on a raised platform when we scurried through the door. He was speaking with Kay Starr, a popular 1940s singer who, one of the station people told us, had once made a million-seller record called "Wheel of Fortune." Her agent was jumping in and out of a chair in front of us, motioning something to the cameraman and whispering things to the producer. Every now and then he gave us a quizzical look as if to ask who we were to be robbing his client of valuable public attention. I slumped down in my seat and kicked off my shoes, glad to be sitting this one out. When the singer finished, she and her agent gave us a last irritated glance before hustling themselves out.

Delia and Alice took their places on the platform, and since it was going well, I just relaxed. On the other end of the oblong room, evening anchormen were preparing for their broadcast. One of the men slipped behind Shirley and me and whispered, "Why not stay and watch the news? We're opening with your press conference."

After the Ford show had finished, glaring studio lights pointed instead at the "Eyewitness" crew. The anchorman began: "Today members of a prisoner-of-war group brought their plea to St. Louis." One by one our faces appeared, fiery statements spewing forth onto the monitor. "How did they make sense of that mayhem this morning?" I asked Shirley.

"Don't question a gift," she said. "Don't you know they're on our side?"

We stretched out on the beds and closed our eyes for five minutes. Twenty minutes later we were leaning on one another inside an elevator on our way down to the hotel dining room. When the door slid open, our hosts, members of Business Executives' Move for Peace, waited with expectant smiles.

I was wishing I could just unwind and enjoy my dinner, but Shirley and I still had an hour radio talk show to do at nine o'clock. A few of our sponsors said they would come with us; the rest would wait in the dining room and listen to the program on a portable radio perched on the restaurant table.

My dinner, wine, and coffee carried on a wrestling match in the pit of my stomach all the way to the station, my anxiety mounting as our taxi whizzed through the streets. I'd never done a live talk show, and this one reached an audience from Minnesota to Georgia.

The station was on one of the top floors of a five- or six-story building. Heading down the hallway toward the studio, I felt like a soldier marching off to war. Somehow I knew this wasn't going to be easy.

The sound room itself was a glassed-in circular compartment in the center of a large open area. Shirley and I and one man entered the glass cage. The rest stayed outside where they could see and hear us. I felt trapped when the door closed; the host was already instructing us to sit opposite him at a round table. A microphone protruded from the counter in front of each of us.

Suddenly a red "On the Air" sign lit up above the door, and the talk show announcer pressed one of many buttons at his fingertips. We all heard the voice of our first phone caller. "In my opinion," he said, "President Nixon is the best friend the prisoners ever had." I told him I disagreed—that the President was only using the prisoners as an excuse to continue the war. He promptly said it was easy to see that I had been brainwashed by filthy radical students in Berkeley, California, and hung up. I let Shirley take the next call.

A woman told her she was going to pray for us; didn't we realize we had to annihilate all those Communists? After that, Shirley and I took turns. A man asked if we'd really gone without sex all those years. A girl from the University of Missouri said that the United States was conducting genocide in Southeast Asia and she was in favor of putting all our husbands on trial as war criminals when they came home.

I was grateful that the callers became more sympathetic to our view as the program progressed. One man said that in listening to us he was struck by the reality of the war all over again. He said he had tried to avoid thinking about it for years, "since there is no one in Washington willing to end it." A woman thought it was a terrible blot on our history that families of servicemen had to travel the country pleading with fellow Americans to care about their captured husbands.

Most people, men and women, expressed a sense of powerlessness. They had no idea why the war went on and on. "It's out of control," one man said. "Now there's nothing we can do about it. It will just go on forever."

When we left St. Louis the next morning, we had no idea if anyone had listened to us or cared about what we had said, but we were glad we'd come. Our good-byes at the airport gates were emotional. We hugged one another and renewed promises to keep up the fight.

A couple of weeks later the Dickson Terry article came out in the *St. Louis Dispatch,* and T. Walter Hardy, Jr., chairman of Business Executives' Move for Peace in St. Louis, sent each of us a copy. Across the top, above the headline, he had written, "We hit the jackpot!"

The story was spread over the entire page, one-third of which was a picture of the four of us. It began, "Four members of Families for Immediate Release swept into St. Louis recently, filled with righteousness and a great sense of purpose. . . . They were young, well-dressed, articulate. . . . All are national coordinators of their organization. . . ."

We were elated with the story, but in the weeks following our trip to St. Louis the war again drifted from the front pages of newspapers and television screens. We were wearing ourselves out trying to keep people interested, but still the headlines were about wage-price freezes, an Attica prison riot, and the President's trip to China.

Several Air Force and Marine fighter bomber units had been shifted to Thailand. Round-the-clock strikes from the new bases were being carried out. Overall, the Pentagon had now committed more than 1,000 combat aircraft to the air war, operating from bases in Thailand and Guam and off aircraft carriers at sea, but the bombing was not as visible to Americans as jungle combat had been. Opposing the war was now like battling a phantom enemy. It was difficult to draw it out into the open.

As I contemplated the situation one morning, it struck me that the President had performed a magic act: He had made the war disappear. The longer I thought about it, the more I resented his trickery. Under 'S' in my telephone book was a number for the State Department. I dialed it and was transferred to Frank Seiverts, special assistant for POW affairs. Though he tried politely to hang up several times, I kept prodding him with questions.

I asked him what the United States was trying to accomplish in Paris. When he answered that we were trying to clarify whether or not the Communists were willing to accept a cease-fire, I mentioned that Point One of their peace proposal called for a cease-fire.

"No, they say there will be no shooting at Americans as they withdraw," Seiverts said.

I asked him if we were insisting that there be no shooting by Vietnamese after we were gone and if we were asking that all North Vietnamese troops withdraw from the South.

"I'm not in a position to know that," he said, "but we want

self-determination for the South Vietnamese, not a coalition government forced on them."

"Wouldn't they be better off with a coalition government than with an unrepresentative leader such as Thieu?" I asked. "Is it worth any more American lives to keep him in power?"

"But they've asked too much for the POWs," Seiverts said. "They say we must overthrow President Thieu."

"The seven-point Communist peace plan does *not* say we must overthrow President Thieu. It says we should stop backing the regime of President Thieu. There is a big difference," I said.

"We must find out what price they are going to try to squeeze out of us for the prisoners," Seiverts answered. "They are using them—you don't like that, do you?"

"Who is using them?" I asked. "Being held at the bottom of a cave in Laos for five and a half years is being used. What I really want to know is: Are we willing to separate Point One of the Communist peace proposal and set a definite date when our withdrawal will be complete in order to gain release of these men? Are we willing to do that?"

"We must find out what withdrawal means—if we can provide military assistance to the South in the future," he said.

"Does President Nixon mean to withdraw combat air support and combat helicopters?" I asked.

"You mean that you think we should not offer that support if it is still needed by South Vietnam?"

"How can we?" I asked. "The Geneva Convention states that 'prisoners of war will be released and repatriated upon cessation of hostilities.' Bombs falling from U.S. planes will not be a cessation of hostilities. This will keep our men captive."

"Would you want us to give up everything all those Americans died for in Vietnam in order to just get back the POWs?" he asked.

"That's not necessary," I said. "We could get a coalition government and also get the prisoners back. Is President Nixon afraid if he offers a withdrawal date for the prisoners that he will have to stop the bombing in Southeast Asia?"

"I think those questions will be answered by the President soon," Seiverts said, and asked me to call again anytime.

At his next press conference President Nixon said, "Looking further down the road, American air power will continue to support South Vietnam until the South Vietnamese have developed the capability to handle the situation there themselves. . . . Air support will also continue as long as there are U.S. troops to defend in South Vietnam."

It suddenly occurred to me what Vietnamization really was: The troops would be there to back up the air support, the air support would be there to back up the troops, and they would all be there to back up President Thieu. Meanwhile, the prisoners would stay where they were—in captivity.

We simply had to work harder than we had in the past; our projects had to be ambitious, our group decided. Our attitude became progressively more aggressive, and with that change came an uneasy suspicion that we might be under surveillance. Perhaps we're frightened by our own feelings of hostility, we laughed, but slowly we began to give credence to our fears.

Shirley had reason to think that her mail had been opened, read, and resealed. The rest of us heard unexplained clicking noises during telephone conversations. To ease the tension, we joked with whoever would eventually listen to our tape: "What a boring job you have. You can tell by our conversations that we're keeping the spicy stories to ourselves. I suppose it's selfish not to tell you about the nasty group sex orgy we participated in last night. . . ."

JoAnn Connor, a Marine wife from Nashville, Tennessee, had joined our group earlier in the fall. She called me on Sunday afternoon to say she had been in Washington, D.C., where she visited Marine Corps Headquarters and asked to see her husband's file. To her surprise she opened the thick folder and found copies of letters she had written to Congress, other government officials, and the press.

"Then I think mine are copied twice, JoAnn," I said. "One for headquarters and one for my Marine liaison officer here in California. The officer gets transferred and is replaced but the file stays and expands. Last month when I stopped at the Marine Corps offices at Alameda Air Station, a new Marine sergeant commented, 'You really surprise me.'

"'Why?'" I asked.

"'How you look. I expected a wild revolutionary-looking type—after all the letters and memos I've read in your file,' he said."

"What the hell," JoAnn concluded, her Nashville drawl exaggerated when making a point, "we must be a prickly thorn in a whole lot of official behinds for them to go to all that bother."

21. UNCONDITIONAL LOVE

NOVEMBER 1971 We'd be damned, we said, if we'd let people lull themselves into believing that the war was over. When we weren't packing or unpacking suitcases, we were meeting reporters on street corners or in coffee houses. This is ridiculous, Shirley commented. How can six or eight of us arouse a nation? Mission impossible, Alice would answer, tossing her hands in the air. Still, we kept at it.

I conducted radio interviews with a phone crooked under my chin while cooking dinners. Dirty laundry had piled up in my utility room, and dust lay undisturbed on furniture throughout the rest of the house. My car chugged down the street as if gasping for a last breath. The boys were so embarrassed by its grunting and squealing noises that they ducked their heads to avoid being seen by friends as we drove through town.

Caught up in the business of reassessing national priorities, I regarded these problems as minor irritations at best. Then one morning I was scraping soggy cereal into the garbage disposal, my thoughts far off in Washington or Paris, when Sean tugged at my arm. "I don't care who's calling you today or what letters you have to write," he said. "You have to take that car in to be fixed. Terry and I have talked it over. We're not riding in it until you do." With that, they picked up their lunchboxes and left me speechless at the kitchen table. I could only push those two so far. I knew they were serious, but I was annoyed at the thought of attending to such mundane matters.

That afternoon I rolled my sputtering old Plymouth into a downtown Oakland garage. I had to be back home in thirty minutes for a radio interview, so I kept glancing at my watch. "It squeaks and moans," I explained to the serviceman as I spotted my bus a block away heading in our direction.

"You figure it out, please," I shouted over my shoulder. I was already on the bus, the door had closed, and we'd lurched forward when I saw the mechanic come dashing out of the garage. Arms swinging, he bellowed, "Hold up. Wait! Wait!"

"Please, stop," I begged the bus driver. He produced some rude noises which I couldn't decipher because he'd covered part of his face with a large hand, but the bus shrieked to a stop.

"You forgot to leave the keys!" the serviceman screamed from the sidewalk. I raised the window, dug into my purse, and tossed my key ring to him. Through the back window I watched him pick it up from the pavement, shake his head, and cross the street. I scooched down in my seat.

I was climbing my front steps when I remembered that the house keys were on the ring I'd thrown out the bus window. At the same moment I heard the kitchen phone ringing. Without thinking, I grabbed a broom from alongside the porch, covered my eyes, and smacked its handle through the door window. Crackling glass flew in all directions. Reaching a hand over jagged peaks, I turned the inside doorknob and pushed. I plucked the phone from the hook and answered, "Yes?"

A male voice told me that he was the manager of the Seattle radio station. "Miss Carlson has been held up today," he said. "She would like to reschedule the interview for tomorrow if possible."

"That would be fine," I said weakly. I replaced the receiver and sheepishly surveyed the damage.

How am I going to explain this mess to the boys, I thought, slumping into a chair. We have to find more people to do these things. How is a group the size of ours supposed to affect the course of this war?

Even my own family doubted the merits of my "extreme" actions—as my young brother called them. My mother seemed to be the only one cheering me on. Her loyalty had held fast since our old Eugene McCarthy days. She nevertheless expressed her antiwar sentiments at peace meetings in the dignified atmosphere of her church guild hall.

The rest of my family didn't actually criticize me. In fact, they seemed to admire the amount of energy I was expending on Bill's behalf. Though they stopped short of endorsing the demand I was making on the President to withdraw immediately from the war, they sent telegrams and wrote letters to Congress supporting amendments that insisted on an accounting for the missing in action. Anything they did, however, was accompanied by an explanation: "After all, Barbara, you're our sister, aren't you?"

But I wanted accolades. I wanted affirmation of my actions. I wanted them to say I was right about the war and that they were proud I'd taken such a public stand.

My brother Bill and sister Jean's husband, with whom I'd argued vehemently about the war in the past, now agreed that we should get out of the conflict. Not because the purpose was wrong, but because we weren't willing to win it, they said. That wasn't enough for me, however. I wanted an act of contrition on their part. I wanted them to admit that the war was *immoral.*

If we'd just gone "all out," they rationalized, we could have whipped "them." If we'd done this or that or another thing, we would have been victorious. What, I wondered. More troops? We'd sent half a million, and what good had it done? More bombs? We'd already dropped more bombs than we had in all of World War II.

On the other hand, if they were in favor of withdrawal now, why didn't that satisfy me? Or wasn't that enough to vindicate my own actions? I wanted them to say I was all right and the war was all wrong, and it bothered me that I needed so much. I knew they cared deeply about the boys and me. They were indignant if our welfare was jeopardized in any way. Why wasn't that comfort enough?

My mother was staying with me when I was turned down for a mortgage to buy our home. The loan manager at the bank had told me that my husband's status made me an "undependable risk." "Besides, we'll need to have his signature," he had explained from behind a vast expanse of polished desk.

I drove home in a blur of angry tears and ran into the house. "I should have lied," I told my mother. "I should have told them he was on active duty."

"Why should you be ashamed of him?" my mother screamed back. "He'd be a hero in another war. You have an allotment. God knows, you pay your bills!" Before the day was over, an outraged family was dispensing words of encouragement by telephone. "Stand by your rights," they were telling me from Michigan, Illinois, and Florida. "I'll come to California and talk to that bank manager myself if they don't come through," declared one of my irate brothers.

They'll always love me whether or not they approve of my every move, I thought, sweeping the last of the broken glass into a dust pan. So who else is there to judge me? My children? Other than complaints about a late dinner or too many chores, they seemed content enough. They aren't handing out bouquets, I acknowledged, but then children don't.

I twisted a wire around the neck of a Hefty bag and was preparing to carry remnants of the window out to the garage when the front door flew open. "Mom, Mom, it wasn't my fault!" Terry shouted from the hall.

It's just one of those days, I thought, and braced for the rest of the story. Sean followed his brother into the kitchen, leaned against a wall, and shifted from one foot to the other. He rolled his eyes and stared at a speck on the ceiling; he wanted no part of what was coming.

"When Matthew's mother calls," Terry continued, "tell her he turned his head or my fist would never have landed on his teeth bands. Besides, he started it!"

The phone rang. It was Matthew's mother. "Mrs. Mullen, you

owe me thirteen hundred dollars," she began. I glared at Terry until the woman ran out of steam and hung up.

"Terry, weren't there any kids in school without teeth bands to hit?" I screamed.

His eyes sparkled; he knew when to pounce on soft principles. "Call her back, Mom. Maybe they'll take my five-speed as a trade. I never use it anymore."

"What do you mean?" I said, sinking back into a chair at the table. "Nothing less than a used car would be a fair trade deal.

"We'll wait for her to call back," I said. "I can't think about it right now."

"Wow, what happened to the door window?" Sean said, his mouth hanging open.

"Let's just say it hasn't been a good day, fellas. Sit down at the table. I want to talk to both of you."

"Now? Do we have to?" Terry said. "Am I in real trouble?"

"Of course you're in trouble for hitting Matthew."

"It was an accident!"

"For not avoiding an accident then. We'll discuss that later. There's something else I want to ask you now."

They each slid into a chair.

"What do you think of your mom? I mean as moms go?"

Terry looked bewildered. He'd been ready to defend his own mishap of the day, but a smile slowly consumed his face. His own misery would be delayed. "You're OK," he said.

Sean nodded his head in agreement. Then thoughtfully, "There are some things I'd change, of course. For one, I should be able to stay up later than Terry."

"How about this POW political work I'm doing?" I asked. "I feel I'm being impatient these days. I don't seem to have as much time for you guys."

"What I don't like," Sean said, "now that you mention it, are baby-sitters. I'm ten years old, you know."

"I hate when you're on the phone—talking, talking, talking," Terry added. "And I have to wait and wait and wait. And all the time you're saying, 'Shush, shush.'"

"That's not exactly what I meant," I said. "But we can work on those things. You understand what I'm trying to do, don't you?"

"Yes," Sean said, and Terry shrugged.

"This war has to end or we'll never see your dad again. But I don't want things to fall apart around here."

"I'm not falling apart," Terry said.

Sean leaned on an elbow and fiddled with a plant on the table. "About Dad," he said. "How do you think he looks now? When I picture him, he's always wearing his uniform. But wouldn't it be old and dirty now? I hope he doesn't have to wear those striped pajamas like some prisoners do."

"They're supposed to give him clothes to wear. I suppose he'd have the same kind of clothes that the people themselves wear in Laos. They are supposed to feed him and give him a nice place to sleep. We have to hope that they're doing that."

"If you and Alice and those other ladies keep getting your pictures in the paper, the President will have to listen to you, won't he?" Terry asked.

"I've been thinking about that all day, Terry. I don't know if President Nixon cares what we say. I don't even know if the American people care anymore. I think they're sick of hearing about this war. That doesn't help us, though, does it?"

"Do you still think he's alive?" Sean asked.

"I can't tell you that he is, Sean. I only know that everyone who knew anything told me they thought he was captured. I believe that he's alive. It's something I feel, that's all. But I can't swear to it. What do you think?"

"I'm still sure he is, too," Sean said. "That's what I've always said, Mom. He's alive, I just know it. But I'll tell you something. I'm sick of worrying about him." He glanced across the table at Terry.

"Sure," Terry said. "It would be neat to have him right here in the house with us, wouldn't it? But what would we do with him? Where would he sleep?"

"He would sleep with me. In my bedroom, Terry. Mothers and fathers sleep together. Or usually. If they love one another, they want to be close to one another. It's nice to talk and cuddle up in bed at night. I really miss that."

"Tell us about when you were in Japan again," Sean said.

"Yeah," Terry said. "About his airplane, too—no, change that, tell about the motorcycle." His eyes were glittering now. "Do you think he'll buy a new motorcycle when he gets home?"

After the boys were in bed that night, I went out to the living room and put a log in the fireplace—one of my prefab, instant fire logs. I've been in a mood all day, I thought, knotting the belt of my terry-cloth robe. I snuggled into the corner of the sofa and lost myself in the jagged blue and orange flames. I needed time to sort things out.

It surprised me that I was still looking for affirmation and how difficult it was for me to accept love without it. As I thought about it, though, my life had been influenced by this quest for approval. Was it possible to quell such a craving? I was the little girl who achieved, who wanted to be well-liked, popular. I had agonized over my appearance—would young men ever think I was pretty enough? I was sure of only one thing—I would be a responsible, mature adult, a loving wife and caring mother. My children would have advantages I had lacked; they'd have a secure home, a father to protect them.

And I probably could have played the role if the plot hadn't taken such an unexpected turn. Would Bill even like the changed me? Would he love me later if he disapproved of my actions now? I couldn't say. He used to call me a gutsy lady. This reputation, however, was based on minor incidents, nothing on the scale of opposing a President.

I got up and poked the log and thought about our first summer in Pensacola when I'd taken to writing letters to the editor of the *Pensacola Journal* outlining my indignation at the practice of segregation in the South, not a popular attitude a few hours away from Selma, Alabama, in 1961. Since most other letters on the editorial page dealt with "Communist trouble-making Negroes," I told them that the elimination of bigotry was the best way to fight communism.

After my third or fourth letter had been printed and I'd had some anonymous threatening phone calls, Bill's commanding officer called him into his office one morning. "I'd appreciate it if you'd get your wife in line and keep her out of local affairs," Colonel Nelson said.

"Why don't you and Irene come over for dinner Saturday night," Bill said, "and you can tell her yourself."

Saturday night was an ordinary, sultry Gulf Coast evening. Bill served ice-cold martinis; after pouring a second into the Colonel's glass, he said, "Barbara, Colonel Nelson wants to discuss those letters you've been writing the *Pensacola Journal.*"

"Really, Colonel," I said, before he could respond, "can you imagine my embarrassment—having worked overseas for the Voice of America, where we bragged about our democracy night and day—to find some of our citizens sitting in the backs of buses? Newborn babies separated from one another in hospital nurseries? Why should you military men be asked to fight for freedom around the world with this injustice occurring right here in our own country?"

Bill fought hard not to smile. "So what do you think of that, Colonel?" he said. "I'm certainly proud of Barbara for bringing this to the attention of the newspaper. What was it you wanted to tell her?"

I waited for the Colonel to speak. He lit a cigarette. "Yes, well, you've got a point. These are just the kinds of things these world Communists look for so they can bitch about our discrimination to the rest of the damn world."

After he'd gone, Bill laughed and I howled and Bill said, "Keep writing the letters, Barby. Just don't leave white sheets hanging out on the line overnight or your husband may die young of a heart attack."

Bill was good-natured about letters to the editor, but how would he feel about public letters to the President? Somehow I couldn't see Bill in terms of disagreements about the war. Whenever I tried to imagine future scenes of that kind, my mind wandered back instead to more innocent days, times free of heady issues.

I got up and poked at the fire again. Soon it would be November tenth, and that jogged me into thinking about my first Marine Corps birthday ball. After all these years I knew the Marine Corps anniversary would still evoke memories for Bill wherever he was, and we would both see one another as we were then, and that pleased me.

I glanced from the fire past my front deck where the moon cast shadows through the eucalyptus and pine trees. It had been a clear autumn night like this in 1959 when Bill took me to that first Marine Corps ball. We'd known one another just six months then. Colored crepe paper had been twisted and draped in streamers from the rafters of a drafty hangar at Iwakuni Marine Air Station in southern Japan. The tablecloths and napkins were also of paper. Many Marine balls would follow, in officers' clubs and swank country clubs: My black cocktail dress would become a long silk gown and Bill's khaki uniform would be replaced by a short blue dress jacket, a white pleated shirt, and red cummerbund, but it was that first ball I remembered.

The fire made a crackling noise. Just looking at it, I felt warmed. I was back in Bill's arms on that dance floor where planes had been parked a few hours earlier. I rested my head on Bill's shoulder; his head was tilted forward so that his lips brushed against the side of my face. "I'm so glad we met," he said, "even if we had to go halfway around the world to do it." A Japanese band accompanied a sultry American vocalist who sang "Love Me Tender"—just for us, we were sure.

Before the evening was out, Bill had taken her place at the microphone. He strained for the high clear notes: "Danny boy, the pipes, the pipes. . . ." A hush had come over the hangar by the time he reached the second verse: "I'll come and find the place where you are lying. . . ."

We will always love one another as we were then, I thought. Whatever happens, nothing will change that. What difference does it make who condones or criticizes me now? I felt alone, but peacefully so. The log in the fireplace suddenly cracked in two; each side continued to burn separately.

The next morning I got up full of energy, making plans. For one, I decided we would have an old-fashioned Thanksgiving. My kids deserved that. I would invite Kay and Ed and Terry's teacher, perhaps my neighbors next door. I felt as if there were time for everything.

I enjoyed that holiday. After dinner we sprawled ourselves out over the living room. We drank coffee and brandy and ate pumpkin pie. I propped myself up against a wall, leaned on some overstuffed pillows, and stretched my legs out in front of me.

The boys were beaming from an abundance of attention all day. Suddenly they ran in from the kitchen, each tugging at the end of a partially dried wishbone. They were in the center of the room when Terry let go of his end and whispered something to Sean. Sean looked at the rest of us for a few seconds as if deciding whether or not to let us in on their secret. "How can we lose?" he finally asked.

"Yeah," Terry said. "We both have the same wish anyway."

22. BOMBS OF CHRISTMAS

DECEMBER 1971

UPI, Livingston, Tennessee, December 23, 1971.

Ten years ago yesterday, December 22, 1961, Army Specialist James Thomas Davis of this small middle Tennessee town became the first American to die in Vietnam. Since then, 45,618 other Americans have been killed in action . . . in the nation's longest war. Another 304,353 have been wounded.

Alice Cronin had just boarded her plane for San Diego, and I felt exhilarated. My spirits were unusually high, considering it was a few days before Christmas. There was nothing to account for it other than an accelerated rate of metabolism—Alice and I had been on the move for the past three weeks.

We'd skipped all the prayer services and tree lightings for the POWs. Instead, we'd contacted every TV and radio station in the San Francisco area, offering ourselves up for talk shows, taping sessions, or live interviews. We'd kept busy. There was no real reason for optimism, and it wasn't the way most of the families were feeling.

Actually, I was feeling guilty because I wasn't as depressed as others. I attributed it to my state of constant motion. I didn't know how I'd have felt if Alice hadn't come, or how I'd feel tomorrow. I didn't want to look facts in the eye and conclude what others had—that we were yesterday's news. Minnie Gartley, our history teacher in Florida, sent me a long typed dispatch about how Eric Sevareid had announced the largest deficit ever in a *peacetime* year on the evening news. If it's peacetime, Minnie asked, why isn't my son home? The White House hadn't answered her letters, she said, and the Defense Department was refusing her phone calls.

A mother in North Dakota whose son was missing in action wrote me:

Most of the time we feel completely alone, and I suspect we are justified. The frustration of never having anyone to discuss things with has nearly done us in. My heart has begun to reflect the agony of the past four years. Something just has to give. You know it is our generation who were willing to "leave the politics to the politicians" and who went on our merry way naïvely believing that if our country said we should be at war, then it surely must have made the right decision, and when they said we couldn't quit once we started, we went along with that, and now we're stuck with the consequences. It's business as usual with most people.

JoAnn Connor called late at night from Nashville. "It's really hard to imagine another year has passed and we're in the same predicament," she said. "Only now it seems even worse, because people think the war is over. I read in the paper this morning that a plane was shot down over Laos—the pilot was finally rescued, but the radar operator is missing. Just seems crazy that it still goes on.

"Chuck was stationed in Chu Lai, and their squadron flight surgeon was on the flight with him. They're both listed as missing in action. Well, last spring the wife of the flight surgeon decided she had had it with the whole bit. She divorced her husband for desertion or something and remarried—against the advice of the Navy and everybody else. I don't know. When this happened, it didn't seem to affect me one way or the other—but now I realize that it actually did. It's like the base at Chu Lai has been turned over to the South Vietnamese, this woman has put it behind her, and it's as though the whole thing never was—except I'm the only person who even remembers."

League women in the Bay Area had simply taken to the Marin hills beyond the Golden Gate Bridge to attend a three-day spiritual retreat. A mimeographed notice told me that the setting would be "remote and beautiful." A minister, a Catholic priest, and a psychologist would share their needs "as another holiday approaches . . . to speak to God together about our situation. . . ."

The letter announcing the retreat was delivered the afternoon that a Navy chaplain came to visit me. Alice had gone grocery shopping for me, I was waiting for her to return and I was reading the afternoon newspaper. Bombing renewal was in the headlines again.

U.S. PLANES HIT NORTH FOR
FOURTH CONSECUTIVE DAY
U.S. AIR BLITZ GOES ON
REDS CLAIM 7 MORE JETS

More waves of United States bombers pounded North Vietnam today for the fourth successive day in the heaviest aerial campaign against the North. . . .

U.S. BOMBING RAIDS CONTINUE

The American air war in Indochina has entered a new phase . . . the air war is one of the largest but least publicized military operations in history, known to the enemy but not the American public. . . .

A knock on the door interrupted my thoughts about America's gifts from the heavens and a lack of peace on earth. Later when I thought about it, I viewed the timing of the chaplain's appearance as ironic. At the time, I was simply surprised to open my front door and have him standing there. So much so that it took me a moment to invite him in.

"I've come over at this time of year to offer some support," he said, smiling and settling into a living room chair.

I wouldn't have known he was a chaplain. Shaved hair, rigid in his uniform—without the insignia he could have been any career officer.

"I haven't been here very long," he said. "You look surprised. Isn't it a usual practice for chaplains to stop by?"

"It hasn't been," I assured him.

"Well," he said, "now that I'm here, is there anything I can do?"

"You can ask your Commander-in-chief to stop killing people with bombs," I said. The words just came out, as if I had no part in producing them.

"That's not the duty of chaplains," he answered, taken aback for an instant. "We don't get involved in policy. We offer support to our men and their families."

"So they'll have the courage to go off to be killed or maimed, I suppose," I said.

He didn't answer.

"Well, how do you feel about this war?" I asked.

"It's not for me to judge," he said. "I answer to God and serve in the best way I can." He brushed an imaginary speck from his right shoulder.

"Didn't Christ judge?" I pursued.

He stood up. "I'm sorry, Mrs. Mullen," he said. "I don't think you understand what our job is. I'll be glad to pray for you and your children and all the POWs."

"Pray for the President, too," I said.

"He didn't stay long," I told Alice later, and she laughed. We'd done a lot of laughing in the past few weeks, assuring ourselves constantly that it was healthy to have a sense of humor, come what may. Of course, we could have simply been going mad; we allowed for that. A small matter, we agreed, as long as we weren't in tears.

We were undiscriminating about the media offers we accepted. We wanted coverage: right-wing, liberal, radical—it made no difference. I did a talk show one night from a radio station in Berkeley which later received the tapes of captured Patty Hearst from the Symbionese Liberation Army. We answered serious questions posed by dignified reporters; we dodged personal insinuations tossed our way by an out-of-breath D.J. on a rock station.

At the end of ten days, breezing along the freeway, we heard our voices on the car radio spliced between background sounds of jets taking off and "I'll Be Loving You Always." Alice declared, "Enough is enough. That's it. We've done it all."

Sometime around the middle of the three weeks I had gotten a call from Bill Cook at *Newsweek* in San Francisco. He said they were doing a Christmas story on POW families, and he would like to meet us the next day in the city.

I'd gotten in the habit of carrying a portfolio from which I could pull an appropriate quote or statistic at a moment's notice, and I had it with me when we met the *Newsweek* correspondent. He was waiting for us in a coffee shop, where we talked informally for a couple of hours. The interview had gone so smoothly I forgot about my "portable Vietnam library," as Alice called it. When we were finished he said he would send a photographer out to the house the next day. It was going to be a terrific article, and we knew it. No wonder we aren't depressed, Alice remarked after he'd left the restaurant.

The day before Alice was to leave, I was scheduled to be a guest on KGO radio, on one of the most popular talk shows in the Bay Area. The week before, however, when Owen Span, the host, had announced his forthcoming guests, he had been besieged with phone calls from League women. Under the circumstances, the station decided that "their" side would have to be presented as well. Maerose Evans was to be their representative, he told me.

Maerose and I were seated in the sound room on one side of a table with our live mikes, the host on the other. Alice watched and listened from behind a window in an adjoining room. Seeing the grim look on Maerose's face, I thought about the first time we'd met, how much we'd laughed that afternoon. The announcer motioned to us that we were on the air.

"We have two guests today who are living through an experience none of us would envy. Their husbands are missing in Southeast Asia. They have different views, however, on how to get them home. We'll have an opening statement from each, beginning with Mrs. Barbara Mullen of Oakland, and then open it up to questions."

"My name is Barbara Mullen," I said, and took a deep breath. "My husband is Marine Corps Major William F. Mullen. For the families of the prisoners of war and the prisoners themselves, this Indochina war has not run down at all. For us, it rages on at the same intensity as ever. We are enduring our fourth Christmas without our husbands since President Nixon was elected. My husband spent three Christmases previous to those, in Indochina. Seven in all. The war is not over until every pilot, GI, and prisoner is back home. The American people have no right to pretend that it is over. They have no right to turn away from the war while their taxes pay for daily bombing raids. As long as those bombs fall, people will die, our men will remain in captivity. The same Americans who allowed those military men to go to war must now bring them home. They must demand that the President set a specific total withdrawal date in Paris and gain a firm agreement from the Communists for POW release."

Maerose began, "My name is Mrs. James Evans. My husband is a Navy commander. He is a career officer, and he wouldn't like me telling the President, 'Do this or do that.' I trust the President. He knows much more than we do about the situation. We just aren't in a position to know what he does. There are secret meetings going on all the time. And if we set a specific date how could we be sure they would give an accounting of all the men who are missing in action? How can we trust them to do that any more than they did after Korea? So many people are just saying 'get out' but how can we? We've already suffered so much. If my husband is dead, I don't want it to have been for nothing. If he's alive, I don't want all his suffering to have been in vain. I say we should trust the President. He's the only Commander-in-chief we have."

After two or three calls I knew it would be an easy afternoon. Opinion was in our favor; I could keep my answers short. Maerose was going on about the Geneva Convention and how neutral countries should help. One minute she would say we couldn't end the war just for the prisoners; the next she'd emphasize how long they'd been there being ill-treated.

I was sorry when the time was up. Alice was ecstatic, telling me it had gone well. I noticed Maerose taking her coat from a hook in the vestibule. I went over to her and asked if she'd like to go somewhere for a cup of coffee. She said, "Yes, I think that would be nice."

We talked about children, empty holidays, our limbo state—anything but the war. She said that although Christmas was only five days away she still had most of her shopping to do. "Me, too," I said. When I'd first met her, Maerose had laughed a lot—a big, hearty laugh. Later on she'd sparked with indignation. But now the luster, even the anger, had left her large, deep-set blue eyes.

She buttoned her coat. "Have a nice Christmas," she said. The restaurant door closed behind her. I wanted to chase after her. I could imagine myself putting my arms around her and telling her I was sorry for her and me and everyone. Instead, I sat there and watched her walk past the window and down the street.

"Well, we got through that one," Alice said, breaking the silence. "Let's go over to *Newsweek*. They said they'd have some early copies for us."

James Wilson, the photographer, was at the *Newsweek* offices when we arrived. "Congratulations," he said. "It turned out great."

Wilson handed me a note that correspondent Bill Cook had written before leaving earlier in the day.

Barbara,
Hope you like it.
A similar story, longer though, is being distributed by

Newsweek's feature service. Both you and Mrs. Cronin are quoted in that also, and I suppose they are sending a picture of you and the boys, since we have several good ones.

I really enjoyed meeting you last week. Keep up the good work.

Peace,
Bill

Alice and I went downstairs in the same building. We each collapsed in a chair in the cocktail lounge, suddenly quite exhausted. We ordered a drink and read the article to ourselves, except for periodic outbursts of approval.

I was glad to see that my photo didn't stare back at me, hollow-eyed and solemn. Alice said it certainly wasn't cheerful, but not as dreadful as others she'd seen. The article was titled "Prisoners of War—They Also Serve." Under the heading were the first two lines of a Christmas poem I had written:

Peace on earth is a lie and death is sadness
They'll never be back, for mankind is madness

The story began:

Mrs. William Mullen of Oakland, a 37-year-old mother of two sons, has cause to inscribe her homemade Christmas card with such unseasonable bitter couplets. Her husband, a Marine pilot downed in Laos almost six years ago, is still missing. The same despair consumes other families of Americans captured or missing in the Indochina war. . . . Now the President is confronted with an incipient revolt among the prisoners' wives that could have political consequences in 1972. . . . "As long as bombs fall in Indochina, my husband is not going to be released," says Mrs. Michael Cronin, wife of a Navy POW. . . . A splinter group left the League this year to form the POW/MIA Families for Immediate Release . . . the new group is already sending out literature and running television commercials.

And its political action in the Presidential campaign is a foregone conclusion. . . . The unabashed goal is results. . . .

"Not bad," I said. "Let's order another glass of wine."

Alice tapped the cover of the magazine lightly with her fist. "This is better than talking to God on a Marin mountaintop, isn't it?" she asked.

The question made me smile. "For me it is," I said.

But now Alice was gone and I had one more TV show to do. After that I would celebrate with the boys—lunch and then *The Nutcracker* at the San Francisco ballet. I had never felt this good at holiday time. When guilt tried to creep into my thoughts, I chased it away.

Gerry Lange introduced her first guest, a tall black man, a dancer who described the difficulties faced by black people in the arts. The third guest was an advocate of gay rights. And there I was sandwiched in between them on the sofa. What the hell, I thought. Maybe we have more in common than is immediately apparent.

When we were finished, Terry followed the dancer into the hall, asking a lot of questions about "show business." Sean pulled me aside. "Hey, Mom," he said, "I don't understand what the other man was talking about."

"I'll explain it at lunch," I said, and whipped them both out into the street. I was happy to be alone with the boys. In the end it always came down to the three of us, and I thought about Alice. Was it harder not to have children? I couldn't imagine what I'd have done without mine.

"I want a cheeseburger, a hot dog, French fries, and a milkshake," Terry told the waitress. He waited for me to voice an objection but gave me a look that said: I waited all morning for you; now I get to order what I want.

Sean appraised his nine-year-old brother with an air of superiority. "I will have," he pronounced slowly, "a ham sandwich and a tossed salad with blue cheese dressing." He was proud of his sophisticated choice.

How I loved these two! They could make the world go away. It was going to be a wonderful afternoon. "Mom," Sean said, "what's gay?"

We got home about seven o'clock. I immediately changed into a comfortable robe and curled up on the sofa. The TV was on and the boys were playing Chinese checkers on the floor when the telephone rang. I thought about not answering it, but I picked it up.

It was Fred Papert calling from our ad agency in New York. "Barbara, I've been trying to get you all day," he said. "We've got two thousand dollars, enough to run an ad in the *Washington Post* on Christmas Day. It should be in the form of a letter to the President from a group of you. We've already had some of our writers on it. What we need is for you to call people for permission to sign their names. We figure we should have twenty to twenty-five."

"I'll try to have them for you tonight," I said. Then, realizing that it sounded as if I were doing him a favor, I added, "Thanks, Fred. It will be great to have it printed on Christmas Day."

I hung up and leaned my head on my arms, flat out on the table. The thought of getting into conversation with families coast to coast the night before Christmas Eve had left me feeling limp. I got out the list and put on a pot of coffee. Three hours later, I called the ad agency back with the signatures. I unplugged the Christmas tree lights before going to bed. Strange, I thought, I don't remember trimming the tree. I suppose we did it before the *Newsweek* photographer came.

Sean and Terry had outgrown Santa Claus, racing cars, and battery robots, but they were as excited as ever about the magic of Christmas. I didn't feel much like a magician, though. The boys were sound asleep, and I was still wrapping presents. "Women are the elves and brownies of the world," I mumbled to myself. I had a new pool table locked in the garage and no idea how to move it from there to the family room.

It was two hours before I gathered enough nerve to wander next door and ask for help. Cars had been arriving at my neighbors' all evening long. "Are there any able bodies in here who'd like to perform an act of brotherly love?" I asked at the door before being whisked into the dining room and handed a glass of something cold and red.

Four of the rollicking guests followed me to the garage, where they hoisted the table a foot off the floor and carried it out the door. So far, so good. They started down the hill, digging their feet into ground muddied by recent heavy rains.

Suddenly the table began moving at a more rapid pace. The men tried to keep up with it. The next thing, I watched as the entire ensemble slid past me and the house. I heard a long squish, followed by a thud. Parts of legs and arms protruded from my holly bushes, the table was balancing at a 90-degree angle against a large tree. Two of the men who were able to move pulled themselves out of the prickly branches and slowly dragged the green slab back up the hill. The three of us inched ourselves and the table into the family room.

By then the other two had escaped from the holly bushes. Limping up the hill and picking thorns from their clothing, all four sauntered back to their party, stretching arms and legs on the way. I made a mental note to lie low in the neighborhood for a week or two.

"Wow, it's neat, Mom!" Terry screamed the next morning. Then he poked his brother. "Poor Santa, he has to come through the mud, instead of snow, in California."

"Yipes!" Sean threw an arm around Terry's shoulder. "Geez, what happened, Mom?" They stumbled against one another until they fell to the floor, howling.

"It's nice, Mom. Honest," Terry squeaked.

"Just cool it, you two. And count your blessings," I warned them. "The table is in good shape. You should have seen old Santa and the reindeer."

A couple of hours later I was drying my hair and trying to get up energy to go to Kay and Ed's for Christmas dinner when a Channel 4 NBC-TV truck drove up. I was surely driven by demons, I figured—otherwise, wouldn't I have sent them away?

Toys were strewn all over. The boys ran through the house, paying no attention to me or to the TV crew. Finally they sat down grudgingly by the tree while the camera rolled and I read part of my Christmas poem. It was soppy, but it would be on the evening news, and that's all I cared about.

On Christmas afternoon our letter to the President, a half-page in size, was printed in the *Washington Post:*

A CHRISTMAS MESSAGE TO PRESIDENT NIXON FROM 25
FAMILIES OF POWS AND MEN MISSING IN ACTION

Mrs. Nixon said last week that the festivities at the White House—rows of decorated trees along the path to the front door, wreaths in the windows, an old-fashioned dinner—were your way of keeping the traditions of Christmas alive for your girls and their husbands. . . .

But now, as you're sitting with your loved ones for your family Christmas, we ask, with respect and anguish, why can't we do the same?

We implore you to set the withdrawal date and end the war. Once and for all.

Shortly after the television newsman had left, my mailman rang the bell. He handed me an envelope and then explained that it wasn't special delivery, but he had brought it over anyway because it was from the White House and he thought it might be important. I pulled a large shiny green card adorned with a gold wreath from the envelope and read:

With our sincere wishes for a
Joyous Christmas and a Happy New Year
The President and Mrs. Nixon

I smiled to myself, imagining that the Nixons and I were reading our mutual Christmas greetings at the same moment.

On December 29 *The New York Times* reported:

The intensified air war over North Vietnam led to a further
breakdown of the Paris peace talks yesterday as both sides
rushed to cancel the session scheduled for tomorrow. There
has been no meeting since December 9 and none is
planned. . . .

23. FOUR YEARS IS ENOUGH

JANUARY 1972 When Sheila opened the door to her Washington, D.C., apartment at midnight, the telegram from Alice and me was waiting.

> WE THINK IT'S TIME TO OPEN A POLITICAL HEADQUARTERS IN WASHINGTON. HOW WOULD YOU LIKE TO RUN IT?

The idea of a Washington political office had been developing over the past month. Ever since Christmas Alice and I had been commiserating with one another about the war that had risen up from the jungle swamps to the skies over Southeast Asia and vanished from view and public consciousness again.

If the bombing war remained secret and hidden, Richard Nixon would be reelected. This realization came to me as I drove out to Alameda Air Station one afternoon. I was thinking especially about a remark JoAnn had made the night before. "Spouting off against Nixon is like trying to cut a rock with a razor blade," she had said. It seemed to sum up our feelings of frustration.

Captain Johnson from Marine Corps Headquarters had asked

me to meet him that afternoon; he hadn't said if the purpose was official or friendly. Either way I thought it would probably be a waste of time. As I drove through the main gate, I was distracted only briefly by a snappy salute from a Marine guard, and I thought about something else JoAnn had said.

Over Christmas she had had dinner with old military friends, a Marine couple she'd known at their last duty station before JoAnn's husband, Chuck, had left for Vietnam. The man had flown a mission over Laos on the day Bill was shot down and told JoAnn that Captain Mullen was alive on the ground. "Tell your friend her husband was captured all right—everyone knew it," he said.

"Alive on the ground," "captured," "radio signals heard"—I thought of the phrases that had directed my life since that day in 1966. What more could Captain Johnson tell me? I knew there would be no new information today.

I hated going to the officers' club, and I avoided it whenever possible. It was like stepping over the threshold into a haunted house. Sometimes I recognized old acquaintances across the room and then felt cheated when up close they turned into strangers.

A Marine uniform stood out among Navy officers at the front entrance, and I guessed it would be Captain Johnson. He thrust his hand out with a smile. "Barbara Mullen? Nice to meet you." Although he'd always been pleasant on the telephone, I wondered what we would talk about today.

Adjusting my eyes to the darkness of the lounge, I followed him to a corner table some distance from the bar and separated from scattered groups about the room. As we sat down, a loud guffaw broke out at the end of the bar. I supposed they were telling old jokes, folklore of the military, passed on to new lieutenants by elder warriors. I suddenly longed to join them in their camaraderie. I remembered being included, laughing, flirting, with perhaps an arm around my shoulder. Not an outsider as I was now.

"Is there anything the Corps can do for you that it isn't doing?" Captain Johnson asked.

"No, nothing," I said. "We're fine. Thanks."

"Are you sure?" he asked.

"Yes, I'm sure. Funny," I said, "I thought maybe you were going to ask me about my political activities."

He didn't want to talk about the war, he answered calmly. "We are proud of our Marine wives, though," he added. "They're the most active for the POWs."

His comment amused me. At least that hadn't changed—the Marines still believed they were "the most." He mentioned that "The Dick Cavett Show" had called headquarters to get my phone number, and then he smiled and told me he had talked to JoAnn Connor recently. She was doing a good job, too, he said. The tenor of his remarks aroused my curiosity. Were we gaining a silent cheering section within the Corps?

I took a good look at Jim Johnson for the first time. He was a career officer, I was sure, of perhaps ten or fifteen years. "How did you get stuck with such dreadful duty?" I asked him. "Do you have a degree in psychology or counseling or something?"

"No," he answered. "I worked for an undertaker."

I stared at him blankly for an instant. Please, God, I thought, don't let me laugh. This man is so sincere. How pragmatic of the Marine Corps.

That evening I called Alice in southern California. "I had lunch with an undertaker today," I said.

"What?" she asked.

"Never mind," I said. "We can't continue to scrape rocks and talk to undertakers."

"What are you talking about?" she asked.

"I think we have to set up a political headquarters in Washington. This is really our last chance," I said. "Can't you come up for a few days?"

I met Alice's plane from San Diego the next afternoon. We drove straight home and got right to the topic. "The President isn't going to make a peace gesture unless he feels threatened politically," I said.

"Are we that threat?" Alice asked, knotting her eyebrows together.

I looked at the two of us in our jeans and sweaters, stretched out on my shag carpeting, and burst out laughing. Soon we both were giggling uncontrollably.

"We'll have to call the *San Francisco Chronicle* to announce our grand political plans," I said, and that set us off again.

"That will have to be the performance of our lives," Alice said. We tossed a coin and Alice lost. She made me stay in the kitchen while she called the newspaper.

A few minutes later she came back to the living room. "They'll come to the house for an interview whenever we want," she said.

"Well, that's done," I said.

Alice smiled. "I guess we can't back down now," she said.

That same evening we sent the telegram to Sheila; our phone rang an hour later.

"I've been fingering this telegram for ten minutes," Sheila said. "I had to compose myself before calling. What's gotten into you two? Where will we get the money? Where will we get the space?"

"We haven't the least idea," I said. "But are you game to try?"

"I'm as crazy as the two of you, I guess," she said. "So why not? You realize I'll have to quit my job in order to do it, don't you?"

After we'd hung up, Alice said she wasn't surprised that Sheila had agreed to do it. She was sure Sheila would have sacrificed anything for her older brother. "Michael's disappearance nearly robbed Sheila of her adolescence," Alice said, "and it has managed to consume her ever since. I suppose a wife and sister are affected differently, but we both love Michael."

The next morning we went to work on both coasts. In California Alice and I got up early. We gulped coffee and Danish while composing a telegram to the Democratic National Committee:

URGENTLY REQUIRE FUNDS TO SET UP POW/MIA FAMILIES FOR IMMEDIATE RELEASE HEADQUARTERS TO EXPLAIN TO AMERICAN PEOPLE DURING ELECTION YEAR THAT NIXON HAS NOT ENDED THE WAR AND VIETNAMIZATION WILL NOT BRING BACK POWS. WE HAVE BEEN TOLD TO KEEP UP

254

THE GOOD WORK. WE WOULD LIKE TO BUT CANNOT
WITHOUT A WASHINGTON OFFICE

Alice and I took turns telephoning people all that day. Bob
Sherman was enthusiastic about our decision, but he fidgeted
over our plans. "Before you put out a press release, be ready to
talk about your plans in detail," he said. By afternoon, aides in
Senator McGovern's office told us there was a possibility we
might get some names from the McGovern "fat cat" list.

That same day, back in Washington, Sheila contacted Rusty
Lindley, who ran the Vietnam Vets Against the War headquarters at 47 Ivy Street, two blocks southeast of the Capitol. A few
hours later Rusty called Sheila back and offered us use of their
offices in the old white frame house free of charge. He said that
John Kerry and others concluded that we were in a better position to make a political impact than either Concerned Officers or
Vietnam Vets.

Sheila ordered new letterhead stationery and had a phone in-
stalled in the Vets' offices before the end of the week. On the day
before our headquarters in Washington was to open, she called
United Press International and Associated Press to make the announcement. After that she carried copies of our press release
over to the Senate Press Gallery.

At the same time Sheila was handing our press release to reporters in Washington, a woman from the *San Francisco Chronicle*
sat in my living room in California, listening to Alice and me reel
off plans for our new political office. "We're going to bring the
issue into the campaign, whether anyone likes it or not," Alice
insisted. "If we don't talk about it, the President won't—and the
American people would be glad to forget the whole thing."

The next morning Sheila got up early in her Washington apartment to check on East Coast coverage of our headquarters opening. We'd made the front page in both D.C. papers. Bob was on
the phone before she'd finished breakfast. "Sheila, get yourself
down to that office right away," he said. "They'll be all over you
today."

The phone was ringing when she unlocked the front door. Cassie Macken, from NBC, said she was on her way over. George Herman, CBS, was also coming. Radio stations called; reporters from all the news services showed up.

"Our plans are to send people into all the primary states," Sheila boasted. "We are definitely anti-Nixon all the way."

Messages of congratulations were called in and delivered to the new office all day from Fred Wertheimer of Common Cause, Henry Niles of Business Executives' Move for Peace, our advertising people in New York, and members of Congress.

A San Francisco radio station woke me at 6:45 the morning after our office opening in Washington. They'd received a wire service bulletin that claimed that the President was to announce a withdrawal date in a speech that evening. Other reporters called me. Would that change our plans for political campaigning, they asked. UPI offered to send a man out to my house to watch the speech with me.

Though I wanted to be proved wrong, I was sure it would be another sham. Nixon would hold out for continued bombing and the same old cease-fire with President Thieu in power. Later in the day the wire services reported that the White House story had indeed changed: The President was actually going to reveal a peace proposal that had already been rejected by Hanoi the previous August.

In Washington Sheila hadn't caught her breath after our headquarters opening of the day before, and she was also being bombarded with questions regarding Nixon's proposed announcement. CBS invited her to come down to the D.C. station to be interviewed directly after the President's speech.

Bob Sherman and his wife, Carolyn, met Sheila outside the CBS building. Inside, all three were directed into a conference room where a table had been set up with a large TV hanging over the far end. Joan Vinson was already there to represent the League. Sheila was relieved to see that Pete McCloskey and Senator Edward Brooke were also seated at the table.

Everyone had been given a text of the speech beforehand, and Sheila quickly glanced over the long and confusing proposal. Her perplexed expression prompted Bob to come to her aid. "Remember," he said, "when reading a Nixon text, always look for what he *doesn't* say, not so much what he does." What he didn't say, they both noted, was that our withdrawal from Southeast Asia would be contingent *only* upon the release of prisoners and full accounting of the missing. The proposal was full of other overstated conditions.

Pete McCloskey fanned himself with the papers and commented briefly, "Well, he does it every time, doesn't he?"

The speech gave details of two U.S. proposals: a secret offer made by Henry Kissinger on May 31, 1971, and a more complex eight-point plan first offered on October 11, 1971, and revised on January 25, 1972.

The May 31 offer was only about twenty words long and appeared simple and clear enough on first reading. But Bob told Sheila that the key word was "cease-fire." "In essence, defeat for the North Vietnamese and Viet Cong—asking them to lay down arms while President Thieu is still in office," Bob said. "There is nothing to say that the Saigon army wouldn't remain intact, along with the security police and the Phoenix program. Withdrawal on our part involves ground forces only in South Vietnam. Air power based in Thailand, Guam, and in the Pacific would remain and General Thieu could use it whenever he wanted."

"The eight-point plan looks even worse," Sheila said. There were only five minutes left to decipher the rest of the diplomatic documents.

Bob agreed with her. "The eight-point plan is worse," he said. "It also proposes a phony election, even phony for South Vietnam. Imagine how likely the NLF would be to step out of secrecy and run for office with all of Thieu's organization ready to pounce. I don't know, Sheila, say what you want, but it looks like one of those gestures to convince the American people in Nixon's favor—period."

At about two minutes to eight the TV monitor came on, and they all had the rare opportunity to witness Richard Nixon preparing to give his speech. He cleared his throat, shrugged, and then produced a smile. "No, not yet," he said to the cameraman as he tried to rearrange his face in various expressions—striving for the appropriate amount of dignity, sincerity, and leadership, Sheila surmised. The task seemed so difficult that even Joan Vinson and Senator Brooke, who had tried to remain neutral until then, began to chuckle at these few precious moments of Nixon theatrics.

Directly after the speech they were all interviewed on CBS camera. McCloskey said Nixon had avoided the real issue, and Senator Brooke made a faint attempt to defend the President. Joan Vinson took the League stand that it was much too complicated an issue for her or anybody to criticize the President. Sheila, listening to Bob's voice in her head, ticked off the reasons why there was nothing new in the revealed offers. She was disappointed, and the American people should be, too, she said.

The UPI man listened to the speech with me in California. Sean sat next to me on the sofa. Concentrating intently, he never let his large serious eyes wander from the TV screen. Terry strayed into the room, shook his head disapprovingly at Richard Nixon's image, and then disappeared.

Early the next morning I dashed out for newspapers before breakfast. Sean and I sat side by side in the middle of the *Los Angeles Times* front page. My first thought was of Terry—he'd be sorry he hadn't hung around for the picture. In addition, I'd have to listen to Sean needling him about it all day.

I looked over the rest of the story in my car. Reading Nixon's quotes in the article, I was struck by our lack of progress over the years and reminded of statements in the past. In 1968 President Johnson had said, "We search every day for peace, but peace with honor."

Now, in 1972, Richard Nixon was telling us, "We have offered the most generous peace terms—peace with honor for both sides."

In 1968 Lyndon Johnson had said, "Make no mistake about it, America will prevail."

Four years later Richard Nixon was promising, "We will not be defeated; we will never surrender our friends to Communist aggression."

Though I hadn't really let myself be hopeful the day before, I nevertheless felt let down. I was thankful when the phone rang and I heard JoAnn's voice. I needed a dose of her Tennessee humor.

"Well, what do you think of this latest hoax by our chief?" she asked. "Everybody and his brother have been calling me. One TV interviewer asked me if I would be willing to set a date, pull out, and leave the South Vietnamese to fall flat on their faces. I said, 'Yes, and on their butts, too!'"

The President's announcement made us even more determined to carry out our own political plans. Sheila was on her own for a while. Operating daily out of our new Washington headquarters, she tried to establish us as an entity to be dealt with during the campaign. She began by calling on Frank Seiverts at the State Department.

Seiverts was the man I'd spoken with at length on the telephone and, according to Sheila, perfect for his job as undersecretary for POW/MIA affairs. He was tall and handsome; his whitish silver hair gave him the right mix of maturity and concern. Sheila called him "a lonely woman's dream knight and protector."

In spite of his disarming good looks, however, Sheila was determined to remain businesslike during their meeting. As he ushered her into his office at the State Department, he congratulated our group on its publicity. He then offered her a chair and asked what he could do for us.

She whipped a piece of paper out of her purse, wrote down the address and phone number of our new office, and handed it to him. "We will expect to receive regular information that is sent to the League," she said. "We also expect to be invited to any meetings with Dr. Kissinger, even though we oppose administration policy."

He reached for the paper and looked at it for a few seconds, as if searching for an appropriate reply. "I can assure you that we will never discriminate against anyone who is a POW/MIA relative," he said.

Gathering her defenses once more to ward off his charm, she said, "If there is anything new at the Paris peace talks, we would also like to be informed of that immediately."

There was a hint of a smile on his face. As she got up to leave, he said, "For your goals, you're doing exactly the right things." At that moment she wondered, as I had when speaking with Captain Johnson, if it was possible that some officials in the administration were secretly rooting for us.

By the time Sheila returned to Ivy Street, Rusty Lindley had come up with an idea. Contacts were fine, he said, but we weren't going to get very far without funds. He suggested that we try to see Clark Clifford. "Don't be ridiculous," Sheila answered. "An ex-Secretary of Defense? Why should he take time to see us?"

But Rusty insisted. The Vietnam Vets seemed to believe that our group could talk to anyone. Sheila wasn't nearly that confident. "Who could refuse to see you?" Rusty asked as he picked up the telephone to dial a number he'd gotten from information. He handed the phone to Sheila.

"May I speak to Mr. Clifford, please?" Sheila asked, all the while wondering why she'd let Rusty talk her into performing such a dubious act.

"This is Sheila Cronin, Washington coordinator for the Families for Immediate Release," she said.

"He's tied up right now, Miss Cronin. May I have the number?" the woman asked.

Sheila hung up the receiver and turned to Rusty. "Well, what did I tell you?"

Within minutes the phone rang. It was Clark Clifford.

She tried to keep her voice from quivering. "I don't know if you know it or not," she said, "but our organization is a group of POW/MIA families who—"

Mr. Clifford interrupted: "Of course, I know your group.

You're going to be a very important pressure in finally ending this war."

Buoyed by these words, she got straight to the point. "I would like very much to meet with you if you have the time, Mr. Clifford." He said he would see her the following morning at his law office.

Sheila was awed by the stature of the man. She guessed he was easily six feet four inches tall; there was also a statesmanlike quality about him that was intimidating without meaning to be. He asked her to be seated across from his huge desk in an enormous chair in which she suddenly felt like a tiny Alice in Wonderland. As if to exaggerate the effect, it was labeled "Official Chair of the Secretary of Defense."

She explained to him what we were trying to do and asked his advice. He approved our plans wholeheartedly, saying our strategy for the primaries seemed to cover all bases. "How are you on funds?" he asked. She grasped the opportunity to tell him we had a small budget and none of the League's giant contributors.

Two days later a check in the amount of $1,000 arrived in the afternoon mail from a law firm in New Hampshire. Sheila knew it could have come only as a result of her visit with Clifford. Our fund-raising letter hadn't gone out yet. She rushed to the phone to thank him. "Mr. Clifford," she said, "we've just received a check in the mail from a law firm in New Hampshire. I know you are responsible and want to tell you we appreciate—"

"Don't thank me," he interrupted. "Don't thank me. Don't talk about anything over the telephone. You can thank me later for everything when this is all over."

That evening Sheila called me. "It was the strangest conversation, Barbara," she said. "Do you suppose he was trying to tell me his line is tapped?"

It seemed an incredible conclusion. "I don't think they would do that to an ex-Secretary of Defense," I said. As outrageous as it seemed, however, we could think of no other explanation for his response. Years later we learned that Clark Clifford was indeed on Nixon's "most tapped" list.

Sheila's next appointment was at the White House with John

Negraponte and others who were members of Dr. Kissinger's National Security Council staff. Though overwhelmed at first by her surroundings—an office in the Presidential Mansion—she soon forgot where she was. She repeated questions over and over until they were unable to hedge on the issue of cease-fire and troop withdrawal. They finally spelled it out: Our air support would continue with President Thieu in power for as long as necessary.

A few days later Henry Niles, national head of Business Executives' Move for Peace, called our headquarters. When Sheila asked him to come to our office to talk, he said that it would be better and safer to meet at a public place. It seemed to Sheila that the whole world was turning into a grade-B movie about frightened people caught in a net of intrigue. On her way down M Street toward the Mayflower Coffee Shop, she imagined that she was in Germany in the 1930s, that two sleek, sinister types in dark trench coats were following her. While she suppressed an urge to giggle, a part of her sensed a real danger. Respectable people like Clark Clifford and Henry Niles wouldn't suddenly lose their perspective, would they?

Niles arrived at the restaurant, noticed Sheila at a table, and walked over to her. The small, elderly man slid into a chair across from her. He talked to Sheila with the kindness of a grandfather giving advice to a granddaughter. He told her that his group would continue to help us. "You're doing a good job," he said, "but be careful."

Sheila called me in California that night, and we laughed about the aura of the meeting. We were dismayed much later to learn that this gentle man, who opposed continuation of the war, was included in the top-ten White House enemies list.

At the time, we wavered between believing that our government was spying on civilians, and making fun of our own jittery nerves. Nevertheless, Sheila made an appointment with Les Whitten in Jack Anderson's office to discuss our fears. I agreed with her that we needed friends in the media who knew what was happening behind the scenes. Her report of the meeting with Whitten made the rest of us feel more secure. "Les is warm and down to earth," she said. "He'll be there if we need him, if things get rough."

Sheila was sitting at her desk in our Washington office a few days later, engrossed in a fund-raising list, when Rusty Lindley said jokingly, "Look at those two men out front. I'll bet they're FBI."

"Don't be silly," Sheila said, then laughed. "Unless of course, they've come over to congratulate us on the fine job we're doing." She was now peering out the window too. "No, it couldn't be FBI," she said. "They're far too obvious."

A moment later there was a knock. She squelched a chuckle and opened the door. Standing in front of her were two tall, short-haired men, nearly identical in their dark conservative suits.

"Good morning," one said. "We're from the FBI. Just thought we'd stop by to see how things are going."

"Come in, sit down and make yourselves at home," Sheila said as cheerfully as possible. But they leaned stiffly against an old desk, side by side, as if separately they might crumble to the floor.

"Well, what can I help you with?" Sheila asked with a purposeful lilt to her voice.

"Who else is using this as headquarters, besides the POW group and the Veterans Against the War?" asked one.

"The Concerned Officers Movement is also here," Sheila said.

"Well," the agent said while fingering a paper on the end of the desk, "how's it going?"

Sheila had begun to enjoy the exchange. She pulled out a bunch of press releases. "We're doing great," she said. "Have a look at these." Just then Rusty's one-year-old daughter wandered out from a back room with a red popsicle in her hand. Most of it had already dripped down the front of her blue overalls.

So far Sheila had been playing hostess; Rusty spoke up for the first time. "Gentlemen, I'd like you to meet the director of Waifs for Peace," he said. Sheila and Rusty laughed, but the agents remained serious and undiverted. One of them took another sweeping look around as if deciding whether or not to leave.

"That's all," he said. "Good day for now." The other followed him out the door.

"God knows what they expected to find," Sheila said as she watched them scurry down the street. "Are we supposed to feel threatened now?"

We didn't know it then, but the telephones at the Ivy Street office had already been wire-tapped. If we had known it, we'd have been angry and possibly made the fact public, but it wouldn't have stopped us. We were hell-bent on opposing the President in the election. We were more concerned with obtaining funds, for instance, than with Nixon's paranoia.

Our telephone conferences between California and Washington concentrated on our lack of money. We were ready to send out a fund-raising letter when Sheila stopped by Senator McGovern's office to pick up their potential donor list. His assistant, John Holum, stopped her on the way out and suggested that our group ask Stewart Mott for a donation.

John said that Mott, heir to a General Motors fortune, lived austerely in a New York apartment. Though General Motors was involved in the production of war goods, he opposed the war and channeled his percent of the profits into antiwar causes and candidates. He would be perfect for our purposes, John added.

Though it was a suggestion that would have seemed preposterous a month earlier, Sheila rushed back to Congressman Leggett's office to place the call. Bob Sherman was on another phone ready to coach if necessary. Stewart Mott listened to Sheila describe our group and its plans; when she finished, he asked, "So what kind of sound business investment does this make you?"

Bob jotted notes furiously onto a memo pad and Sheila recited them into the telephone. "Well, Mr. Mott, we feel that the war issue is withering and that we are the most effective antiwar lobby around. We've gotten excellent press so far, and we feel we can take the POW issue away from Nixon and turn it around to a patriotic reason to end the war."

He said, "Thank you. I'll take it into consideration."

"I blew it, Bob," Sheila said, a bit stunned.

Within a week, however, a sizable check arrived, and Mott promised to continue to help us with newspaper advertisements and travel expenses. Entrenched now in our Washington headquarters, with a few promises of funds, we felt invincible. It was time to get on the campaign trail.

Valerie Kushner and a few others were going to travel to New Hampshire with George McGovern, the Democratic front runner, but Sheila and three other women from the Washington area would accompany Pete McCloskey into the first primary state where he would oppose the President for the Republican nomination.

Their days in New Hampshire were full from morning to night with radio/TV/newspaper interviews, bean suppers, open forums at supermarkets and country stores, press conferences, and informal get-togethers over coffee. On the last day, at one of the local high schools, Congressman McCloskey had to leave for Boston to film the William F. Buckley show, "Firing Line," and Sheila was asked to fill in for him as a luncheon speaker.

The group was the Manchester Exchange Club, a Republican businessmen's group. Sheila called them "a bunch of hard-nosed Nixon supporters" and admitted later that she had been "scared to death." After a bountiful luncheon, though, she looked out over the room and knew what she wanted to say. "My brother is having pig fat for lunch today," she began, and the rest came easily.

Sheila called me at 1:00 A.M. when she returned from New Hampshire. "We worked our tails off up there," she said, "but we've shown them we weren't bluffing."

"You'll have help from here on," I promised. "We'll cover all the primaries. Nixon has had four years. That's enough."

The next Sunday eight POW wives from the East Coast appeared on a Mike Wallace segment of "60 Minutes." Each made a similar statement: "Get out now." "Withdraw now." "Out!" "The President has to end the war or lose the election."

24. BREAKING POINT

FEBRUARY 1972 Bob Sherman turned the key to his Paris hotel room and went directly to his typewriter. He wanted to transcribe his notes on the meeting he and Congressman Leggett had just had with members of the North Vietnamese negotiating team quickly while they were fresh. They'd met with Nguyen Minh Vy, second-ranking man in the North Vietnamese team, and Le Chan, head of the North Vietnamese news service, for several hours. Disclosure of a secret meeting between Xwan Thuy, head of the North Vietnamese delegation, and Henry Kissinger had been discouraging. Reportedly, Kissinger had told the Communist diplomat, "You should be under no illusion that we will withdraw simply in exchange for the prisoners."

Bob reached into his briefcase and took out his note pad. He sat down at a desk by the window and typed his report:

. . . After discussing the outlook for peace negotiations, Congressman Leggett asks Nguyen Minh Vy to grant him a personal request. He then asks for information on Major William Mullen.

He shows Vy four sheets stapled together: first, basic information on Barbara's husband, followed by a POW/MIA

Families for Immediate Release letter to the President and a press release, both signed by Barbara. Congressman Leggett explains that Barbara has worked with us. That she has heard nothing about her husband. And asks if they can help her.

They look at the first page with interest but as soon as they see the word Laos, they say there is nothing they can do. I ask them to take a minute please to read the letter and to keep it for a reference. The number-three man glances at it briefly and gives it to Vy to hand back to me. When Vy looks at the letterhead, he says the name of the group should be POW/MIA Families for Immediate Release and End to the War, not Families for Immediate Release. He hands the papers back to me as if he considered the matter finished. He then says instead of writing to him, the wives should be asking Nixon to end the war.

I panic. An opportunity could be going down the drain because of a stupid misunderstanding. Congressman Leggett points out that what he had just given him *was* a letter to the President, but Vy has gone on to another thought and is speaking again. He says, "We used to receive a flood of mail on the POWs from families and elsewhere, but now it is much less and this is much better." He smiles.

I don't smile back, but instead launch into the most impassioned speech of my life. I explain about the group and describe Barbara. "She recognizes the unhappiness of the war for both sides. In fact, she realizes what she has endured not knowing if her husband is dead or alive for six years is trivial in terms of the whole war. Nevertheless, if you could find out about her husband it would build tremendous goodwill."

Their faces express concern. I can't tell if it is real or simulated. They talk, animated, among themselves in Vietnamese for a minute—which they had not done before. Then Vy turns back to me and says, "She should contact the Pathet Lao."

I say, "We've tried to do that. We requested a meeting

with the Pathet Lao through every channel some time ago and have never had a reply."

Vy asks who we wrote to. I tell them we wrote to Prince Souvannouvong in Sam Neua and Sot Pethrasi in Vientiane.

"Those are good addresses," he says.

I say, "But we got no answer. You must have contacts you can use. I wish you'd take a minute to read these letters." I hand the letters back to him.

They have another three-way conversation. Their brows are furrowed. I wish I knew what they were saying. They turn back to me. I ask them to please keep the letters. If they don't have time now to read them, perhaps they will later. But they interrupt and say, "We have faith in you." I think, what a strange remark. It stops me cold. Are they going to help Barbara? They hand the papers back to me.

"You should write again," Vy says, "send this letter to them."

So that's it, I think. Maybe they're going to slip the word to the Pathet Lao to respond to Leggett. And maybe they're just stringing me along. I'll write and try.

A short while after Bob returned from Paris, Sot Pethrasi, spokesman for the Pathet Lao Communists, made a public statement from Laos regarding American prisoners there. Speaking in fluent French, he explained that our bombing had so disrupted the Pathet Lao communications that it was impossible to compile a list of prisoners. He would not reveal the location of any prisoners but said they were held in mountain regions so remote that they were difficult to reach under the best of circumstances. He said that he had accepted mail for prisoners from their families, but held little hope of its being delivered. "We no longer have a postal service. We no longer have a route. What can I do? That is the reality."

Bob's notes on the Paris meeting, and the Pathet Lao statement heightened my own frustrations. Would we ever find men held in mountain regions so remote they were difficult to reach? Could those men wait yet another year for yet another President? Working on the election, months off, was beginning to seem like a useless exercise. To think that was a betrayal of the other women; I was losing my will at the wrong time.

It was a Saturday afternoon when the desire to escape overwhelmed me. I couldn't pace around the house another minute. I was tired of thinking and waiting and thinking. I told the boys to pack up—we were going to take a vacation. "In February?" Sean asked, wide-eyed. "What about school?"

Terry had already raced into the bedroom and was tossing things into a suitcase.

Measured against our survival, their missing a week of school seemed unimportant. Ordinarily, I'd have felt guilty doing it, but even in retrospect I viewed the trip to Strawberry Hill as an involuntary action, a necessity. As soon as I turned the hairpin curve and saw the spacious old lodge nestled there in the motherlode country of the Sierra Nevada Mountains, I knew we were doing the right thing.

Through the wide windows of the main room with its exposed beams and huge stone fireplace, I looked out at snow-covered trees and a frozen brook. Beyond us in the white hills were toboggan slides, saucer runs, and skee-doo trails, all yet to be discovered. We're in another land, I thought, for a short while, where we can't be hurt. I was glad I'd left no phone number.

We'd brought two changes of clothing. At lunchtime we hung our soggy pants, sweaters, and socks on doorknobs and radiators to dry before we headed back out. The boys reveled in the fierce activity. Terry drove our toboggan at full speed. Behind him on the slim conveyor, Sean and I grasped the sides. The only sound was wind whistling past us and Sean's voice booming from behind me, "You dumb shit, Terry! Slow down. You're killing us!"

The skee-doos would be fun, and safer, I told myself that night, thinking of the next day's plans—I would do the driving.

I steered us slowly and carefully up to the top of a white mound and then gasped as I viewed the crevasse below. By the time we reached the bottom, our acceleration carried us up another hill and then down again. Before I could change course, we were heading for a tree. I pulled on the wheel, turning the skis under us only slightly. We swung to the left just enough to avoid hitting the trunk head-on and collided from an angle.

I peeked out from a snowbank a few seconds later. The skee-doo had come to a stop a few yards away and flopped over on its side. I heard Terry screech from somewhere, "Yahoo, cool, Mom!"

Sean, unseen behind the overturned skee-doo, blasted a hoarse reprisal. "I'm going to get killed on this trip! Mom, didn't you hear the man tell you how to drive that thing?"

Terry surfaced from a cover of white powder, a wide grin on his face. "Let's get right back in, Mom. That's what you always tell us. Do it again so you won't be afraid."

"Well, I changed my mind, Terry. We should be afraid of some things, for good reason, no doubt. If you think I'm getting back in that vehicle of death, you're crazy."

Terry let out a howl. He rolled over and over down the embankment. Sean was still grumbling and brushing himself off.

"Stop laughing, Terry," I warned. "Have a little respect for your mother."

At the lodge that night I drank some wine by the fire after dinner while the boys played pool. Later, looking at them asleep, stretched out on the bed next to mine, I felt suddenly warm and thankful. I pulled the heavy quilts up over them. A lot had gone right, after all. Maybe the fresh air had revived me enough to try again.

I'll give it one more fight, I told myself as we drove down from the hills, leaving the highlands behind and passing through the foothills. My resolution began to waver about the time we reached Oakland, however. At home, my energy drained further as I listened to phone messages on my answering machine.

One was from James Stewart, a congressional candidate from the Palo Alto district. When I called him and heard the magnitude of a project he had in mind, I wanted to throw my bags back into the car and return to the mountains. I tried but couldn't match his enthusiasm. The project was to involve every candidate for President, he said. A statement from our group would be endorsed by the candidates; university student-body presidents would enlist student workers for candidates who supported it.

When he stopped to take a breath, I commented that it sounded very ambitious. He said we could launch the whole thing at a press conference by March. Larry Diamond, student-body president at Stanford, would direct university activity; the Quakers would coordinate the project nationally. "You'll have to get endorsements from the Presidential candidates and the agreement of your group, of course," he added.

I couldn't remember agreeing to participate in the project, but then I supposed I just hadn't had the stamina to object. At any rate, I was sitting in a large wood-paneled room of a Victorian house in San Francisco a few weeks later waiting for our first planning session to begin. I gazed around at the group assembled in the American Friends headquarters. Dennis Allen, a Quaker, handed me a copy of a statement he'd written which our group was to sign. It seemed to be a position paper on the war. Then Stewart's assistant, a young earnest-looking woman, said that she had also brought a statement. Larry Diamond, the young man from Stanford, reached into a briefcase and produced his version of the words that were supposed to be ours and would be the bulwark of this national effort.

Soon a three-way debate regarding the statements was under way. I listened as a mildly interested spectator, finally commenting dully, almost to myself, "We can write our own statement." They stopped talking and looked at me blankly, so I added, "We're the ones who have to sign it, aren't we?"

They seemed to take note of me for the first time. "Yes. You can if you want to," Stewart's assistant said. I wasn't sure I did want to. It might require a vitality I didn't possess, but at the same time, I wasn't going to let someone else speak for us. Hadn't it taken us years to wrestle our freedom of speech from the clenched fists of government officials?

I had difficulty carrying out my share of the assignments as the weeks went by. I forced myself to write the statement and to call the headquarters of the Presidential candidates. I got an endorsement from each of them—Shirley Chisholm, Hubert Humphrey, John Lindsay, George McGovern, Edmund Muskie, and Pete McCloskey. Seventy-two student-body presidents of leading colleges and universities had promised to manage the program on their campuses. But I was thankful when the day to launch the project arrived.

We were sitting in a restaurant on Fisherman's Wharf after our press conference at the Fairmont Hotel. Everyone seemed pleased with the way things had gone. I was pleased, too—that the press conference was over and I'd managed to get through it.

Jim Stewart, the congressional candidate, and Larry Diamond were excitedly planning follow-up work. "We'll have to organize the students on every campus at once," Diamond was saying. "We'll send a mailing to community and church groups telling them how to raise funds and how to distribute the statement. They'll need to contact political candidates in their areas."

Jim Stewart was all wound up. "Business Executives' Move should launch a campaign to contact prominent financial figures," he said. I couldn't seem to keep my mind on the conversation, wanting only to finish lunch and head back across the Oakland Bay Bridge.

I got up each morning brimming with ideas for the primaries and deeds to accomplish that day. Of ten good intentions, however, perhaps one was crossed off by nightfall. While I moved at a sluggish pace, Sheila was running a marathon in Washington. She was organizing people for the primaries and making appearances herself wherever possible—a demonstration sponsored by Another Mother for Peace, a press conference with Joan Baez, a Martin Agronsky program.

John Holum had offered her a paid job in the McGovern campaign as a way of helping us financially. She stopped in there daily and then went on to our office to work. At McGovern headquarters she saw Valerie periodically. Sweeping through the building, Valerie floated in and out of Frank Mankiewicz's office just long enough to check on her next scheduled public appearance.

Shirley, Alice, Delia, Sally, and so many others were doing

media spots, giving speeches, appearing with candidates. I was sorry I wasn't contributing as much, so I gave myself pep talks and tried harder. And yet I was beginning to believe that our struggle was futile.

The majority of people agreed with me about the war, and yet it went on. One afternoon Abigail Van Buren wrote in her column:

> Over the years one of the most frustrating aspects of being "Dear Abby" has been my inability to provide solutions for some problems. One in particular . . .
> I refer to letters from individuals and organizations urging me to ask my readers to write to Hanoi, asking that our prisoners of war be released, or humanely treated. . . .
> My dear readers, you are appealing to the wrong person. You should be appealing to your congressmen, senators, and President Nixon to bring an end to this senseless war in Vietnam.
> If *our* country were being bombed, would *you* agree to release the enemies' war prisoners?

I read in the same newspaper that President Nixon had proclaimed another Week of Concern for the POWs. "Bullshit," I muttered wearily as Sean walked through the door.

He set his books down on the table. "What did Nixon do this time?" he asked, swinging the refrigerator door open.

I walked over to him and ran my fingers through his curly brown hair. "Oh, the same old stuff," I said. "How would you like a snack?" Somehow it's impossible to dishevel him, I thought, yet Terry manages to look like a throwaway kid most of the time.

The next morning Frank Marianno, a network TV reporter, called to ask if I would do a joint interview with Julie Butler during a ceremony to commemorate Nixon's POW week. I said yes and then questioned my decision. Suddenly it seemed a foolish endeavor. But then, how could I refuse if Julie, Maerose's assistant, would be there representing the League? She's probably doing it for the same reason, I thought. She's doing it because I am.

My communication with the Bay Area League women, such as it was, had detected a weariness much like my own lately. I was sure they were all getting bone-tired, too.

Julie, the reporter, and I met on top of a grassy hill overlooking Presidio Army Base in San Francisco, where flags were raised to the top of poles and a band played "America the Beautiful." Marianno talked with Julie first. She asked that people pray and write letters to the signatories of the Geneva Convention; there was also to be a roll call by states of all the POW/MIAs at the entrance to the Golden Gate Bridge later in the week, she said.

Marianno asked me what I thought of the ceremony, and I told him I thought it was useless. "All we have to do is end the war. We don't need flags or bands or roll calls."

Neither Julie nor I projected much enthusiasm. We'd done it too many times. On the way to our cars Julie admitted that she was finished. She asked if I had learned how to pull my phone out of the wall jack. "If you haven't, Barbara, you should try it. If you really want to hide, pull the drapes and lock all the doors, too. I'm still holding that in reserve."

I really wanted to quit, more every day. But there I was dressing for a McGovern reception at the St. Francis Hotel. At least make it through the June primary, I kept telling myself. Don't let the rest of them down. I fastened an earring and took one last look in my full-length mirror. I was wearing my best public uniform—long skirt, white wool top, and gold belt. I brushed my brown hair behind my ears and down my back. Bill had never seen me with long hair. Strange, that suddenly made me feel sad. It seemed more important than the political event I was about to attend. I forced myself to leave the bedroom, gave instructions to the baby-sitter, and drove off in the car by myself.

A special gold invitation entitled me to attend a private cocktail party beforehand. I searched around the St. Francis until I located the specified room, took a deep breath, and pushed the door open. The first person I saw was Warren Beatty and then Julie

Christie. Behind them was a dazzling array of glamorous personalities. Half of the room was speckled with glittery show people, the other half important California political figures.

Past all of them, I saw a large man in a Christian Brothers robe. He was leaning against a wall at the far end of the room. I pointed myself in his direction at once and, looking straight ahead, made my way through the crowd and across an expanse of luxurious burgundy carpeting. I stopped directly in front of the priest and confessed, "I'm not a movie star. I don't know what I'm doing here, but I figured maybe you weren't one either—a movie star, that is."

"I'm Father Riga from St. Mary's College," he said, stretching out a large hand, "and I promise you I'm not a movie star." His eyes smiled above a full beard; brown robes stretched around his ample frame. "Since there are now two of us," he said, "let's have courage. How about circulating around and allowing these people to meet us?"

I tagged after him. Who would tempt fate by ignoring him? "Dennis Weaver," he said, "this is Barbara Mullen and I'm Father Riga, . . ." as if it were an important announcement. Dennis Weaver, taller and more handsome than he appeared on film, smiled warmly. I was glad we'd started with him.

Others seemed ill at ease when Father Riga explained my situation; I tried to make them more comfortable. Julie Christie smiled up at us through the mass of tight curls that framed her face. By the time Father Riga finished telling her my story, however, she looked stricken. She kept saying, "I'm sorry."

I found myself studying the carpet and gazing up at the glittering chandeliers. Everything in the room seemed to sparkle but me; I felt light-headed and not quite grounded. I heard myself talking to people, but it was as if I were listening to someone else's voice. Windows stretched the length of the room. Through them I stared out at the twinkling lights of San Francisco skyscrapers and tried to regain a sense of reality. Father Riga soon drew me back into the conversation.

When it was time to troop down the stairs to the grand ballroom, I slipped my arm under Father Riga's and he escorted me to the front table. He sat on my left. On my right was Warren Beatty and next to him Julie Christie. Father Riga leaned toward me and asked if there was anything special I'd like him to include in the invocation. I told him from what I'd seen so far, he was not short on words. We were laughing when George McGovern began greeting everyone at the front table.

Father Riga opened the affair eloquently with poignant words that brought us sharply back to the real reason we were there. Beyond the glamour, I conceded that these were dedicated people. A California congressman, Phil Burton, introduced each of us to the filled room. After that McGovern spoke. The ballroom was alive with excitement. I supposed hopes were high again. For me, though, the election seemed very far off.

I've been very fortunate to have met such good people, I told myself as I left the ornate ballroom and walked through the hotel lobby. It was beginning to drizzle, and I suddenly felt very alone when I got outside. I paid the man at the garage and drove my car out into the San Francisco street.

It wasn't long before I realized that I'd turned a wrong corner somewhere. I was blocks from where I ought to be. I kept driving and still nothing looked familiar. It was a route I'd taken hundreds of times. I clenched the steering wheel tighter and tighter. Cold perspiration began to drip down from my armpits under my white wool sweater. I turned the inside light on and looked at my watch. It had been forty-five minutes since I'd left the hotel.

It was raining hard now. The wipers swayed back and forth; lights from other cars glared on the wet pavement. I was ready to pull over to the side of the road, lock the car doors, and have a good cry, when suddenly, through sheets of rain, I saw a faint outline of the Oakland Bay Bridge directly ahead of me.

I turned into my driveway half an hour later and whispered, "Thank you. Thank you." I leaned my head forward and let tears drip down onto the steering wheel.

25. DRAWN SHADES

APRIL 1972 The California primary was two months off, and I didn't know if I'd last that long. When I was to make an appearance in support of George McGovern, I spent the previous day preparing myself emotionally for the event. My body felt heavy with imagined weight. I came directly home after the rally or interview to rest.

My only motivation was allegiance to the other women in our group. I'd have felt less guilty if they hadn't been working so hard. The Families for Immediate Release headquarters had paid off. Our group members had shown up in all the primaries, some traveling with George McGovern and others speaking on behalf of local peace candidates.

Sheila called me every few days to report the actions and movements of various women. I grew weary just listening to her voice alive with energy on the telephone. She probably hadn't had a full night's sleep in four months, and still she kept at it.

One evening in the middle of her recitation she told me that the League was sponsoring a symposium at a Washington hotel and she had decided to participate. "Political action will be my topic," she said excitedly. "It's a great opportunity; the press will be much more interested in our view than theirs."

4444444

"Why bother?" I said. I couldn't comprehend why she wanted to do it. And yet, presenting our case to the press and the American people had always been our goal. I knew my response disappointed her, so I added, "You're right, Sheila. Go to it. Pay no attention to me. I'm just going through a bad period."

The symposium at the Washington Holiday Inn was about to begin. Sheila was already seated on the speakers' platform when she spotted Carolyn Sherman near the front of the filled auditorium. A few minutes later Bob slid into the seat behind her, and Sheila smiled down at them, happy to know there were at least two friendly faces in the audience.

Sybil Stockdale, the founding mother of the League, opened the symposium with a speech containing veiled references to those who would go political and destroy the unity. Sheila spoke next. She talked about harsh political realities: the war was supported by politicians and would be ended by politicians; the prisoner issue had been exploited by administration politicians from the beginning. At the end she paused and said, "We are the most used women in American history."

The floor was then thrown open to questions. Someone asked Sheila about illegal bombings in Laos and Cambodia. As she started to respond, Joe McCain, whose father was an admiral and Commander of U.S. Naval Forces in the Pacific, interrupted and shouted, "Sheila, don't answer. You know your brother would be appalled and ashamed by your activities."

"At least I'm not ordering bombing raids on him like your father is," Sheila returned.

Joe McCain then unleashed a verbal tirade against Sheila. After a few minutes Bob Brudno, a POW brother, decided to intercede. He said something to quiet Joe and then tried to stand up quickly. As he did, his chair toppled over backwards with him in it. Sheila ran down from the podium and bent over to help him.

A League officer then came to the center of the platform and adjourned the disrupted meeting. Sheila, Bob, and Carolyn left immediately. Reporters pounced on them as they left the auditorium, but Sheila was too disturbed to speak with them. They hurried out to the hotel lobby instead, where suddenly Joe Mc-Cain, the admiral's son, reappeared and stepped directly in front of Sheila. "Sheila," he said, "when your brother gets home, you'll be sorry. He's going to hate you for this."

"I just want to make sure he comes home, Joe," she said.

Though I listened to Sheila's story with sympathy that evening, I was glad there had been three thousand miles between me and the confrontation. The event marked a turning point for me. I knew I could no longer exhibit my own anger that way. All I wanted was to burrow into a hole like a groundhog and come out on the first day of peace.

That same evening I decided to invite JoAnn Connor to visit me in California. I thought about her Tennessee humor—the way she had of dismissing the President and the brass with an earthy phrase or two. I smiled, thinking of our last phone call after one of Richard Nixon's haughty statements regarding his difficulties with finding an "honorable peace," and JoAnn's response: "Well, how could he? I'm sure that man couldn't find the outhouse in a fog."

A couple of weeks later I waited eagerly at the airport for her plane to arrive. I tried to imagine what she would look like. In our circumstances it wasn't unusual to meet someone personally with whom you'd already developed an intimacy by long distance.

Somehow I was sure I would know her—I picked her out of the crowd as soon as she came through the gate. Her hair was unconstrained, falling freely to her shoulders; she wore a blouse and casual skirt and sandals. A stranger might not have guessed she was a career officer's wife, and I wondered how much she had changed—how she might have looked back in 1965.

I leaped forward to claim her and whisked her out of the airport. At home we talked for five days and part of the nights, moving from the kitchen to the living room and back to the kitchen. "I invited my new liaison officer and his wife and children all over for dinner one night," JoAnn said. "He was curious as hell about me, so I thought I'd show him I was more or less a normal human being in spite of the efforts of our government to disrupt my life and send me to the nuthouse."

"Have some more wine," I said. After the second day we began to look at ourselves apart from our unending circumstances, something neither of us had done before. We tried to imagine what we might do with our lives if we were freed, and wondered how much longer we could exist in this uncertain state.

Having dangled a toe into these strange waters, JoAnn plunged deeper. "There must be more interesting men to fight with than Richard Nixon," she said.

We were having dinner that evening in a popular restaurant; there was a crowded bar behind a brass rail a few yards from where we were sitting. The sounds of animated conversation drifted across the room. I sipped my brandy and glanced around. "Sure," I said, "but who's going to bother with a couple of women who are legally bound, free one day, not the next?"

JoAnn laughed. "Plenty of them, no doubt. We'd probably be considered safe and wanting."

Long after JoAnn was back in Nashville, the questions posed by our discussions provoked me. A toe in the water was not total submersion, but would that be just a matter of time? Was it time to call fate the victor?

It didn't help that it was spring, a time of transition when events marked the passage of time. Bill's thirty-seventh birthday had just passed on March 28; he was thirty when he left for Vietnam in 1965. I was sent an invitation to his twentieth high school reunion, and his classmates asked me to send them a letter they could print in the front of their reunion program. I could only think of a few words:

I wouldn't want it to seem that I was speaking for Bill. I don't know what his feelings are now about this war. I couldn't possibly describe his longing for his dear mom and dad and his gram. And how could I know the depth of his sorrow at having missed every event in the lives of his growing sons, who were babies when he left? He wanted to share all the firsts with them: baseball, ice skating, a first crush on a little girl. They're nine and eleven now, and he's missed all of these. . . .

Sean was graduating from the sixth grade, yet it seemed he had just jumped into the van that took him off to kindergarten. As the ceremony began, the children marched onto a platform in the elementary school gym and sat in chairs in rows. Sean came forward, having been chosen to make the welcoming speech. He looked tall for his age, dressed in navy blue pants and a light blue blazer. We'd had his curly hair trimmed. No longer a little boy, he was beginning to look more like Bill.

"For the graduating class of Montview Elementary School, I want to welcome all our mothers and fathers to this important event," he began. As I listened to his husky young voice, I wanted to stop time, to halt the ceremony. It wasn't fair. Sean would now go on to junior high school and his young childhood would be lost to Bill forever.

The war was escalating again. The United States had begun work on a seventh air base in Thailand. Bombers and fighter-bombers in Southeast Asia conducted massive air strikes daily. Families were receiving the same news I had been given six years earlier.

I pinned the last statistic onto my bulletin board that I could ever bear to read. May 1972: Total POW/MIAs, 1,723. Killed in action, 55,000. Wounded, 453,000. Under it were several layers of yellowed pieces of paper from 1967, when the figures were barely beginning to tally.

Nothing would change until Nixon was defeated in November. That was five months off, and I knew I didn't have five months left in me. I woke up the morning after the California primary; McGovern had won the Democratic nomination. I was alone when the telephone rang. I walked over and pulled the cord out of the wall jack. I had no desire to know who was calling.

I wanted to be concerned again with ordinary things. I'll spend the summer doing things with the boys, I thought. I'll make them chocolate fudge brownies with walnuts from scratch and take them to the beach at Santa Cruz. I'll paint the family room white and re-cover the furniture.

Then suddenly my frenzy was gone as quickly as it had come on. I felt limp, not hysterical. Perhaps I'll lie down on the sofa a few minutes, I thought. Then I'll really dig in.

But I didn't move. When the boys came home from school at three o'clock, I was still in my robe.

"What's wrong, Mom? You sick?" Sean asked.

"I don't know," I said. Terry shrugged, and they both left the room.

It was nearly dark when I wrenched myself up from the pillows and dragged one leg after the other into the kitchen. I took four franks from the refrigerator, boiled them, and stuffed them into four rolls. I poured two glasses of milk. The boys ate quickly; when they thought I wasn't watching, they each grabbed a handful of Twinkies and disappeared into the family room. I pretended not to notice and found my way back to the sofa.

There wasn't a sharp pain to soothe; there was nothing. At night I sat in the dark in my living room and stared out at shadows of trees in the canyon. During the day I closed the drapes.

I hadn't been dressed for five days when Helen stopped by. She was a neighbor, the mother of three. She had come through a divorce, gone back to the university, finished, and was now teaching English. She was also coming alive socially. She'd even begun to date. She'd passed me by, as I felt everyone else had.

She'd been trying to call, she said, and had gotten worried. "Have you eaten?" she asked, frowning as she appraised my appearance.

I didn't want anyone to see me like this, especially Helen. I picked at a bologna sandwich she'd made. "I'm going to call Dr. David and make an appointment for you," she said.

Helen was one of the most self-confident women I knew. It always surprised me that she kept a psychiatrist on reserve. Dr. David was on call both in her head and in Berkeley. "One should have an analyst around like a spare tire in case of a blowout," she explained. "I haven't seen him for a long time, but I'd run all the way out there on foot if I felt an emergency pending."

I didn't care about pending emergencies. I probably already had one. "How could he help me anyway?" I asked. "My situation is unsolvable."

"Maybe he can't," Helen said, "but at least you'd have to take your robe off and get dressed to drive out there."

I didn't care if he could help. In fact, I was sure he couldn't. I not only didn't mind if the sun came up or went down; with the drawn drapes I wasn't aware of either. I wasn't eating. I threw newspapers in the trash without unrolling them. I scarcely talked with the children. They kept a distance and gave one another knowing glances.

They plugged the telephone in after school so their friends could call them, and it terrified me. I told them to say I wasn't there. What if I picked it up by accident and someone asked me a question requiring a clear answer? I wasn't sure I could put a sentence together. Then letters started arriving. People who had tried to call wanted to know if I was all right. "Where have you been? What's happened? There are important projects we have to discuss." Discuss—I could scarcely find the bathroom.

I called Dr. David early one morning. He said to come along; he would fit me in. I slumped down in a chair in his cozy little wood-paneled office. I was determined he would have to coax me to speak. Then I would defy him and all his professional colleagues to come up with a word or a shot or a pill that would eliminate the cause of my damned depression.

I wished he'd had a sinister mad-doctor look. If he had, I'd have held out longer. Instead, he was smaller than I, with a neat mustache and kind eyes. He smiled patiently and waited for me to say something. He would have waited forever, I guessed. Finally, I admitted in a whisper that I didn't know why I was there. No one could help me, I said. "I'm not a wife. I don't need to be a wife to be a woman. But I'm not allowed to be a woman." I knew I wasn't making sense. I gave up and mumbled something about not really existing. "I don't exist," I said. "I don't think I'm really here."

"You do exist," he promised me. "You're sitting there in my chair." Then he said something about how I deserved to get something out of life.

"Easy for you to say. You're used to talking to people who can get on with their lives. They're divorced, so it hurts. A husband dies and that hurts. But they are faced with a reality." Now I would really set him straight, I thought. "They're alone. Sooner or later they can face it. What can I do? My husband may come home next year—or five years from now. What do I say then? 'Sorry, fella, I have this new life and you don't fit into it'?"

"Don't face all that right now," Dr. David said. "You need to do something for yourself right now."

"I just want to live like a normal woman again," I said. "How can I do that? What would I tell people?"

"It seems to me you've waited a long time to give yourself some happiness," he said. "Take one thing at a time. And tell people anything you wish."

I tried calling Sheila and Shirley and Delia, but always hung up before they could answer. I had a whole wastebasket full of crumpled letters I'd written and rejected. Finally one morning I let the ringing continue until I heard Alice's voice.

She listened and then admitted that her own state was not much better. "I'm close to folding myself," she said. "I may be in your position tomorrow, for all I know."

It was no time to bow out, I apologized. With the election coming up, it wasn't even logical.

"Logical," she said. "Is this war logical? Is what they've done to us logical? If I get up in the morning and remember my name, I think I've outlasted them."

I laughed and said how much better I felt just talking with her. "Will you phone everyone for me—Sheila, Sally, and Delia and Shirley and Bob and Carolyn?" I asked. "I just can't do it myself right now. Tell them I'm sorry."

"They'll understand, Barbara," she said. "We've all been so worried about you."

When Alice called back, she said, "Shirley is writing you a letter for the rest of us. If you have any sense, you'll follow her advice."

I smiled from beginning to end as I read Shirley's letter a few days later. It was typical of the way we dealt with things. We found a way to laugh.

Dear Barbara,

I have a wonderful solution for you. I have given this considerable thought, and have visualized you complying completely, and the sight is a tonic, believe me. Ready?

First, fill up the goldfish bowl to the top. This is very important. Now get all the files on MIA/POW stuff you have and put as many in your arms as you can hold. Got the picture? There you are, pretty as can be, barefoot (I forgot to stipulate you *must* be barefoot), arms loaded and standing at the doorway of an empty room contemplating what direction to run off in. Fling your arms high over your head, the object being to use your strength to fling papers, clippings, pictures (especially that dumb one from St. Louis) and stickers, stamps, clips, etc., as far from you as possible. Just to be certain you have flung your damnedest, spread anything on the floor that seems to be stuck together.

OK? Now go back into your bedroom and get the rest of all those files and do the same thing, only start off in the other direction when you fling! Don't even stop to contemplate what you have done or you may suffer a regret or two. Now, to continue this mad junket—go get the fish. Holding the bowl in one arm, dip your fingers into the bowl and jog around the room, on tiptoes, dipping and flinging the water all around the room, trying to saturate all the papers, but being careful not to run out of water so the poor fish doesn't know he's being depleted of his vital substance. Are you still running? Don't you begin to feel better, knowing those papers are now getting more and more useless?

Stop sobbing! It is all for the best, Barbara, and there's no use in punishing yourself any longer. If a newsman calls whilst all this is going on, just take some of the now-wet, soggy, papier-mâché and stuff it into the phone and tell him he has never sounded so good.

The boys will want to get into the act at this point, and you might as well let 'em. Now sit down a bit. Rest up and watch the kids have a go and let them enjoy themselves. Do not, I repeat, *do not,* let the kids have any of the drippy paper. We have a special detail for it. Get a good-sized box; pack it in wet layers with the paper; address to Frank Seiverts at the State Department; put a return address somewhere in North Vietnam, and mail it. Can't you see him when he gets it? He, the CIA, and the National Security Council and the Defense Department will go wild thinking a new peace proposal has come on a slow boat through a monsoon! Or that we've been working out of Hanoi all along. It was worth all that, wasn't it?—and besides it gets it all out of your bedroom and dining room. And that *was* worth it.

See, Barbara, life does have its little compensations, doesn't it? I just baked some POW/Nixon cookies. You put them in the oven, turn off the heat, and they're ready whenever you want to heat them up again.

Have some joy somehow. It's time.

Love,
Shirley

26. A TASTE OF FREEDOM

Definition of grief: Essentially the emotional and related reactions that occur at the time of and following the loss of an
important person in the emotional life of an individual who
has reached the state of development where he has the ca-
pacity for object love. Grief is the emotion that is involved in
the work of mourning, whereby a person seeks to disengage
himself from the demanding relationship that has existed
and to reinvest his emotional capital in new and productive
directions for the health and welfare of his future life in
society.

The excerpt was from a document written for the Defense Department by Professor Ludwig J. Spolyar at the University of
Minnesota. His study, several mimeographed pages long, was entitled, "The Dynamics of Grief of Wives of Military Personnel
Missing in Action."

I opened it eagerly the day it arrived. It seemed a good omen,
following on the heels of my visit with Dr. David and my eman-
cipation letter from Shirley. As I read paragraph after paragraph
of verbose instructions, however, I was soon struck by its complete irrelevance to the missing-in-action dilemma. It applied only
to a cycle of grief for the dead. Had that been our problem, most

of us would have already clawed our way through the grief process.

There was only one way to disengage from our "demanding relationship," and that was divorce. Legally, in some states, that was possible after a number of years on the grounds of desertion. Legally allowed, but emotionally impossible for most women— how could a man be accused of desertion because he was captured by an adversary in a war? Professor Spolyar's advice that emotional capital should be reinvested "in new and productive directions for the . . . welfare of one's future life in society" was as inapplicable. Would he have us tell a returning husband that we were sorry, we'd reinvested our emotional capital elsewhere?

The study elaborated: "A person should live in terms of the future rather than in terms of the past . . . a person may have completed their grief work so effectively and emancipated themselves prior to any finalization of death that it may serve as a safeguard against the impact of a permanent separation. . . . The final phase should result in a readjustment to reality and a future life of social normality."

I read the document repeatedly, trying to glean a flicker of insight that would help me. What if the wife had, as the professor advised, emancipated herself prior to finalization of death only to have her husband reappear, living and breathing? "Readjustment to reality"—the final phase, he called it. Any of us could have eventually unlatched that hinge to freedom with the knowledge that the loved one was dead. The truth was that the experts had no solution. There were no studies to cover the "perhaps death" grief cycle. In fact, it was no cycle at all. It was a wheel missing part of its rim, stopping always in the same place, prior to completion of its revolution.

"It's just a party," Helen said. No big deal. It would be at her house, some drinks and food. "What's the harm?" she asked.

What's the harm, I asked myself. As I saw it, I had two options. I could shroud myself in gray, deny I was a woman and sit in the house forever, or I could get up and go out.

I was still considering the former even as I took panty hose from a bureau drawer, fastened a long skirt at the waist, and pulled a newly purchased bright pink sweater over my head.

I hadn't looked at myself through the eyes of a man for a long time. Would he see that vacant stare in the eyes, the one I recognized in Maerose and all the other women? I practiced smiling in front of the mirror for a minute, first widely, then more subtly, crinkling my eyes, then holding them wide open. I couldn't remember how. There was a way you did it with men that was different. Wouldn't the first man who spoke to me see through the contrived cheeriness?

I lifted my hair on top, then brushed it lightly and tucked it behind my ears. I then fastened two round white earrings and re-examined the image. I couldn't remember whether the latest style makeup required more rouge or less; to be safe, I brushed another stroke on each cheek. I still had no confidence in the result, but I consoled myself. At least, my figure had finally become stylish. Perhaps I would no longer be referred to as "that tall thin one." During my years of hibernation the Marilyn Monroe goddess had transformed itself into an elongated sylph, which helped. I didn't feel sylphlike, though, I felt fifteen years old and self-conscious, as if I were on my way to my first Knights of Columbus dance. But Helen would be there, and I would study her moves.

I'd cultivated Helen's friendship over the past few months. I watched her carefully. Helen was worth watching. She gave parties, joined groups—singles, encounter, career. Her appearance changed dramatically as she altered it for each occasion. If I queried her between costume changes, she would answer with a question, "How can you find yourself without looking?"

I wanted to believe that there was a real me waiting to be discovered, too, nothing like the one I'd been living with the last few years—one who could act on impulse, do things just for fun. I parked my car, got out, and straightened my long skirt. I practiced my mirror smile while rehearsing a series of phrases I hoped would carry me from the front door to wherever Helen was stationed in the house.

I picked up my casserole dish from the front seat and trudged down the path to Helen's house. I hadn't questioned the request for a baked dish earlier, but now it seemed out of place. I couldn't remember bringing cooked food to events in my single days. You don't come to a party on impulse with a pot of macaroni in your hands, I thought.

When I opened the door, a man with drooping eyes looked at me expectantly and asked, "What's the casserole?" He tagged after me into the kitchen.

"Tuna," I said.

"We have two tunas already," he said, as if waiting for me to change my answer.

"Well, I'm tuna number three then," I said, using my practiced smile for the first time.

"I like Spanish rice," he said.

"Sorry," I said, peeking past him and into the dining room and living room where all but my hungry friend were gathered. What the hell, I thought, and edged my way around small groups of people, all of whom seemed to know one another, and sat next to a gentle-looking man who was either resting or as unfamiliar with the ritual as I was. His face lit up when he noticed me. "I keep trying these get-togethers," he said, "but it doesn't help."

"Help what?" I mistakenly asked, after which he reviewed the past twelve years of his life, during which his ex-wife had put him through hell, he said, none of which was his fault.

As soon as he turned his head to pick up his glass from the table, I whipped myself up from the sofa. He hardly noticed; another unsuspecting woman had slipped into my place.

After I'd been at the party an hour or so, I cornered Helen in the kitchen. I told her it was different from the old days; that I'd been listening to accounts of divorce and children and custody battles all evening. "Is it me?" I asked her. "I thought I'd be defending my honor by now. I believe I could walk through here naked without notice."

Helen told me not to worry. There was this problem of the walking wounded, she explained—they spot a newcomer and pour it all out again. Then she looked brighter. "Don't give up," she said. "Underneath, some of these men are very nice people. We're going to have great times together. Give it a chance."

By the time I got home and peeled off my panty hose and placed my big white earrings on the nightstand, I'd managed to alter my first impression of the evening. I was even feeling proud of myself. I thought of the experience as an initiation. I acknowledged that it hadn't been much of a test. Nevertheless, I hadn't been singled out as peculiar, and I felt a sense of accomplishment.

For weeks after that, I followed Helen around just the way I had my sparkly girl friend Shirley in high school. I was getting better at the posturing, turning out a double entendre, promising something I needn't deliver. It was easy to learn superficial behavior, but this world of options still frightened me.

What I really craved was the tenderness of a caring relationship, but that was out of the question, as dangerous as a walk through a minefield, I believed. The alternative was a casual encounter, and the thought of that made me cringe. I'd never tried one-night stands, and I suspected I wouldn't be very good at it.

Old married friends and family suddenly overflowed with unrealistic advice. "Barbara, just accept an invitation to go out to dinner now and then. There's nothing wrong with that." As they saw it, a gentleman, stimulating and handsome, would appear long enough to wine and dine me. At the close of the evening, he would kiss me on the cheek sweetly, implying ever so subtly a wish for more than the kiss on the cheek, but he would never insist on more. Of course it followed that I could summon him up again, when needed.

I harbored no such fairy-tale illusions myself, which is why I was consumed with ambivalence when it came to accepting an actual date with a man. Why, then, was I going to the parties, joining Helen's clubs, I asked myself. In order not to face the issue, I searched for anything that would allow me to label a man unacceptable: a word of improper grammar, hair too slicked down, too fluffed up, white socks, dark socks. If he remained attractive in spite of my relentless picking, I became anxious. If, however, a presentable man didn't seem interested in me, I was hurt, but secretly relieved.

Finally I ran out of excuses. As I ran a lipstick over my lips, I promised myself if I was pursued at the singles' party that evening, I would commit myself to a future engagement. My only requirement was that he speak the English language moderately well and not have a record of mugging old ladies. I was going to do it.

When I returned home, the deed had been done. I had a date lined up for the following Saturday night. I tried all the next day to remember what he looked like. I wouldn't have recognized him in a group of ten. Was he blond, brunet? I couldn't recall.

Saturday came, and every time I pictured myself walking out the door with him I ran into the bathroom. I'd had a case of diarrhea all day. What if my neighbors saw us leave, I worried. What would they think? And what about Sean and Terry? I put off talking to them until late afternoon. They leaned on elbows on the table, appearing totally absorbed, as I ran through a long explanation ending, "So I'm going out to dinner with a friend—a man friend."

"You mean you have a date," Sean said.

"Well," I said, trying to collect myself, "I wouldn't call it a real date."

"Why not?" he asked. "Sounds like a date."

"It's OK. Mothers who don't have husbands always go out on dates," Terry added, looking pleased with his knowledge.

"But that part is hard for me because of Dad," I said.

"I guess Dad wouldn't mind," Sean said, "unless this creep wants to kiss you and be lovey and stuff."

"Do you want him to kiss you, Mom?" Terry asked.

"Wow," I laughed. "Kiss me. To tell you the truth, I can't even remember what he looks like."

"Geez, Mom," Sean said. "What if he's freaky looking?"

"He should be handsome," Terry said. "'Cause you're pretty. So he should be handsome." Terry was at the stage when he thought his mother was beautiful. Sean had passed through it.

Sean now felt it was his duty to tell me I "looked dumb" much of the time and to call attention to my faults. "What's wrong with your hair?" he would ask. "It looks doofey. It's not normal. It's too curly on the ends."

My nerves got shakier as the time of my date's arrival approached. Why was I doing this? I'd had more confidence when I waited for my first date to the spring concert in the eighth grade. I tried to chase the boys outside, but they sat like two stuffed animals on the sofa, waiting with beady eyes to look him over.

He was blond, after all, it turned out, but not up to the boys' expectations. It was written all over their sober faces.

I hoped my jitters were temporary, but they hung on all evening. My conversation over salad and steak was stilted; the wine didn't help. My movements were awkward. Why not relax, I asked myself. Give him a chance. Look at him. He has a strong face, an easy smile; he's dressed nicely; his suit isn't polyester; he's talking about something other than sports, and he actually has a sweet manner.

But nothing helped. The hours stretched before me like a drive across the Great Plains. I snuck a look at my watch at eleven-thirty. Early, but still a respectable hour to call it quits.

All the way home in the car I made small talk and worried over how I would discard him at the door. He would expect to be invited in, I supposed. I hesitated on the porch, and he reached an arm around my waist; his hand gently urged me toward him. He touched my chin and caressed my cheek, and then our lips touched. I hadn't been kissed for so long; if anything, I expected to respond too readily. Instead, I felt nothing but embarrassment. I pinched my lips tightly together. The harder he pressed and the closer he held me, the more I resisted. It seemed my body had become as unbending as a sheet of steel.

He finally backed away. His good night included no polite pretenses about the likelihood of further engagements. I closed the door and leaned against it as if to ensure that he wouldn't change his mind and try to open it again, though that would have been the last thing on his mind. He was probably halfway down the

canyon by then, counting his blessings and heading for the nearest barroom. I unglued myself from the door.

By the next morning I had not only forgotten what he looked
like, I'd also managed to look upon the experience as not quite
the flop it had been. By afternoon I was fairly glowing with the
realization that I'd spent an entire evening with a man. I was
ready to try again, but next time my approach would be different,
I told myself. I had to look at this problem objectively. I would
have to think of myself as two people: one who would live in the
present, another who would be there waiting for Bill when he
returned in the distant future.

Whatever happened to me, therefore, would occur in a vacuum; it would have no meaning. I convinced myself that it would
work. Now that I had rationalized what I was determined to do,
however, fear put on a new face. I was afraid that I'd adjusted
too well to the lack of sexual activity in my life. I'd read that
abstinence lessened desire, and I became obsessed with a wish to
disprove that. My problem was that the years had magnified the
importance of the act itself, as if fidelity to Bill were imperative to
his survival. One thing I was sure of—if I had an affair, it would
have to be light-hearted. I would keep it neat and compartmen-
talized.

My next concern was that times had changed too much for me
to catch up. If I'd been divorced like Helen and other women I
was meeting, it would have been easier, I thought. They seemed
motivated by a strong desire to prove to themselves and ex-
husbands that they were still desirable. I had no such fuel firing
me. I simply wanted to feel like a sensual being again.

I accepted dates that turned into pawing sessions, evenings of
meaning yes and saying no. I felt as if I'd been thrown twenty
years back in time to back seats of cars after high-school basket-
ball games. I'd come home worn out, throw my clothes on the
bed, and take a hot bath. I'd pour cupfuls of sudsy bubble bath in
the water and argue with myself. "What are you waiting for—
sainthood?" followed by, "That was close tonight. Before long,
you're going to slip into bed with one of these characters."

I might have had an easier time readjusting if men had accepted my situation. I had to be truthful; the boys would tell them anyway. One night Terry explained, "My mom is only going somewhere with you because she needs friends, but my dad is away so it's OK with us."

The same man, hearing my entire story later, was overcome with righteousness. "I wouldn't touch you if I could," he said. "It would be like manhandling the flag."

There were two other common responses: A man would see a sexually starved woman and offer his services, or he would suddenly become fatherly, protective, and solicitous. In the first instance, I didn't want to accept favors; in the second, I became the old me and lapped up his sympathy. In any case, these reactions to my predicament were not what I needed to help me discard my ambivalence and inhibitions.

I knew a day would come—perhaps not soon, but eventually—when I would want to make love with someone; I was excited and yet terrified at the prospect. I'd gone so long without drawing strength from the physical touch, the closeness and warmth of another person. I'd forgotten the fulfillment, the precise moment of completion. I had purposely anesthetized my feelings. What harsh rules I've imposed on myself, I concluded. Bill would have been much more compassionate.

The foliage around my home seemed greener, the sun warmer that summer. When my children played raucously, I smiled. They were mine to enjoy when and how I wanted, not sparingly during stolen moments. Today was all that mattered; it was all I could count on. The war was a distant rumble.

Just as I was wallowing in my moment-to-moment enjoyment, Mrs. Benson came to call. She'd been sent by the Neuropsychiatric Research Unit of the Center for POW Studies in San Diego. I backed my chair away from the table as she spread her papers across it. I eyed her warily while she sat there asking endless questions and talking about the problems of severe readjustments that the prisoners would experience when they returned.

She filled in blanks and wrote long paragraphs in specified sections until finally she seemed satisfied. She would have enough information when she finished her cross-country swing, she said, to answer the needs of our families when the time came—when that time was, she had no idea, however. Her job was to ready us for the homecoming of the prisoners.

I mulled over this new incursion into my life after she left. I soon heard from others who'd also been subjected to the probing of "project homecoming" representatives.

JoAnn called me after her briefing. "One thing you can bet in this election year," she said, "they intend to leave us with the impression that this administration has done so much that all the prisoners might come walking out of the jungle any minute. I think I'll tell the Marine Corps, if Chuck ever gets back, they know where to find me. Otherwise, just let me be."

Though I, too, ridiculed Mrs. Benson's mission, her talk of imminent releases had left me feeling unsettled. The part of me that was Bill's wife daydreamed again about prisoners returning to the open arms of wives and sweethearts.

My coping system was dependent upon my ability to become interchangeably two separate people I had created—the woman who waited for her husband and the one who lived for today. Suddenly, beyond my control, I felt that the two were merging. Though I continued to spend evenings with other men, a familiar tune or remark transported me in time to Bill and another place.

I heard the report on the radio at night: An Australian freelance photographer who had been held for twenty-nine days by Pathet Lao guerrillas had been released. In the morning I went out for newspapers and read all the accounts of his confinement. He repeated conversations he'd had with his captors about American pilots shot down and captured in Laos.

The guerrillas told him that in Sam Neua Province the entire population lived underground because of intense U.S. bombing. They said there was a bakery in Sam Neua that made bread especially for the American prisoners, because the Pathet Lao realized Americans were not used to a rice diet. The Australian asked the

Lao Communists how many American pilots they held, and they answered that there was no way to know the exact number, but there were at least 200.

I realized one of them could be Bill, and my world was shaken again. I didn't know how much longer I could walk the emotional tightrope I'd rigged for myself, but I sensed not for long.

27. PEACE IS AT HAND

JULY 1972 Helen was confused by yet another change in my behavior. She had listened intently to my brave words about starting over and believed me. We continued to plan adventures together. Sometimes I'd go through with them and other times I'd back out with contrived excuses. One night I called at the last minute to tell her that I wouldn't be joining her in San Francisco that evening. "Please make up your mind," she said. "How much longer can you live with such uncertainty—not knowing what you really want?"

It was a legitimate question. I was feeling more torn every day. Becoming politically active again would mean withdrawing from new friends, gambling that they would be there later when I needed them. I would have to become the missing-in-action wife again. I would have to reenter limbo.

I fought doing that, and yet as the Democratic Convention approached, I found myself calling Sheila at the Families for Immediate Release headquarters in Washington again. Sheila, Shirley, Valerie, and Minnie Gartley would be at the Democratic Convention. Knowing this made my decision to stay away more difficult.

In the middle of the night I'd find myself planning a press

conference—what our group should say, how McGovern should respond. In the morning I'd call Bob Sherman and I'd be full of ideas. Afterward I'd pull the phone from the wall jack again.

During the week of the convention my mood swung from pride to regret: pride in the women as I read reports of their press conferences and interviews, and regret that I wasn't sharing it all with them.

Valerie delivered one of the speeches seconding the nomination of George McGovern. As I waited for her to appear on television that evening, I remembered the day two years earlier when I first heard of Valerie Kushner, the Army doctor's wife who told a congressional committee that her husband was more important than President Thieu's corrupt regime.

TV cameras panned around the convention hall, honing in on McGovern people who seemed to be wearing perpetual cool grins. The delegates shouted, whistled, and applauded after each speech.

Finally Valerie's turn came. She explained why prisoners' wives were backing George McGovern. "This war has done to us in a very personal way what it has done to the rest of the country," she said. "In 1968 both candidates promised to end the war, and we believed them. But the baby I was nursing when I heard those promises is four years old now. He still has never seen his father, and still the war goes on. . . ."

Reporters commented later that her words were poignant, that her speech moved everyone who heard it. She had brought the war home, they said, in a way none of the politicians could.

I felt reassured at the end of the Democratic Convention. McGovern would clobber Nixon in November, I told myself. It was just a matter of waiting. But then, a couple of weeks later, the Republicans replaced Democrats on the TV screen, and I became jittery all over again.

There were glimpses of Tricia and Eddie Cox and Julie and David and Sammy Davis, Jr., and scores of tributes—one to Pat. Afterward, red, white, and blue balloons fell from the rafters. They showed movies of the President's trip to China, and more balloons were dropped. Vietnam was referred to only indirectly;

the Young Republicans said they were disgusted with the peace demonstrators on the other side of town.

I couldn't imagine what they were going to do for two more days, but on Sunday night the "Youth for Nixon" gave a party. As they skimmed across a dance floor to oldies-but-goodies songs in Bermuda shorts and button-down shirts, I thought about young men the same age who were sloshing around in rice paddies on the other side of the earth. "Can't give up and let the Commies take over," declared one of the Nixon youths in a crisp cotton striped shirt, shorts, and loafers when a reporter asked him about the war.

The images were upbeat and optimistic. They were of good times and patriotism.

McGovern and his staff and backers had hammered away at the war issue all through the primaries. Vietnam had returned to the front pages of newspapers, and I had begun to take for granted that a peace candidate would win. The morning after the Republican Convention, however, it occurred to me that Richard Nixon might actually be reelected. The vision of that convention floor, especially those red, white, and blue balloons, floating effortlessly and joyfully over the tops of all those bouncing heads just wouldn't go away.

Whether I liked it or not, I had a stake in this election, and I couldn't stand by during its eleventh hour. Perhaps there was still a chance to change the outcome. As much as I despised reentering the political arena, I knew I would despise myself more if I remained passive.

Sheila's morale slipped along with McGovern's poll results after the Republican convention. One thing after the other seemed to plague McGovern's campaign, from his ill-fated choice of Thomas Eagleton for Vice President, to divisions among special-interest groups. Problems within the campaign itself overshadowed news of a break-in at the Democratic National Headquarters by the Nixon Reelection Committee. McGovern tried but failed to focus media attention on the real issues. As McGovern faltered, donations to

Families for Immediate Release fell off. There was never enough money to cover expenses.

In a state of desperation Sheila called to ask for my help. "My energy is depleted," she said. Her voice was trembling. "I've gotten so tied up working for McGovern and the POWs, I don't know who *I* am. I've almost become my brother. I don't regret it, but I have nothing left to give.

"We're in the last leg of our fight, Barbara," she said. "Could you dive in actively again—until the election? You don't know how I hate to ask."

The next day I plugged my phone back in full-time and Sheila took a temporary rest leave. She said she would speak at rallies, at rock concerts, in nightclubs, anywhere, but she no longer had the stamina to organize the families.

I didn't know where to start myself. How could I, the reluctant participant, cheer the team on? I hoped Sally Alvarez would give me encouragement, but when I called her she told me she was struggling to show up at McGovern functions herself. "At times I think it would be better if I just didn't wake up at all. I feel all-out sad, and like ninety years old," she said. I could hardly believe this was the woman who had set the warmongers straight, from the lowliest official to Dr. Henry Kissinger himself.

I was thankful the groundwork in most of the states had been laid, that our group was a known entity to the McGovern staff. I made one or two calls of encouragement a day, but for the most part we were all on our own.

On Labor Day weekend I traveled north to the seacoast town of Fort Bragg. Sean and Terry and I were guests of honor in the town's annual Paul Bunyan parade. We rode down Main Street in a convertible plastered with "McGovern" and "POW wife" signs. Red, white, and blue streamers tacked to our float dragged behind us like a bride's train. When the parade began, I felt like a strange species on display. As we passed the local bank and drugstore and five-and-dime store, though, I suddenly felt as if the whole town had gathered us up in a tender embrace, and I began waving back at people who lined the streets. They were blowing kisses and holding two fingers in the air to form the peace sign, and I wanted to believe that this was the real America, that the negative commentators were all wrong.

When I returned to San Francisco, I felt invigorated. I did talk shows, radio tapes, and newspaper interviews. The McGovern people bolstered one another with talk of a miracle that would turn things around. Realistically, however, they knew the chances of winning were growing slimmer every day.

Senator McGovern was having a hard time campaigning against a President who seldom came out of the White House. The press complained that Nixon wasn't answering questions about Vietnam or anything else. At the same time, the *Washington Post* was beginning to reveal the extent to which the break-in at the Democratic headquarters by the Nixon Reelection Committee was only the tip of the spying and sabotage iceberg. "The major purpose of the subversion activities was to create so much confusion, suspicion, and dissension that the Democrats would be incapable of uniting after choosing a Presidential candidate," the *Post* reported. I was amazed at how well the strategy was working. McGovern was kept on the defensive, shadow boxing, never landing a punch.

But then Radio Hanoi broadcast that three prisoners would be released to the custody of Cora Weiss and Dave Dellinger, and I hoped our miracle had come. The families of the three prisoners were invited to come to Hanoi to accompany their sons and husbands home. Minnie Gartley's son, Mark, was one of those to be released; the other two were Lieutenant Norris Charles and Major Edward Elias.

It was the opportunity we needed to gain the attention of the U.S. electorate. We knew Minnie would use the dramatic event to full advantage. Our history teacher would speak frankly.

"Just don't be afraid," Shirley told Minnie as she was about to board her plane at Kennedy Airport. "Remember, we love you."

A reporter asked Minnie if she feared government displeasure with her trip. "No," she said, "I'm doing what my heart tells me."

Another newsman asked Olga Charles, Lieutenant Charles's wife, what she was bringing her husband. "Myself," she said. "I'll be the best present he could have."

Major Edward Elias's wife, however, was not going, because the State Department disapproved of the trip. JoAnn called from Nashville to tell me she was disgusted with Mrs. Elias's decision. "If they told me not to go to Hanoi to get Chuck, I'd have hung up the phone," she said. "That Mrs. Elias is a typical military wife—when the Air Force says pee, she pees!"

During their first four hours in Hanoi, the women had to run for air-raid shelters several times. Olga Charles, after the fifth run, commented, "And I was silly enough to think they'd stop bombing while we were here."

"At a ceremony in Hanoi," reported the Associated Press, "an American mother joyfully clasped her prisoner-of-war son, and an American wife embraced her husband in a room hot with glaring television lights."

When asked how he felt, Mark Gartley said, "I am elated at the prospect of gaining my freedom, but at the same time I realize that as long as this conflict continues, the dissension and unrest in the United States will go on, more pilots will be killed or captured, and many friends now in detention camps will be unable to go home. I cannot be truly happy until they all come home, too. . . ."

The three told how they tried to be optimistic in camp about when the war would end, but the longer they were there the harder it was. Mark said, "One guy kept saying, 'Just think, two more weeks and we'll all go home.' But he's still there. I have seen men go from black hair to gray hair to white hair."

When interviewed along the way, Lieutenant Charles said, "I hope I have made it clear that I am a McGovern man. . . . I feel that only by ending this war will all the prisoners come home. . . ."

The released prisoners were en route when I got a call from Bob Sherman, who was now one of McGovern's speech writers. Bob said that the POW release story was breaking and they wanted me to appear with the senator the following evening in San Francisco. I should meet staff people at a cable car in front of the Alioto Restaurant on Fisherman's Wharf, he instructed, and then join McGovern on the balcony of the restaurant where he would address the gathering.

The crowd on the wharf was growing by the time we got there. "I'm suffocating to death," Terry screamed dramatically. About the same time, a mild rain turned into a downpour. Squishing our way around puddles, we squeezed through the crowd until we reached the cable car where we were to meet the McGovern staff. Clutching each boy by a hand, I tried to climb aboard, but a campaign volunteer stopped me.

I hung onto the rail with one hand and Terry's coat sleeve with the other. "I'm with the campaign," I said. "Barbara Mullen— POW wife. Weren't you told?"

"Please, lady," he said, "just join the crowd. McGovern will be speaking from the balcony soon."

"What's going on, Mom?" Sean asked. "When do we meet McGovern?" Water dripped off the end of his nose. Terry's jacket was soaked.

"I guess someone got mixed up," I said. "Let's try to walk up the hill to the garage if we can get through this mob."

It was almost midnight when we got home and I called Bob. It was three in the morning at his end, but he seemed to take it in his stride. "You can afford to be calm," I said. "You're not drenched to the skin."

"OK, Barbara, let me see if I can contact John Holum and see what happened," he said. "He's with McGovern. They'll only be in San Francisco till tomorrow, and we have to get some mileage from this prisoner release. Stay up awhile, will you? We'll get back to you."

About twelve-thirty John Holum called, full of apologies. "Could you be at the Jack Tarr Hotel by nine in the morning?" he asked. "McGovern would like to do some newspaper interviews with you. Just answer questions, informal like—the two of you together."

John had said to ask the receptionist on the mezzanine for Dick Dougherty, McGovern's press secretary. When I got there, the receptionist was surrounded by a crowd of people. Intermittently she was scribbling notes, answering the telephone, and chewing on the end of her pencil.

Finally I got her attention. She shoved the pencil behind an ear and said, "Just a minute. I'll try to find Mr. Dougherty."

Dick Dougherty appeared a few minutes later. "Just follow me," he said, and made a special point of smiling.

So far, so good; at least he seems to know why I've turned up, I thought, and trailed after him. He brought me into a small suite of offices, where I was told to make myself comfortable. I sank into the nearest chair but was sure it was not within my ability to be comfortable just then. I watched groups of people rush in and out of the close quarters and its anteroom for ten or fifteen minutes. "Mr. Dougherty," I said, finally asserting myself, "I typed up a rough draft of the sort of answers I thought I'd give the press. Would you mind giving it a glance to see if it coincides with what the senator will say?"

He took the paper from me but was immediately interrupted when Frank Mankiewicz wandered in. Dougherty then set my draft on a desk and brought Mankiewicz over to meet me.

"Hello, there," Mankiewicz said. "Good to have you with us. We can use your help. We'll be with you in a few minutes."

Mankiewicz leaned back in his chair and stretched a foot across the end of the desk. He seemed to be enjoying himself. He made three or four phone calls. Each conversation was laced with jokes. In between, he was getting people to promise all sorts of things. All the while he talked, he kept eyeing my plaid skirt and tailored blouse, appraising the product to see if it would sell, I guessed.

Just then, Mankiewicz's attention was diverted. Hubert Humphrey had walked through the door. Mankiewicz put his hand over the phone and with a sweep of the other hand made a quick introduction. Senator Humphrey shook my hand and slid into a chair beside me; he seemed glad to have a place to alight. "How would you like a cup of coffee?" he asked, and smiled pleasantly.

"I'd love one," I answered.

When he came back with the coffee, I said, "Senator Humphrey, we've met before."

"In Washington?" he asked.

"No," I said, "at a tiny airport in northern Michigan, back in 1966. I was scared to death, but I approached you anyway. I asked if you would try to get me some information about my husband. His plane had been shot down ten days earlier."

Humphrey's expression changed immediately. He suddenly seemed morose and gazed off across the room. Was he recreating the scene? "Yes, I remember that day," he said finally.

"Have you heard anything?" he asked after a moment.

"Yes and no," I answered. "I learned enough details to know he could be a prisoner of war—no more."

"Such a long time ago," he murmured, more to himself than to me. And I wondered what personal regrets might lie behind his abrupt change of mood.

"The only thing about the circumstances that has changed over the years is me," I said. And then, trying to lighten the heavy gloom I'd created, I smiled. "I'm not as frightened as I was that day."

Gary Hart and others popped in and out; I was no closer to finding out what I was to do, when George McGovern walked in. He seemed strangely removed from the frenzied activity around him. He looked relaxed, more like a friendly neighbor who had just strolled in than a Presidential candidate, I thought. But Mankiewicz moved with a sense of urgency for the first time, and I realized with a start that he was picking up my draft answers from the desk where Dougherty had tossed them. He handed the paper to McGovern, who asked, "Is this from Dougherty?"

Mankiewicz answered, "Yes."

McGovern now thought my one-in-the-morning notes were a draft release from his press secretary. Before I could explain, Dick Dougherty reappeared and said, "Senator Humphrey, could you accompany Barbara Mullen?"

McGovern had already left; I didn't know which reporter or reporters were about to interview us.

Senator Humphrey took me by the arm. As we reentered the lobby, making our way down a center opening that had been cordoned off, I felt as if I were marching to the altar with Hubert Humphrey about to give me away. But quickly enough it came over me that we were heading up an aisle indeed, but it was leading us straight to a platform. Bright, hot TV lights pointed at the area. When I blinked, Senator McGovern came into view. In a split second I would be up there with him. My mind flashed, "He must be giving a speech, and I'm going to be at his side."

When we reached the platform, Senator McGovern received me from Senator Humphrey. I felt McGovern's hand on my shoulder and then heard the Presidential candidate announce, "I'd like to introduce Barbara Mullen, the wife of a man presumed to be a prisoner of war for six and a half years. She and her organization have done an extraordinary job of trying to end the war and gain the freedom of the prisoners. She would like to address you this morning on behalf of those goals."

Jesus, I thought, as I looked out at all the familiar faces of a national press corps—greats from the networks and wire services, notable columnists. I hadn't a word planned for this. Please, if there is a God, I prayed, let my mouth open up and issue forth some understandable words.

"I'm supporting Senator McGovern because he will bring an end to this murderous war." There, one sentence out. I thought of another. "He will also bring men out of prison cells after years and years of confinement. Think if you had been caged in an eight-foot-by-eight-foot square since 1966. Think how you'd feel hearing bombers night after night, their venomous excrement from the sky reminding you that it was not yet over.

"Three of those men were released this week. I hope President Nixon will allow them to speak when they return. I hope our own military will not take away the freedom just given back to them by the North Vietnamese. They have earned the right to tell their story. Everyone has spoken for the POWs. It is time they speak for themselves. Will our President be afraid to hear what these three men will say?

"We are proud of the wife and mother who went to Hanoi to bring their own loved ones home. The President has had four years to do it himself and has failed. I urge the American people to vote for Senator McGovern."

Papers rustled; news people rushed off. Senator Humphrey was again by my side. This time I was glad to have his arm. He guided me through the crowd. I looked back; Senator McGovern was motioning thank you.

Senator Humphrey suddenly held my hand tightly and leaned toward me. In my ear he whispered, "That was eloquent. Eloquent. And courageous."

I was at the top of the stairway leading down from the mezzanine. Several people had already surrounded Humphrey, and Frank Mankiewicz was standing in front of me. "Thanks, thanks so much. It was great," he said.

I walked down the stairs in a daze. I hadn't even asked him why I'd ended up being the main speaker. I wandered into the bright California sunlight, down a San Francisco street away from the Jack Tarr Hotel, and turned into the nearest coffee shop. It was filled with laborers, secretaries, and businessmen on morning break. Life just goes on, I thought. A waitress swished a damp cloth over the counter and nodded. "Just coffee," I said.

A large AP picture of McGovern and me appeared on the front page of the *Oakland Tribune* that afternoon. We looked as if we were about to embrace at the end of an old Bette Davis movie that would then fade away into a star-filled moonlit sky. The story began: "Sharing the podium with the Democratic Presidential candidate was Mrs. Barbara Mullen of Oakland, coordinator for Families for Immediate Release. . . ."

I finished prying a knife loose from a mass of peanut butter and jelly that had cemented itself to the kitchen counter just as Sean ran into the room. "Look at the newspaper, Sean," I said. "There's your mom on the front page with McGovern."

"Geez, Mom, that's awful," he said, laying it on the table. "You look like you're going to kiss him on the nose."

My previous day of national politicking would have seemed no more than something I'd imagined were it not for a call from Captain Jim Johnson at Marine Corps Headquarters. "I saw you

on the national news last night," he said. "You did a good job.
You have every right to express your opinion on this war and the
election, you know."

"Thanks, Jim. I appreciate that," I said.

When the plane with the three released pilots landed at Kennedy Airport in New York, they were met by a high-ranking delegation of military men and Pentagon officials. An argument broke
out when Roger Shields of the Defense Department informed
Mark Gartley that his request for two days' leave with his family
before being examined and debriefed would not be approved.
Minnie insisted that the military fulfill its part of the release
agreement. "We just want him to ourselves," she said, "free of
the government, the Navy, and the North Vietnamese for a few
days."

"He's an officer in the United States Navy," Shields answered.
"He has to come with us now."

Minnie couldn't speak; she began sobbing, and her son reached
an arm around her shoulders. "My mother hasn't cried in years,"
he said. "You may have pushed this too far."

Pentagon officials told the men to change into uniforms and
then ushered them off the plane before the press was able to
speak with them.

About two weeks later Mark Gartley came to Washington and
called Sheila. She went to see him in a motel in Alexandria. He
said he had heard Sheila's brother's name on occasion, but they
had never been in the same camp. He said he couldn't talk about
very much because he had military orders telling him not to. She
began to discuss the political situation with regard to the election
and the war, but sensed a mounting tension. She changed the
subject, welcomed him home, and left.

On Monday, October 23, reports out of Washington indicated
that some sort of cease-fire accord was near. Hints of this were
also coming from Saigon, Cambodia, Laos, and Hanoi. Nothing
about this surprised me. I'd expected speculation about peace a
week before the election, and I listened with a cynical ear. As

details were revealed, it sounded like the coalition government proposal that the President and Dr. Kissinger had turned down many times in the past.

Reportedly, Hanoi was willing to accept a cease-fire, provided that Saigon agreed to a three-sided interim government that would rule the country for about six months until general elections were held and a new government and constitution were created. The tripartite group would consist of Viet Cong, South Vietnamese, and neutralist elements in equal numbers.

On Tuesday, October 24, Henry Kissinger returned from talks with President Thieu in Saigon. The next day the headline read: THIEU WON'T ACCEPT ANY CURRENT PEACE PROPOSAL.

"After this last fight," Thieu said, "the war will fade away."

On Thursday, in the early morning, Hanoi's international radio issued the full text of a statement on the state of negotiations and asked that the Viet Cong, the United States, and South Vietnam immediately sign the agreement along with them, the North Vietnamese.

"Peace is at hand," Henry Kissinger promised over the radio and TV later that morning. I should have thanked God for those words, but I didn't believe them. I felt that Hanoi had forced Kissinger to verify its own public statement. I knew now that Nixon's election was guaranteed, and I resented that Henry Kissinger and Richard Nixon would take credit for an unsigned peace treaty that offered nothing we couldn't have gotten years earlier.

The October 31 target date originally set for signing slipped by. On November 1 Nixon said the United States was not about to be rushed into signing the peace accord. The day after that the administration insisted that another negotiating session was needed to put the accord into final form, but a North Vietnamese spokesperson said, "Everything has already been agreed to. The agreement can be signed within minutes."

Once more Richard Nixon had managed to dangle a promise of peace before anxious voters. Bob Sherman tried to console the women in our group, saying if it weren't for efforts such as ours and McGovern's, the war issue wouldn't have survived the campaign, that President Nixon would have dropped it like a hot potato. Even if that were true, it wouldn't change the results of the election now.

In California, the projections had already been made before the polls closed on election night. Sally Alvarez called, but we were no help to each other. I wanted to call Sheila or Shirley or Alice all evening but somehow couldn't pick up the phone. In her apartment in Washington Sheila sat alone. Someone had given her a candle in the shape of Nixon's head. She lit it and numbly watched it burn away.

28. THE LIST

JANUARY 1973 A bleak gray sky hung over Washington, where gala Inauguration Day preparations were underway for President Nixon's followers. Thousands of others who attended Leonard Bernstein's Inauguration Eve "Mass for Peace During Times of War" were quiet and somber, the beauty of the concert serving only to intensify a feeling of futility for many.

I had spent the past month in my house reading letter after letter from dear old friends who were as finished as I was. There was nothing left to do. The mistrust of Nixon, disappointment in the American electorate, and the horror of the bombing, renewed in late December, were all-consuming. The administration gave no excuse for the bombing this time. Perhaps, some said, this brutal weapon was being used to force changes in a peace accord rather than as an instrument of war. We could only guess and wait.

When it was reported early in the day on January 17 that the President was going to reveal a final peace agreement, I hardly paid attention. But my phone rang all day: Bill's folks, my family, then Sheila and the other women. CBS asked Sheila if they could film her reaction to the President's announcement on TV that evening. News people called me requesting telephone interviews after the speech. There was a different feel to the news bulletins this time, and in spite of myself I was getting caught up in the excitement.

By the time a TV camera circled the Oval Office and slowly moved in on the President, I was too nervous to sit down and watch. I paced across the carpet, casting half-glances at the TV set. I hoped he would end the war but hated him for using the announcement as a demonstration of personal triumph. He looked straight into the camera and at us. He started with platitudes. Why didn't he get to the point? Ready to defend myself against a barrage of propaganda, I was only half listening when his next words slipped out.

"There will be a total release of all American prisoners within ninety days," he said. I was afraid I had heard him wrong. As he continued, I tried to grasp the full meaning. Who are "all the prisoners"? Do they know who and where and how many?

Sheila, Shirley, Alice, Bob, and Carolyn called me and called one another after the speech. I heard from Sally and Delia Alvarez. "I can't believe it," was answered by the same phrases, time and again. Finally, when everyone had calmed down a little, they expressed concern for me.

"I can't enjoy the thrill of the news thoroughly until I know if it includes Bill and the rest in Laos," Alice said.

Then Bob called back and said he would find out as much as he could about the agreement with regard to Laos. He was worried that it was the same proposal Kissinger had revealed before the election which had not mentioned Laos.

This agreement had better include Bill, I thought. He was as much a serviceman as Michael or any others who happened to be shot down over North Vietnam. When the phones stopped ringing that evening, I contemplated the full implications of the announcement and a calmness flowed over me: At last the killing would stop. I felt no personal elation, however. I had an intuitive sense that none of this would affect Bill or me in any way, and I couldn't explain why.

NBC called Sheila that evening to ask if she would be inter-

viewed by Barbara Walters the next morning on "The Today
Show." She agreed, saying to herself, "Thank God, my swan
song. This is it."

When Barbara Walters asked what she thought of the peace
agreement, Sheila answered, "I don't see how a dishonorable war
can be ended honorably. One can only say that it was ended—
that we got out," and then she added, "I hope the peace accord
covers the men missing in Laos and other parts of Indochina as
well as Vietnam."

The North Vietnamese and Viet Cong were to give us the "list"
of POWs on Saturday, January 27; Henry Kissinger explained
that the North Vietnamese would be responsible for giving us the
names of "all" the POWs.

I decided to go away for the weekend—somewhere where I
could be by myself when the news came. I didn't want to talk
with reporters, well-meaning friends, or family. I needed privacy
in a place where I could not be reached by telephone. I would not
be at the mercy of that silent instrument again! I would be in
charge this time. Captain Johnson at Marine Corps headquarters
said I should call him every two hours on Saturday until they'd
received the list.

Before leaving, I put a note on the kitchen table for the baby-
sitter:

> The boys' piano lessons are Saturday at four. Terry is going
> to a birthday party for one of Helen's boys on Saturday night
> and needs a present ($4.00 in the envelope). The boys are
> both playing football at Montclair Park on Sunday after-
> noon. Their school bus picks them up at 8:30 Monday
> morning. Don't forget the sack lunches. Thanks.

That takes care of the weekend, I thought, but what about
Monday? How will the world look Monday morning, I wondered.
I threw my bag in the car, kissed the boys good-bye, and drove up
the coast toward Mendocino.

As soon as I got to the lodge, before carrying my bags up to my room, I called the Marine Corps from a public telephone. They said that they didn't know how long it would take to transmit the names from Paris; I should call back at four o'clock.

I was glad to be alone. I would sit downstairs in the main room of the chalet and collect myself. Two couples sat at opposite sides of the room, engrossed in their partners, unaware of me or anyone else, which suited me fine. Tremendous wood beams pointed to the sky, giving a spacious effect. I felt I had room to breathe. At the same time, a stone fireplace whipped up flames from below, emitting a protective warmth. I sat in a chair by the fire for an hour or so until I felt calm enough to go for a drive.

I stopped at a coffee shop and ordered a sandwich, but the bread felt like dry cotton balls in my mouth; I left the sandwich half eaten on the plate. I checked my watch every few minutes. At four o'clock I called the Marine Corps from a pay telephone in the restaurant.

"Not yet," Captain Johnson said. Headquarters must have been frantic with people calling. I wanted to wait longer before calling the next time, but I dialed them again as soon as I reached the lodge.

I called three more times. By nine-thirty I was prepared for another "not yet," when Captain Johnson asked, "Barbara, are you OK?"

"Yes, fine," I said, but I felt my heart pounding.

"Bill's name was not on the list."

"OK," I said, surprised by the sureness of my voice. "It's best to know."

"Yes," and he paused. "I was really hoping to tell you something different."

"We had to know," I said. "Have Bill's folks been contacted?"

"We're sending someone over from Weymouth Air Station," he said.

I hung up and dialed the Massachusetts number. I was amazed at how well I was doing. "Oh, Barbara," Mary answered. "These two officers came to the door. They brought a telegram. I couldn't look at it. Dad read it and he told me Bill's name wasn't on the list. Dad doesn't care what they say. He doesn't believe it. The men left a minute ago. Wait. Dad wants to talk to you."

"Barbara, don't pay any attention. I know our Billy is alive. To hell with their lists," he said. "You keep your chin up now. Here's Mary again."

We'd always been able to end with a consolation: "Don't get down. We'll hear soon. . . ." Now we had heard, and I couldn't think of another thing to say. This was it. I felt weak; I couldn't seem to catch my breath. Suddenly I gasped and choked out a few words. "Mary, I can't talk now. I know how you feel. My love to you and Dad. I'll call you tomorrow. I'm so sorry."

"Take care of yourself tonight, Barbara," she whispered in a raspy voice.

"You too," I said, but was not sure she heard. I had never broken down with either of Bill's parents before.

I felt my way up the wood stairs to my room, hanging onto the railing all the way. I threw myself on the bed and cried—all the tears held back for years, hidden from children, hidden beneath layers of hopes and prayers, dried with the heat of hostility and reasoned arguments. At last I was able to cry.

It was 4:00 A.M. when I pulled my sweater and slacks off and crawled under the quilt. As soon as daylight came, I got up and dressed and drove up the coast a short distance. I parked the car and walked to the edge of a steep embankment. Perched on a flat piece of rock, I sat motionless for hours, watching swells of blue-green water move smoothly toward shore before crashing against the rugged cliffs, thereby causing their own destruction. I felt cast ashore, along with them. I'd lived so long with my dream—a myth, really. I'd looked at other possibilities, but always, down deep, I knew now I'd believed Bill was alive.

After several hours I felt drained, almost cleansed. Surely I could manage as I had been; I'd already been alone such a long time. I would still be alone—not waiting for someone as before, but alone. I got up to leave and remembered I hadn't eaten all day. It was late afternoon, and I suddenly felt very hungry.

After dinner in the lodge dining room, I went to bed and fell into a deep, heavy sleep. I woke up early, filled with an intense desire to go home. I wanted to see Sean and Terry.

It was only seven-thirty when I stopped at a roadside restaurant for breakfast. I glanced at newspapers on a stand near the cash register and thought, They can't hurt me anymore. I may never read a newspaper again. I'd begun to turn away when a headline jumped out at me—LAOS POW LIST NOT INCLUDED.

I felt dazed and light-headed; I held onto the counter for a moment. How could they? I ran back to the car. Later I couldn't remember driving the rest of the way home.

I was glad no one was in the house when I got there. The baby-sitter had left, and the boys were in school. On the kitchen table were three loose-leaf notebook pages of messages, and on top was a telegram from the Marine Corps:

JANUARY 30. THIS IS TO CONFIRM THE INFORMATION PROVIDED YOU BY YOUR CASUALTY ASSISTANCE OFFICER THAT YOUR HUSBAND MAJOR WILLIAM F. MULLEN'S NAME WAS NOT ON THE LIST RELEASED TO OUR GOVERNMENT ON 27 JANUARY 1973 OF PRISONERS HELD IN SOUTHEAST ASIA. THERE WILL BE NO ACTION TAKEN TO CHANGE HIS STATUS FROM MISSING UNTIL WE HAVE HAD AN OPPORTUNITY TO ANALYZE ALL INFORMATION PROVIDED OUR GOVERNMENT AND OBTAINED FROM THE RETURNING PRISONERS. YOU WILL BE KEPT INFORMED OF ANY FURTHER DEVELOPMENTS.

R. E. CUSHMAN, JR., GENERAL, USMC, COMMANDANT OF THE MARINE CORPS

Why "prisoners in Southeast Asia"? UPI knew the list hadn't included Laos—why didn't the Marine Corps? I was certainly going to find out, and I was going straight to the White House to do it. I got a number from information and dialed. "I want to speak to Dr. Kissinger about the list he didn't get from Laos!" I told the first voice that answered. He said that someone would contact me immediately, and I shouted into the phone, "Now! Not tomorrow!"

James Murphy, a deputy assistant at the State Department, called me within minutes. "Mr. Murphy," I said, "I was told by the Marine Corps that the list didn't contain my husband's name, but I understand that we didn't get *any* names of those held in Laos."

"The list should be coming from the North Vietnamese on those in Laos," he said. "We hope they will give a list to Dr. Kissinger."

"What do you mean, you hope?" I asked. "Do you mean there is nothing in writing requiring a list of POWs in Laos?"

"It's not in writing, but it is understood that the North Vietnamese will be responsible for getting us the Laos list. There is a four-party commission."

"But it's not in writing? Nothing in the peace treaty states that all the POWs in Indochina will be released as the President promised? Dr. Kissinger said he had a guarantee that all the prisoners would be released when he announced the signing."

"No," Mr. Murphy said, "it's not actually stated that it covers Laos."

"You mean this four-party commission has no written authority to go into Laos, to find out about those men, to get them released? Who belongs to this four-party commission?"

"North Vietnam, the Viet Cong, South Vietnam, and the United States," he said.

"What good does that do in Laos?" I was trying hard not to lose control, but my voice was trembling.

"Well, we have to trust that the North Vietnamese will get us that information," he said.

"You mean we should trust the North Vietnamese, whom President Nixon has told us not to trust for years? Is this the airtight agreement he boasted about—after all our waiting? How about the MIAs—will they be accounted for in the sixty-day period, while our withdrawal takes place as he promised?"

"No, but . . ."

"Do you want to know how many letters I have from our President saying that the men would not be abandoned? What does go on in Laos? Is there no treaty there?" I asked. "Does the war just go on there? If we continue bombing there, do we expect them to give us information on those men?"

"We're not clear on that," he said.

"Not clear? Does this peace agreement that our President and Dr. Kissinger signed include Laos at all?" I asked.

"No, it doesn't," he said.

I hung up and dialed the Marine Corps and asked for Captain Johnson. A Marine sergeant said Captain Johnson was unavailable. The Corps was sorry, he added; they hadn't realized on Saturday night that the list did not include men in Laos.

I stared at the phone after I'd replaced it—how long I wasn't sure. Was I supposed to live on their crumbs of hope again? I hadn't moved from the chair by the kitchen telephone when the phone rang again. It was my sister Shirley. "Barb, are you OK?" she asked. "I don't know what to say. I've been listening to the news all weekend. I can't believe there was no list from Laos. We tried to call you Saturday."

"I just never thought it would be like this, Shirl. I let myself go through all this grief over the weekend. I don't know what I'm supposed to do now."

"How could they put you through such hell? They must have known none of those men in Laos was on the list. Especially since we're still bombing the hell out of the place. I just can't tell you to keep the faith any longer, Barb. Let us know anything we can do. Anything," she said.

I found another telegram under my pages of messages. This one was from my brother Floyd, and was just two sentences:

IN PAST WARS WOMEN HAVE SEARCHED POSTED LISTS PRAYING NOT TO FIND A FAMILIAR NAME. IN THIS CONFOUNDED WAR WE HOPE YOU WILL. OUR LOVE. FLOYD, YOLANDA, ANNIE

The following Thursday, February 1, the so-called list of prisoners in Laos was handed over to our government by the North

Vietnamese. It consisted of six names, all of whom were men whose planes had been shot down near the Laotian–North Vietnamese border. The men had been held captive in North Vietnam. Our government was calling it "the POW list from Laos," yet none of the nearly six hundred servicemen missing in Laos was on it. The list hadn't come from the Laotian Communists.

My anxiety had been building all week. Each bit of news substantiated my worst fears—that our government was simply writing these men off. What else could it mean if our government had accepted this list of a mere six men out of six hundred? That evening I received another telegram from the Marine Corps:

I REGRET TO CONFIRM TO YOU THAT YOUR HUSBAND MAJOR WILLIAM F. MULLEN'S NAME WAS NOT ON A LIST RELEASED ON 1 FEBRUARY 1973 TO OUR GOVERNMENT OF PRISONERS HELD IN LAOS. THE INFORMATION YOU WERE PREVIOUSLY PROVIDED REGARDING ANY CHANGE IN STATUS REMAINS UNCHANGED. YOU WILL BE KEPT INFORMED OF ANY FURTHER DEVELOPMENTS.

R. E. CUSHMAN, JR., GENERAL, USMC, COMMANDANT OF THE MARINE CORPS

Americans thought the war was over. Many POW families were rejoicing. A reporter from the *Montclarion,* a local weekly newspaper, called and I let her come over as much to have someone to talk to as anything else. I rambled on and she listened. I told her it was disheartening to see the media talking about peace. "The President says we can now go on to other things. Yet I'm sitting here, no different than I was six years ago, knowing no more. After four additional years of bloodshed, President Nixon has no agreement covering Laos. This is not an 'honorable' peace, as he claims. The world thinks the war is over, and my boys have no hope of a returning father."

I sent a telegram to the President and asked, "What about POWs in Laos? The Laotian Communists have talked about them for years. They've described their treatment and their condition.

As far back as the summer of 1969, Sot Pethrasi, the Pathet Lao spokesman, claimed they were holding 158 Americans. What kind of cover-up is this?"

When no one answered my queries, I asked the State Department to send me a copy of the actual treaty which the Republic of South Vietnam, the Provisional Revolutionary Government, the United States, and North Vietnam had signed. After reading the sixteen mimeographed pages applying to the release of captured personnel, I knew for certain that Laos was not covered by the treaty. The Protocol concerning prisoner return stated that it was binding only on "the four parties participating in the Paris Conference on Vietnam." Article 1 began: "The parties signatory to the agreement shall return the captured military personnel of the parties . . ." and Article 13 ended, "The Protocol shall come into force upon signature of the Protocol, each party shall publish the text of the Protocol and communicate it to all captured persons covered by the Protocol. . . ." The "list" I had waited for that weekend in January was never meant to include Bill.

Senators Cranston, Tunney, and McGovern, Congressman McCloskey, people at Another Mother for Peace and Common Cause, and all my old friends were compassionate, but no one knew how to help. In an attempt to clarify the administration's position on the prisoners in Laos, Bob Sherman and Congressman Leggett wrote Secretary of State William Rogers:

> I am troubled by what appears to be a serious shortcoming in the Vietnam agreement, and by an internal contradiction in Dr. Kissinger's description of it.
>
> On January 25 Dr. Kissinger said, "American prisoners held in Laos and North Vietnam will be returned to us in Hanoi."
>
> Neither the Agreement nor the Protocols at any point mentions American prisoners held by the Pathet Lao.
>
> In his January 24 press conference, Dr. Kissinger said, "The only protocols that exist are the protocols that have been made public. . . . There are no secret understandings."

> Clearly there is a contradiction here. . . . These questions are literally matters of life and death for the families of men lost over Laos. Please let me hear from you within a week.

Congressman Leggett's answer from the State Department reaffirmed that there had been no agreement in writing for the release of the men in Laos. The administration, however, didn't mention this omission when explaining its peace treaty to the American public.

On February 17 the Communist Pathet Lao said, "We will not free our American prisoners of war unless there is a cease-fire in Laos. If they were captured in Laos, they will be returned in Laos after a cease-fire there."

A cease-fire was signed in Laos between the U.S.-backed Laotian nationalists and the Pathet Lao on February 21. American participation in the Laotian war had always been secret, and they were not signatories to the cease-fire now. During a thirty-day period both Laotian parties who had signed the treaty agreed to set up a coalition government. Fifteen days after the signing, complete lists of prisoners held were to be exchanged between the Laotian nationalists and the Laotian Communists. The nationalists would then give the list to the United States. Sixty days from the signing—by May 21—the Laotian Communists were to release their prisoners.

Pathet Lao officials who were asked about the POWs said, "They will be released as prescribed in the agreement, but we cannot give a number."

I waited through the fifteen-day period and hoped that our government would hold them to their promise. When questioned, Secretary of State William Rogers said, "We just don't know yet how many are held captive in Laos."

The specified fifteen days came and went, but no list was received. Nevertheless, to my dismay, Ron Ziegler announced a few days later from the White House that *all* the lists had been received and *all* the American POWs would be released by March 29.

I knew Ron Ziegler's words were a lie—all the prisoners would not be released. In a letter bursting with fury I asked the Commandant of the Marine Corps how our government could abandon men because they had become missing in the wrong place. "How could none of the nearly six hundred men in Laos be alive?" I asked. "In North and South Vietnam, one-third of the men shot down turned up as prisoners. On that basis, there should be several hundred prisoners alive in Laos. Where are they?"

The Commandant's reply promised me that these men would not be forgotten.

In a syndicated column Guy Wright shook himself loose from the cloud of euphoria that enveloped the nation. He wrote:

> The time has come to ask a dreadful question: Are we really getting all our POWs back from Indochina? Or has the enemy secreted some away? And if so, has our own government acquiesced in this deceit? . . .
>
> When the cease-fire went into effect, the Vietnamese Communists listed 587 U.S. prisoners, military and civilian, whom they were holding in both the north and south, and 68 who had died in captivity.
>
> At the time American officials expressed astonishment at the brevity of the POW lists, which were only 40 percent of what they expected.
>
> They promised to press the enemy for a fuller accounting. But except for an occasional stray, the enemy figures haven't changed.
>
> It is our own government's attitude toward those figures that has undergone a transformation. From indignation and disbelief it has switched to resigned acceptance, with tongue clucking toward anyone who doesn't go along. . . .
>
> . . . Then there's the prize puzzle of Laos, where we

listed hundreds of men missing. . . . Even more incredible, the Pathet Lao listed no one who died in captivity.

Unless a better accounting is forthcoming, it will be difficult to avoid the conclusion that "peace with honor" involved swallowing some peculiar scorekeeping where the counters were human lives.

29. SOME CAME HOME

FEBRUARY 1973 Captain Jeremiah Denton, tall and thin, but holding himself erect, descended the stairs. He saluted fellow officers and walked as far as a microphone at the end of a long red carpet. He thanked God and country and everyone for his freedom and said, "I think more than ninety-nine percent of us would say faith in God got us through it. Perhaps our communion with God was improved by the rigor of our circumstances."

One by one, they disembarked from the plane. "We lived on loyalty," said the second man when he reached the microphone.

"You had to have a sense of humor," said another. "For instance, that light at the end of the tunnel; we looked at it for a long time."

They had lost weight and were pale but managed to walk unassisted. The stories of the brutalities they had suffered would not be revealed until later. Physically frail from eight years of captivity, Everett Alvarez, nevertheless, carried his slight frame with dignity. At the end of the carpet he spoke quietly. "People just don't realize what they have until they've lost it," he said.

They had landed at Clark Air Force Base in the Philippines. The names, called out one at a time, were familiar to me—Alvarez, Sally's son, Delia's brother; Closkey—Shirley's brother;

Mulligan—Louise's husband; Stratton—Alice's husband; Butler—Julie's husband; Glenn—son of Mrs. Curtis Glenn of Oklahoma.

The networks had canceled all regular programming to broadcast their arrival. The boys sat next to me on the sofa and watched in silence, as I did. It was a glorious occasion, yet I could only mourn the wasted years leading to it. Absorbed in the drama, I didn't think about its effect on Sean and Terry—what must be going through their minds. When the last man had departed the plane, Terry put his hand on top of mine and said, "Don't give up yet, Mom, I think Dad's still in the back of the plane. He's probably hurt and needs someone to help him out."

After other programming resumed, Terry kept staring at the screen. Sean took note of my own immobility and stood up. "Come on, Terry," he said, "this is only the first plane, you know."

Lieutenant Commander Everett Alvarez, Jr., arrived at Travis Air Force Base the following Saturday, February 17. From there he was flown to Oak Knoll Navy Hospital in Oakland, where he met his father, Sally, Delia, and the rest of his family. After an emotional greeting a reporter asked him what kept him alive. "Faith in my country and faith in my fellow prisoners," he said.

I talked to Sally a few days later. "We've had you in mind every day, Barbara," she said. "Come over, please, as soon as you can, to meet Everett. He's fine. He won't be home with us for a couple of weeks, but he's gaining weight and seems in good enough spirits. Thank God."

"I will," I assured her, all the while wondering if I could bear to do it. I felt like a character in a tragic drama who had been left standing alone on the stage.

As if she'd read my thoughts, she added, "I want our friendship to be the kind that lasts our lifetime, no matter what roads we travel. If you need us or me for anything, just ask."

Alice called me a few weeks later to tell me that Michael would be released with the second group. "Now that he's coming, I don't know how I waited all these years," she said. "Another week seems eternity. I'm feeling so much for you, though, Barbara. It hurts knowing that Bill isn't coming back now with the others."

"Don't let that interfere with your wonderful moment," I said.

"I can't believe it's not resolved in Laos," she said. "I never thought it would turn out like this. I can imagine the pain you feel. God knows, you've been a loyal wife and a caring mother. You and Bill deserve for him to be coming back with the rest."

"I can't talk about it," I said. "You just have a happy reunion with Michael. Get on with your lives now."

"But I care about you—whatever happens. Remember that," she said.

I knew she cared, but I couldn't share her joy, and I didn't want to spoil it for her or minimize it for her. I wanted to be alone, to numb myself to the events that were unfolding. How could my friends know how much it hurt to hear about the homecomings?

The day Michael was to arrive in the United States, Sheila, an older sister, and a younger brother flew to San Diego to meet him. They drove to Alice's house and found her in a frenzy. Sheila assured her that her red knit dress was becoming, demurely proper, yet deceptively seductive. Alice had just finished shaving her legs and had managed to nick herself several times. In the limousine on the way to the airfield, she removed tiny pieces of toilet paper from her cuts and wiggled into panty hose.

At Miramar Naval Air Station a military welcoming committee led the whole family into a brightly decorated lounge where other wives, mothers, fathers, and children waited. Windows looked out on the runway. The atmosphere was tense. Most people seemed unsure how to behave. They accepted glasses of champagne served by waiters and tried to relax. Spells of elation and anxiety intermittently replaced each other.

Outside the terminal, WELCOME HOME signs were sprinkled throughout a gathering crowd. Alice's friends held a long banner—twelve-inch red letters shouted WELCOME HOME MICHAEL CRONIN. Microphones were set up at the end of a red carpet as they had been when the prisoners disembarked in the Philippines.

A voice from a wall speaker announced that the plane would be a few minutes late. More champagne was passed around. The families sipped in moderation—no one wanted the precious moments on the runway blurred in any way.

Sheila went to the ladies' room, where a little girl, about five years old, was primping in an organdy ruffled dress in front of the mirror. Sheila smiled at the youngster's serious concern over her appearance. "Who do you know who's coming home?" Sheila asked her.

"My daddy," the girl said. "Of course, I was born after he was shot down."

"Don't worry," Sheila said, "he'll be very pleased with you."

As they left the rest room, the loudspeaker announced the arrival of the plane carrying the released prisoners. As if the body of people had en masse sucked in its breath, the room suddenly became quiet.

Off to the left, the plane came into view, and the families were led outside and told to stand on one side of the red carpet facing the crowd. The plane came to a stop alongside the carpet; each man deplaned. His name was announced, he shook an admiral's hand and walked to the microphone. As soon as he had uttered his grateful thank-yous to the world, his family surrounded him.

When one man turned from the microphone, six children broke loose from their mother and ran to him. He embraced his wife and hugged his older children, and then his wife went over to a little girl in an organdy dress who was observing the confusion from a few yards away. Taking her by the hand, the mother brought her over to her father. He leaned down, picked her up, held her high in the air over his head, and then squeezed her to him.

When Michael came down the stairs, Sheila noted that he looked gaunt and older, but all she cared was that he was alive. He reached the microphone and smiled for the first time. "It's great to be back in the greatest country in the world," he said.

Alice burst away from the rest of the family and ran to him. He nearly lost his balance as she threw her arms around him. Seconds later the others ran toward him, too; he hugged each of them separately. At first he almost seemed bewildered, unable to comprehend what was actually happening, but then his large blue eyes filled with tears. Sheila looked at him and suddenly realized that none of them would ever know the hell he'd been through.

The night before the third and last group of POWs was to be sent home, the U.S. government made a request through the Joint Military Commission that POWs in Laos be released. The last U.S. combat troops were to be pulled out of South Vietnam that coming weekend.

Phuong Nam, chief spokesman for the Viet Cong delegation, accused the Americans of trying to delay the last troop withdrawal since "there is nothing in the cease-fire agreement or its protocol on prisoner releases which permits the American government to ask the Provisional Revolutionary Government or the Government of North Vietnam to also release POWs held by other countries in Indochina." In fact, he said, it was an illogical request.

Plans therefore went forward for the last group to be released by the end of March. Many, however, were still unaccounted for—Maerose's husband, Margaret and Sam Beecher's son, Mitch Jones's husband, Carol Hanson's husband, JoAnn Connor's husband, Joan Vinson's husband, and on and on. But Americans didn't want to think about those still missing, the wounded lying in veterans' hospitals, or tombstones spread across our country. They wanted an escape from news of a dreadful war they had never understood. They threw out a red, white, and blue welcome mat for the prisoners who had returned. Travel, hotel accommodations, automobiles, ski lessons, lifetime passes to pro baseball games, summer cruises to the Greek islands, vacations all over the United States, record albums, money in savings accounts, and spa memberships were offered to the men and their families. Their children were taken to Disneyland, showered with Mattel toys and an array of other items.

A bit incongruous, I thought, that children of men who hadn't come home were being ignored completely. We hadn't heard a word from the POW Studies Center in San Diego, either. What had happened to the stacks of questionnaires and elaborately laid-out plans? The vow that MIA families would not be forgotten?

At the center of the festivities, Richard Nixon immersed himself in the sweet bouquet of fine heroism emanating from the released prisoners. The President beamed as he offered a toast at the Defense Department and declared, "History will vindicate my Vietnam policies." On the way out of a Pentagon luncheon he stopped to speak with people behind a roped-off area. How good the uniform now looked, he said, recalling that so many brave men had done so much for their country, for peace in the world. "What do you think of our POWs?" he asked the group.

A man in the crowd answered, "God bless you, Mr. Nixon." The President smiled broadly and shook hands along the ropes.

A woman shouted, "Thank you for bringing them home, Mr. President."

"In the right way," the President interjected. "They served and they wanted to come home in the right way, standing tall and proud. Their sacrifice was not in vain."

In solitude, I asked, Wasn't it his own policy that had kept them confined to cells, added hundreds to their numbers, and allowed unknown numbers to die in captivity? Their return was substituting for the battlefield victory that had eluded the President, and there was nothing I could do about any of it.

I hadn't seen Margaret and Sam Beecher of Indiana since the day we'd picketed the White House together. Their son had not returned, and she wrote me now:

> I would be less than honest if I did not say this has been a most difficult month and a half. It has been wonderful to see my many friends' husbands and sons returning. Sam and I share their joy. But our lives can never be the same.
>
> I trust you are all right. I have thought about you and all your hard work and the impact you had on so many people with your organization. . . .

Colonel Scott Albright, who represented the League, made a trip to Saigon near the end of March, after the last prisoner release from Vietnam. When he returned, he stated, "Most of the MIA casualty sites cannot be seen or photographed from the air. Nearly all of those in Laos and many elsewhere are in what is still hostile territory—which means we must receive permission through negotiation to go in or to send someone else in. Many, if not most, of the sites are in dense jungle areas, some of it three-canopy jungles. Many crash sites are known to be booby-trapped, and many have unexploded ordnance on board. Few can be reached over ground."

On April 6, ABC News reported that the Pathet Lao had killed their POWs because they lacked the facilities to detain them. The next afternoon, in Washington, Brigadier General Russel Ogan, director of the Defense Department POW/MIA task force, answered questions about the prisoners in Laos. We can only speculate on the report of executions, he said, because our government honestly doesn't know what has happened to these men. When asked if we had ever received a list from Laos, he stated, "Some officials of the Pathet Lao have said that there are no prisoners and that 'there are many graves along the Ho Chi Minh Trail.'"

On April 13, Dr. Roger Shields, of the Defense Department, said, "There is no basis for these stories," when asked about reports that many airmen in Laos were summarily executed by the Communist Pathet Lao.

If there was no basis for the stories, where, then, were the prisoners? Early in the morning and late at night I agonized over unanswered questions. With our CIA swarming over Laos throughout the war, why didn't they know those POWs were disappearing—if they were disappearing? If they had known, would they have told us? Would the American people then have allowed more pilots to fly those suicide missions?

A Western journalist conducted an interview on April 24 with Sot Pethrasi, spokesman for the Pathet Lao Communists. He asked Pethrasi, "Since hundreds of Americans are listed as missing in Laos, is it possible that there may be prisoners in remote areas about which you previously knew nothing?"

"It is not possible," Pethrasi answered. "They came to

massacre us and we had to defend ourselves. . . . If they had wanted to stay alive, they should have stayed in the United States. That was their fate if they were unlucky."

"Is it possible that villagers, angered by the bombing, may have killed American fliers who reached the ground safely?" asked the journalist.

"No, that is not possible. They were bombed and they were angry, yes, but they are very disciplined. We have a very good organization. In all villages we have people, and they give orders to the villagers that they must not kill prisoners."

"Did any of them die in captivity?" the journalist inquired.

"No. All our prisoners were well-treated," Pethrasi insisted. "I do not know that any died."

"It is known that many men reached the ground safely. Are you quite certain in your own mind that there are no prisoners?" pursued the journalist.

"What I say is clear. It cannot be clearer," Pethrasi answered, and added, "You seem very interested in these criminals."

"Yes, I am interested," the reporter replied.

I was distressed by the contradictions. If the prisoners were not killed by villagers and did not die in captivity, where were they? We had, in truth, sent men into a secret war, unprotected by a treaty of peace later. It was nearly summer and the men in Laos, as far as anyone knew, had either been executed or were still held in caves in mountain hideouts. I recalled how two years earlier, at the San Clemente White House, Dr. Kissinger had promised us, "We will settle an overall agreement for the accounting and return of all men everywhere in Indochina." But in the end, it appeared, Bill was being deserted by his own government.

In the late spring I heard from Vivian Johnson, my McGovern co-worker, in Fort Bragg. She said that the memory of our days in Fort Bragg and the Labor Day parade were still vivid in the minds of townspeople. She asked if the town could dedicate a freedom tree and a plaque in Bill's honor. She insisted it wasn't in memoriam; they hadn't given up on Bill. All the same, I knew that's what it would seem to be. I agreed, thankful that at least someone had remembered him, and I asked that the dedication include all the disabled veterans and other MIAs of the Vietnam conflict and that the theme be one of peace.

The ceremony was conducted on a sunny afternoon. The mayor presented the plaque to the town and a tree on which the plaque would one day rest was planted in front of an old railroad station.

An Air Force officer had flown in from a base near Sacramento to make the dedication speech. "Few if any of these men had such high-flown thoughts as 'Give me liberty or give me death,'" he said. "Rather, they died with words unspoken or words that were brief and urgent. They gave their lives for various immediate reasons: for a comrade, because theirs was an obligation to serve, or simply because at that particular time and place their country asked them. . . ."

Underscoring the ambiguity of the occasion, a city official ended with a promise. "Somewhere in Laos it is presumed that there are prisoners of war," he said. "Could Major Mullen be among them? We must be sure that the search for him and others shall not be abandoned."

On May 24 the released prisoners of war were briefed by the President, Secretary of State Rogers, and Henry Kissinger, while Mrs. Nixon gave a complete tour of the executive mansion to their wives. Afterward, on the south lawn of the White House, the President and Mrs. Nixon gave a festive party for the men and their wives to celebrate the return of "all" the prisoners.

Perhaps those men in Laos were alive—perhaps they were dead. One thing was certain—the President didn't know which.

30. NEXT TIME

Over the years, many had prophesied the outcome. Three and a half years earlier, on an icy cold day in New Hampshire, Edmund Muskie had said, "All of the lives, all of the wounded, all of our millions of dollars will have no effect upon resolution of their political problems when the time comes because it simply isn't possible for this country, powerful as it is, militarily, economically, politically—it is simply impossible no matter what our intentions, however good they may be, to settle the political problems of Vietnam. It just will not work. So all of this has been wasted, and when we finally leave, they will find their own way to settle their problems and we may not like the result when it comes."

A few months later Edward Kennedy, speaking at the Press Club in Washington, had said, "The present government of South Vietnam will immediately wash away in the stench of its own inconsequence and incompetence and corruption when the Americans leave Vietnam."

And now that it had happened there was hardly a ripple of concern. The worst consequence nationally was a deflated spirit. Our resources had been drained by a surrogate enemy; our real defense capability had been weakened by our Asian escapade. Yet no one wanted to talk about the conflict. It appeared that our longest war would have the shortest memory.

It had been more than two years since the book on the prisoners of war had been closed—the chapter on Laos having never been written. In some ways it was as if the war had never happened. There were times I wondered if I had imagined all of it. Yet it had changed my life forever. I was a single mother, working, caring for twelve- and fourteen-year-old sons. I was calling myself a widow—no one wanted to hear that my husband was still missing in action.

The week Saigon fell, a UPI man tracked me down at my office. My son had given him the telephone number, he said. He asked if I would like to comment on the imminent defeat of South Vietnam. His very question seemed to threaten my privacy; I wanted nothing to jeopardize my present existence. If they didn't care about Bill, why should they bother me?

I told him that there was nothing left to say. It was all in vain unless we'd learned something. All the sacrifices—the dead, the wounded, the missing—couldn't alter the result. "It was their country, wasn't it?" I said. "A costly lesson."

When Nixon resigned the summer before, I was unable to summon the slightest compassion for the haggard-looking man on television who rambled on about his mother and morals. He left the White House in his helicopter as the remaining Americans were to escape from the roof of our embassy in Saigon. As I watched him disappear like a fly in the sky, out of vision, I thought how little his suffering was in comparison to that of hundreds of thousands who fell victim to his decisions. He was being punished for the misdemeanor, not the felony. I felt no vengeful pleasure in his demise, however. It was too late for that.

The war should have been over, finally, now that South Vietnam had surrendered. But there was one unresolved issue. The missing-in-action files remained open, lying around on desks, rather than stacked away in archives with the rest of the unpleasant memories of a nasty war. A class-action suit by some of the families had prevented the military from making any more "presumptive findings of death." There was only one way Bill could be declared killed in action, and that was by my hand. The responsibility had been handed back to the next of kin. Until it was done, our own lives remained as tentative as ever.

Some had taken the difficult step. Maerose had held a memorial service for Jim the previous fall. Mitch Jones had done the same a month earlier and then moved to Texas to make a new start. JoAnn Connor had gone back to school and was now a librarian. Carole Hanson had changed her husband's status and married one of the released POWs.

The fortunate ones whose loved ones had returned tried to leap over the gap of years that had separated them. Julie Butler was expecting another child. Sheila was a social worker in a large hospital. Valerie's husband was in private medical practice. Shirley Culbertson was doing work for volunteer social organizations. Louise's husband was running for Congress. Minnie's son was secretary of state for the state of Maine. Alice and Mike Cronin were expecting a baby.

Maerose and the other League women had worked relentlessly and loyally on projects I had thought irrelevant. She never understood my ability or desire to challenge. And now that it was over, I found myself worrying about all of them, those who had challenged and those who had not, hoping they'd find happiness in spite of the lost years.

Soon after the phone call from UPI, my privacy was invaded by another voice from the past. A letter arrived from the POW Studies Center in San Diego. Three years had gone by since Mrs. Benson had visited me that afternoon bearing her long questionnaires and promises. I understood the center had provided the returnees and their families with a good deal of counseling and assistance, but as far as I knew, wives of the missing men had never heard from them.

This new communication asked if I would set aside another afternoon to spend with one of their representatives. Attached to the letter from Marina Hynds, a psychologist, was another 26-page questionnaire. Besides a couple of pages of inquiries about our physical health, the form asked for personal information on other topics: recent sexual difficulties, drug addiction of a family member, a new close relationship. The covering note instructed, "We would like you to complete the Recent Life Changes form prior to our visit."

A week or so after the forms arrived, the psychologist called to set a time for the interview. I asked her why they hadn't gotten in touch before this—when we needed them. "This is different," she said. "We're compiling information now. We're doing a comprehensive follow-up on both the women and the children involved in order to record the ill effects of long separation on their physical and mental state of health."

"You mean you want to see what damaged children I have and how crazy I am in order to complete your study?"

"Well," she said, "we'd like to see what the effects have been and record them. So next time we can do a better job."

"Next time!" I said. "Mrs. Hynds, will you please go to hell!"

In April 1976, a year after the fall of Saigon, Sean turned fifteen and Terry was thirteen and a half. Ten years had passed since the day Bill's plane was shot from the sky. Though I would never be free as long as he was listed as missing, it seemed against all the principles of nature to declare one's husband dead with a stroke of the pen. I only had to sign a consent form; it was as easy as allowing a child to have a measles shot. A diabolical plot, I thought, to delegate this guilt-ridden task to the one least able to do it. How we worshipped the printed word; it could cancel a person.

Major R. H. Dietrich was current head of the Casualty Section; I'd never spoken to him before Bill's status was to be changed. How many "heads" of Casualty had there been? Where was Captain Johnson now? Or Colonel Abblitt, my first, back in 1966? I wondered. I signed the forms and mailed them to Major Dietrich. Once he processed the forms, Bill's status would be changed to deceased; I would legally be a widow. Without proof of death, however, the Marine Corps would keep him on its missing-in-action list.

I waited for the telegram. It was delivered on May 5.

I DEEPLY REGRET TO CONFIRM THAT THE STATUS OF YOUR HUSBAND, LIEUTENANT COLONEL WILLIAM F. MULLEN USMC HAS BEEN CHANGED FROM MISSING IN ACTION TO DECEASED. THE EXACT DATE AND PLACE OF LIEUTENANT COLONEL MULLEN'S DEATH ARE NOT KNOWN. BASED ON A REVIEW OF YOUR HUSBAND'S CASE AND THE LACK OF INFORMATION THAT HE SURVIVED, IT IS PRESUMED THAT HE IS DECEASED. ON BEHALF OF THE UNITED STATES MARINE CORPS I EXTEND OUR HEART-FELT CONDOLENCES IN YOUR BEREAVEMENT.

LOUIS H. WILSON, GENERAL, USMC, COMMANDANT OF THE MARINE CORPS

I felt no different the day after I received it from the day before. When Bill's mother and father asked if a memorial mass could be performed in his hometown of Brockton, Massachusetts, rather than on a military base, I didn't object. It didn't seem to matter to me one way or the other. Once I had agreed, however, I began to look forward to it, thinking that perhaps a memorial mass would help me to believe that he was dead.

On May 9, 1976, ten years and ten days after he'd become missing, the service was held in a church where Bill had been an altar boy as a child. Priests had come and gone. It was a large parish; none remembered him now.

The Marines, once more in their splendid uniforms, were waiting on the sidewalk in front of the church when we drove up. Perfectly creased blue pants, red stripes down the sides, strode toward our car. A pair of spotless white gloves reached into the back seat to help me out. None of these men attached to a nearby Navy reserve base had known Bill. Many of his old Corps buddies, in fact, had already had memorial services of their own.

A moment of regret passed over me as the major offered his arm to escort me into the church and down the aisle. I should have tried to find old friends, I thought. Bill should have had a flyover with a missing plane. He would have liked that.

Bill's mother and father sat in the front pew with Sean and Terry and me. I was proud of the boys. They were both tall for their age and quite handsome in their grown-up suits. Sean looked so much like his father now. It surprised me when I glanced at him hurriedly—it was like seeing Bill again. Terry was like him in other ways—he was open, spontaneous, and happy most of the time.

The priest came over to where we were seated before the mass began. He held Bill's mother's hand. When he turned to leave, she said, "Father, this is Barbara, Sean, and Terry."

He nodded and went up to the altar. I wanted this to be something for the boys to remember. But when the priest began his eulogy, he spoke of "the boy" who died for his country, and I sensed that something was wrong. I knew Sean and Terry couldn't think of their father as "a boy." Bill was a career officer of thirty when he went to Vietnam.

The priest said we should remember the suffering of his parents whose son never returned. When the eulogy was finished I realized that he hadn't mentioned a wife or children. I wanted to run up to the priest in his fine vestments and beg him not to be done with it, to cry out, "He wasn't a boy. He was a husband, a father. These teenagers are his."

The highest-ranking Marine officer, however, was already coming up the aisle. He had a questioning look on his face. No doubt he was confused by this strange memorial service that had ignored the wife and children. He took my arm and we started back down the aisle. Another Marine waited for Bill's mother and dad and the boys. Two enlisted men carrying the flag followed all of us out of the church. This isn't happening, I thought. It can't be over. I don't feel anything at all.

We went back to Bill's parents' home, but I found it difficult to make small talk with guests. I wanted to start the day over, go back to the church, begin again. People asked if I had been disappointed in the service; I kept my answers vague. Bill's mother was busy arranging the buffet lunch. We had been through so much together; I couldn't bear to tell her how unfulfilled I was feeling.

Bill's relatives and old school friends were there, but no one was present to remind me of the life Bill and I had together. Later, after everyone had gone, I left the house and drove to the nearest drugstore. I hadn't realized how much I'd relied on the mass to put things to rest. Even as I dialed the parish number on a public telephone, I wondered why I was doing it. There was no way to repair the damage now. A woman answered and said that Father Linahan was having his dinner. I explained who I was and said that it was urgent.

He came to the phone, and I told him I was the wife—I paused and said "widow"—of the Marine for whom he had conducted the memorial mass.

"Who?" he questioned, and then said, "I didn't know that the young man was married."

"How young would he have been, Father? He became missing in 1966. His sons are in their teens now." I tried to control the trembling in my voice.

"Whenever the Marines mentioned 'Mrs. Mullen,'" the priest said, "I had taken for granted they meant the mother. I just never thought he might have been married. We think of a serviceman as a young man, a boy." The priest said that it was a grievous mistake. Had he known that the serviceman was married, the mass would have been directed at the widow and the children. He said he would have talked of our love and devotion. He would have mentioned Bill's continuing love for us where he is now. And he would have said some special uplifting things for the boys.

"Yes, that's what I wanted," I said.

I regretted that I hadn't done it at a military base, but it was too late now. Bill deserved the pomp and circumstance, bands, ticker tape, the flyover. They all deserved it—these Vietnam heroes.

I hated to return to the house. I couldn't tell his folks how distraught I was. Bill was their boy who had gone off to war, and

340

that was what he would always be. The bizarre circumstances of
the years were what had thrown everything out of chronological
order.

A few days later Bill's mother and dad took me out to the family cemetery plot to show me a tombstone. On a large marble
stone were the chiseled words "Lt. Col. William F. Mullen, Jr.,
loving son of Mary and William." What about loving husband,
loving father? I thought. I wanted something for me. I needed a
finality that never seemed to come.

The next day I called the Marine Corps in Washington to ask
if Bill was eligible for a plot at Arlington Cemetery.

A month later the Marine Corps sent me a photograph of a
plain white marker upon which was engraved:

IN MEMORY OF

WILLIAM FRANCIS MULLEN

LT. COL.

U.S. MARINE CORPS

VIETNAM

1935–1976

The picture of the marker reminded me with a twinge of Irish
fatalism that Bill had always asked me to listen to the beautiful
second verse of "Danny Boy": "But if you fall, as the flowers are
dying and you are dead as dead you well may be, I'll come and
find the place where you are lying and kneel and say an Ave there
for thee."

Thinking of all the lost Bills and Larrys, the Hamburger Hills,
and the rhetoric, I wondered where and during which bungled
chance for peace he might have died, if indeed he had died.

Not long after the marker was in place, I called the Marine
Corps again to ask if Bill's medals were being held somewhere. It
seemed irrational that I should care, but I wanted someone to

say, "Hey, boys, in spite of that ill-fated war, your dad was of the right stuff, he was courageous and appreciated."

The Marine Corps said that of course there were medals and they would send them on to a local Marine contingent. A Marine captain, belonging to a small Marine Corps unit at a local Air Force base, called a few weeks later to say he had the medals. He asked us to pick them up the following Friday.

The boys dressed in their best, down to the leather shoes. But in the car they hardly talked. This is contrived, I thought. They're probably just going along to pacify me.

A sergeant behind a counter took our names and dialed a phone, joking with whoever had answered on the other end. "Captain Foley says he'll be right out," he said, still smiling.

The building was one of those "temporary" structures made of corrugated material that looked as if it wouldn't make it through a rainstorm, but had withstood the elements since 1942. The walls were painted what Bill called "sick green" because all the infirmaries and hospitals were covered with it. The chairs had straight wooden backs and arms; on the seats were worn plastic cushions. The place reminded me of a dispensary where I had taken the boys when they were babies in Pensacola, Florida.

Captain Foley could be heard laughing down the hall. At the same time, he clapped a passing fellow officer on the back and motioned to us. "Hi, there, come on with me," he said.

When we reached his office, he told us to sit down and asked the boys about school and what sports they liked. Then he took off on a discussion about the Red Sox, which seemed to be his favorite baseball team. Neither of the boys were contributing much to the conversation. An enlisted man came in with some papers which the captain signed. The young Marine asked if I'd like a cup of coffee and then told the boys where to find a Coke machine down the corridor. It began to dawn on me that there was no real presentation ceremony planned. Finally I said, "Captain, can we see the medals?"

"Yes, they're right here," he said, and pulled a large manila envelope from a drawer. He emptied the contents on the desk and several odd-sized velvet boxes tumbled out along with a sheet of white cardboard. The medals were pinned to the cardboard. "I guess they're all here," he said.

Just then the boys came back into the office with opened Coke cans. I realized, seeing them in this military environment, that their hair was much too long. I supposed I should have forced them to have it cut. They're being too polite, unnaturally subdued, I thought, and I questioned again why I was putting us through this.

"If you have a camera, I'd like to have a picture taken," I said.

Terry gave me a cold glare.

"Sure, we have a camera out front. Just a minute," the captain said, and dashed out.

"Let's get out of here," Sean whispered stiffly. "As soon as he gets back."

The captain lined us up in a row. Just before he clicked the camera, I shoved the medals into Sean's hand. The captain then went back to his desk and gathered the leather boxes into a pile on the desk and pushed them back into the envelope with the back of his arm. He crinkled the envelope at the top like a bag and handed it to me.

When we got back into the car, the boys crawled into the back seat together. They weren't speaking to me or to each other. We'd driven past the guardhouse before I tried to cut the icy silence. "Sean, take the medals out of the bag and read what the tags say, will you?"

I couldn't think why I didn't just let it drop. I watched Sean through the rearview mirror. Two or three minutes later he stuck one of his hands into the bag. "This one is from the Republic of South Vietnam," he said, trying to mask his own curiosity. He glanced at another. "The Purple Heart, Mom." He looked at the rest of them without reading out loud and then set the bag on the seat next to him.

Terry sighed and looked out the car window.

I wanted to say something to reestablish my credibility with the boys. The occasion had been a disappointment to them, though they weren't going to admit it. Start somewhere, I thought; nothing can make this day more awkward than it is. "We don't know when or how he died," I said. "We don't even know if he died. But we do know we tried every way we could to bring him back. If I didn't believe that, I just couldn't go on. We all have to be proud of that."

"OK," Sean said. "OK, Mom. All right."

Jesus, I thought, this is going terribly.

All the way home I mulled it over. I can't find an ending, a period, paragraph—a reason. Maybe I never will, I thought, slamming the car door in the driveway. The boys rushed ahead to the house, then Sean stopped suddenly and hollered, "Hey, Mom, you left the paper bag in the car."

A couple of weeks later, Bill's effects were delivered. The driver set them down in the middle of the living room floor—two cardboard boxes and a gray-green footlocker stamped in white 074230 MISSING IN ACTION. Though the words still gave me a chill, they could no longer dilute a harsh truth: Bill hadn't returned.

I walked around them for an hour or so, wanting to open them, but afraid to do it. With the boys out, there would never be a better opportunity. I crouched down on the carpet, unfastened the lock, and slowly raised the lid of the wooden footlocker.

Strewn over the top shelf were a razor, a used bar of soap in a plastic box, and a dry toothbrush. I picked them up and set them carefully on the carpet. A large color photo of two boys about two and a half and four years old lay on top now. Alongside it were dozens of snapshots and hundreds of airmail envelopes addressed to Bill in my own handwriting. A colorful pamphlet was wedged between the letters. "New York World's Fair, 1966," was printed across its front cover. I remembered sending for it, mailing it to him. A surge of excitement passed through me; I could almost feel again the anticipation of our longed-for rendezvous in New York; then a musty odor rose from the box, reminding me of the years.

I lifted the top shelf out and set it on the floor. This had been his bureau in a tent or a wooden hut at Chu Lai. I touched the underwear he had worn and held it against my face. Once more the years seemed to fold back. I reached down farther into the box. Near the bottom my hand found a white T-shirt wrapped around an oblong object. I opened the leather box. Inside, tarnished and mildewed, was a lonely Air Medal. Like knights after the Holy Grail, they'd been taught to chase after these medals. How subdued and powerless it was now, robbed of its glory, lying neglected in this lifeless container.

I was about to search further when Terry flew through the front door. "Mom, our team won. I was the hero of the day, and all the girls thought I was terrific. As usual," he added.

"No, you weren't," Sean said.

They both stopped short when they saw the locker and the boxes. "Hey, is this Dad's stuff?" Sean asked.

Terry pounced on the footlocker. I curled up in a chair while they pulled things out, held them up, and dropped them to the floor. "Can we try them on?" Terry asked.

They threw their jeans and T-shirts on a chair and crawled into fatigues and flight suits. They stuck their feet into combat boots and clomped up and down the hall. Soon friends were brought in to view each article. Before long, it turned into something that resembled a ritual that would verify that their dad was a real person. He wore clothes, brushed his teeth, shaved.

They ran out the door wearing heavy leather boots and khaki shirts. "You can use anything but the leather flight jacket," I had said. Sporting insignia of simpler days on its sleeves, it was a chronicle of Bill's military career. The last patch sewn on was that of the First Marine Air Wing, Vietnam. Surely he had expected to wear it proudly in future years. I could picture him in it, the fur collar turned up casually at the back of his neck.

I went to bed early that night, thankful that the arrival of Bill's belongings had gone well. We are going to make it now, I thought. No regrets. I've done all I could. A peace had come over me; it had been growing all day. What I was looking for I already had. We tried, I thought, and fell off to sleep.

Suddenly, in the middle of the night, Terry cried out from his bedroom. "Mom, come here, please." He sounded like a small child again. I found him rolled up in a ball, hugging his pillow.

He was crying, and his body was shaking. Between gasps, he blurted out, "You lied to us. You always said he'd come back!"

I put my hand on his shoulder, but he wriggled away. "We couldn't give up, Terry," I said. "What if we had given up and said he was dead and then found out later that we were wrong? I always told you I didn't know. We still don't know. He just never came back. I tried to do the right thing."

"I wanted my dad back and all I got was a bunch of his old junk," he said. I wondered how a thirteen-year-old could be expected to understand this irrational conclusion.

"Would you like to wear the leather flight jacket to school tomorrow?" I asked. "It might make you feel better. I know your dad will somehow know you're wearing it and it will make him happy." Without answering, he turned toward the wall and pulled the blankets over his head.

The next morning Sean watched quietly as Terry donned the prized garment. I was surprised that Sean didn't object. Terry, the shaken youngster of the night before, stood in front of the hall mirror. He turned to one side and then the other and Sean said, "Shit, it's really neat, Terry."

Terry picked up his books, gave me a confident half-smile, and bounded out the door. His brother followed. I stood at the window and watched the jacket with its drooping shoulders and too-long sleeves disappear down the street.

EPILOGUE

<u>CAPE COD, MASSACHUSETTS, APRIL 1985</u> One small light has been left on in the corner of the living room. I am alone and in a mood to remember things tonight. It is nine years since Bill's footlocker came back from Vietnam, but I can see myself clearly that morning after the boys left for school. As if in a slow-motion film, I am moving about the living room, picking up one article at a time and tucking it back into the container. I find a black leather aviator's logbook under a pair of fatigue pants and set it to one side. When I finish the packing, I sit down and flip to the last page, where a final entry in Bill's neat handwriting reads: "Aircraft A4E, Date—April 28, 1966."

I close the book. Looking back at the footlocker, which was deposited unceremoniously in the center of my living room the day before, the word "efficient" comes to mind. It should have been stamped FINAL DELIVERY, I think. Ropes that had been tied around the wooden box are now lying on the carpet beside it. As I am deciding whether or not to retie them, it occurs to me for the first time that I might never know what has become of Bill. Perhaps the conclusion is no conclusion. I don't know how I'll ever accept such an ending with grace. Surely I'll go on thinking of

Bill at odd hours of the day or night and wonder if he is alive. I
am afraid that the uncertainty will always haunt me.

My gaze is still fixed on the crate. So this is it, I think. It isn't
much, along with those meaningless legal papers, on which to
base the rest of my life. But it's all I have.

In the shadowy darkness my mind continues to drift back over
the years. I picture Sean and Terry, not as the tall young men
they've become, but as toddlers encased in padded snowsuits
chasing each other down a path to a mailbox, stumbling and getting up. The first one lifts himself on tiptoe, and his hand
reaches into the box to retrieve a letter from Daddy. An instant
later they have been transformed into teenagers. I am facing
them from a chair across the room, and they are sitting next to
each other on the sofa. I am telling them of my decision to re-
marry. Sean asks several questions: "Will the stepbrothers and
-sisters live with us? What will we call our stepfather?" Finally
Terry speaks. He says he doesn't want to leave California and all
his friends.

Even now, years later, I feel guilty for subjecting them to another complex set of circumstances just as they are grappling
with their adolescence. As it turns out, however, their adjustment to a new step-family is not as difficult as I'd expected. I'm
still thankful that they made it through those teenage years without serious problems. Probably just luck, I think.

Sean is now enrolled in the graduate school of politics at San
Francisco State University. In 1984 he worked on the floor of the
Democratic National Convention and then served on Joan Mon-
dale's press-advance staff throughout the Presidential campaign.
He talks for hours about political issues—how countries of the
world must solve their differences by peaceful means. He is impa-
tient with other twenty-four-year-olds for whom the Vietnam
War is a chapter in a history book.

Though Sean and Terry were only youngsters during the
1960s, I believe they are nevertheless a product of the sixties,
idealists now living within a generation of pragmatists. But I am

glad that this is so. I hope they will always have the strength to follow their convictions.

I'm also pleased that they both seem to have a special vitality for life. Their father would like that too, I think. He'd enjoy the raucous activity that brings the house alive whenever they're here. On nights like this when I'm alone, I almost miss the chaos myself. Terry will be home this weekend, though, and I'm looking forward to seeing him. He's driving down from his college in New Hampshire in order to speak at a Vietnam Veterans breakfast in the morning. I may wait up for him tonight, since I'm not feeling sleepy yet.

The only sound I hear now is the rustling of wispy seashore pines as they sway easily in a slight breeze outside the windows of our old captain's house. How fragile they are, I note, compared to my tall eucalyptus and sturdy redwoods. I'm surprised how much I continue to miss those giant trees and my canyon home. Until I met Ed Keenan, I planned to live in California forever, but that intention changed as our relationship grew. Being loved again was exciting and all the more precious because it was unexpected. In spite of this, we delayed making a permanent commitment. I kept allotting time for matters to straighten themselves out. Communication with the Marine Corps, however, had come to a halt; I received no additional information about Bill.

Finally, several years after our first meeting, Ed and I were married. I remember how drastically life changed for Sean and Terry and me after that. We moved to Massachusetts, where Ed's business was located, and I became an instant stepmother to Ed's seven children. At first I was stunned by the new role; then I grasped onto it as if it were a lifesaver in a high sea. I was determined to have it all—husband, family, work, perhaps additional education. I was driven by a desire to make up for lost time. In retrospect, I laugh at my own naïveté. I'd taken on unimagined responsibilities, and my aims were far too ambitious.

Tonight, though, as I sort things out, I realize that I have achieved some of my goals. Ed and I have more time for each other now; I'm writing every day, and I've just earned a master's degree. Next year I'm thinking of teaching some college courses.

It is getting late, but I don't want to go to bed yet. I'm looking forward to the future this evening, but I'm also enjoying my memories, and I'm thankful that at last I can do both with ease. I go to the kitchen and pour some brandy into a glass that was a wedding present twenty-five years earlier, and I return to the living room. I am feeling warm and hopeful now. I take a sip of brandy and let myself drift back into the past once more. A scene comes to mind as though it had occurred this very morning. Bill is a young man again. He is laughing, holding one of the children high above his head. He lowers him to the ground, throws an arm around my waist casually, and I lean on his shoulder.

Early the next morning I am sitting at a table in a Veterans of Foreign Wars hall in Hyannis, Massachusetts. Two or three hundred people have come to a breakfast meeting organized by the Cape Cod Vietnam Veterans to help POW/MIAs in Southeast Asia. The Vietnam Veterans are wearing odd pieces of old uniforms—a camouflage jacket, khaki pants. One has a medal pinned to a blue windbreaker jacket. I am touched that after all these years they refuse to forget their comrades who are still missing.

At the front table Terry is seated between members of two other MIA families. A mother and father in their sixties tell how their young son, a Marine enlisted man, became missing during a search-and-destroy mission into Laos in 1969. Their identical sweat shirt jackets are covered with pins and patches, which plead HELP THE MIAS, REMEMBER THE POW/MIAS. A sister of an aviator shot down over Laos has just asked that letters be sent to President Reagan and Congress on behalf of the MIAs.

I am nervous, wondering what Terry will say. He arrived late last night, and we haven't had time to talk. He walks to the center of the table, where his nearly six-foot-five frame towers above a small podium. He is wearing a white shirt open at the neck; his beige sports coat nearly matches the color of his hair, which is curly now like Sean's.

"My father, Lieutenant Colonel William Mullen, a Marine Corps pilot, was sent to Vietnam in 1965," he begins. "One year later, two weeks before he was supposed to come home, his plane was shot down on a bombing mission over Laos.

"In 1973 almost six hundred POWs came back from North Vietnam. President Nixon and Dr. Kissinger, however, had signed no agreement for release of the prisoners in Laos. There are five hundred sixty-six servicemen still missing in action in Laos. None of the men shot down there was ever released.

"After 1973 Dr. Kissinger tried to buy the prisoners in Laos from the North Vietnamese for three and a half billion dollars in aid, but Congress refused to vote the money. President Nixon became involved in Watergate and the missing men were forgotten in the years that followed.

"I don't understand how our country can allow men to be captured in a war and then desert them. Some of these men would have been held for fifteen to twenty years by now. The United States should tell the world about this tragedy. President Reagan should send the Secretary of State to Laos to talk with the Communist government there. We should ask ourselves what the life of a serviceman is worth. And, if necessary, our country should pay any amount to get those men released.

"Our government continues to receive information from refugees, satellite photos, and U.S. intelligence sources that report that live American prisoners have been sighted in Southeast Asia. No one knows how many men could have survived, but even if one is still alive, we owe it to him to bring him home.

"I hope people who care will make others believe that this terrible thing has happened and demand that our government get them released somehow. We found a way to bring the hostages home from Iran, and these men have been held twenty times as long.

"I want to say something personal now. I was only two and a half years old when my father left for Vietnam. I never really knew my father. But I do know some things about him. He is tall, his hair is dark and curly, and his eyes are blue. He was a fine pilot. He laughed a lot and had a lot of friends. He was a good baseball pitcher, and he played the piano. He loved to sing;

his favorite song was 'Danny Boy.' I know a lot more things about my father. But I never knew my father.

"If my father is dead, I want him brought back and buried at Arlington with the rest of the dead heroes. Because no matter what anyone thinks of the futile and tragic war in Vietnam, the men who fought there were heroes.

"If my father is alive after all these years, he must think we've forgotten him. I want him to know that we haven't. There is still time to bring him home. If others are alive, we must bring them all home.

"My wish is simple. If my father is alive, I want to know him, not things about him. If he is dead, I want to be able to put a flower on his grave."

The following is a statement by former Director of the Defense Intelligence Agency Lieutenant General Eugene Tighe, U.S. Air Force (retired), as quoted in the *Congressional Record*, 1985:

During my tenure in the DIA, the MIA/POW issue was a key issue for me and of high priority. I ordered a daily update every morning on my desk. I saw more information daily than any man in the world. The evidence is clear to me that there are Americans being held against their will in Southeast Asia.